To Gordon
From

HORSE AND HOUND
FOXHUNTING COMPANION

HORSE and HOUND

Foxhunting Companion

SELECTED AND INTRODUCED BY

FOXFORD

FOREWORD BY

THE DUKE OF BEAUFORT

COUNTRY LIFE BOOKS

Part of the proceeds from the sale
of this book are being donated to the
Hunt Servants' Benefit Society.

Published by Country Life Books
and distributed for them by
The Hamlyn Publishing Group Limited
London · New York · Sydney · Toronto
Astronaut House, Feltham, Middlesex, England

First published 1978

ISBN 0 600 34571 8

Filmset in England by
Photocomp Limited, Birmingham
Printed in England by
Butler & Tanner Limited, Frome

Foreword by The Duke of Beaufort

KG PC GCVO MFH

Today is May 1st. In previous years from 1919 to 1939 I would have been dressed for hunting and on my way to the Meet to try to catch a May fox in one of the hilly parts of the country over which my hounds hunt. Times change, and in World War II the hilly land was ploughed; and so today the spring corn is showing in many areas. So that May fox rests in peace, and I hope he is bringing some form of food to his vixen wife.

Throughout my life I have been extremely lucky in being able to enjoy foxhunting. I was blooded before I was a year old by my father when he killed a fox with his doghounds on the doorstep of the South Door of Badminton House. He taught me most of what I know about foxhunting, which has helped me tremendously, and I believe the writings in this *Horse and Hound* book much resemble his views on the greatest of all sports. Michael Clayton has certainly chosen a grand team of experts to do the writing, which will be much enjoyed by all the book's readers. Finally, may I take this opportunity of thanking him personally for many excellent and interesting articles which appear regularly in *Horse and Hound*—long may it continue!

Beaufort

May 1st, 1978

Contents

AUTUMN

WINTER

SPRING

APPENDICES

ACKNOWLEDGMENTS

*

Drawings by John King

Photographs by Jim Meads, Brackley

Seasonal engravings by
Thomas Bewick

*

List of Authors

Introduction by Foxford

WE have always been fortunate in receiving articles and information for our weekly hunting pages in *Horse and Hound* from leading figures in the sport.

The paper has been reporting and strongly supporting the sport for nearly 100 years; our centenary year is 1984.

Foxhunting, although the "traditional sport of the countryside", is at the same time a vital, living activity which commands the intense interest and participation of many people throughout the year.

True, the hunting season proper starts on November 1 and ends in March or April, but the local Hunt's summer programme is essential if good sport is to be achieved in the winter season ahead.

To the foxhunter, the Hunt's puppy show is one of the most important fixtures of the year, and he will probably visit one of the major hound shows during the summer months as well.

Horse and Hound charts the foxhunter's year in full, and therefore it was appropriate to produce articles from our pages to cover the entire 12 months of activities associated with the Chase.

Foxhunting has had to adapt to the vastly changed conditions of the latter 20th century, and it has done so most successfully. Although the sport's traditions remain important, and are paid due deference here, the emphasis in this Companion is on contemporary foxhunting.

It is always a problem in a sporting paper to ensure that the newcomer or novice is given plenty of information and encouragement, whilst at the same time ensuring that the "in" group at the heart of the sport finds regular material which fills its specialist needs.

I hope, judging by the loyal support of our readers, that we have managed this, and I have endeavoured to perform the same role in this book.

The techniques of hunting are fascinating; its lore provides a lifetime's subject for study. It is true that different people enjoy the sport for a variety of reasons.

But as Jorrocks exclaimed: "Tell me a man's foxhunter, and I loves 'im . . ." There is a basic fun in foxhunting which binds together all who follow hounds regularly.

Its challenge to the young as a risk sport, one of the few remaining in the English countryside, is as strong as ever; its appeal to the naturalist and the country lover remains absorbing to men and women of all ages and from all parts of the community.

A sense of humour is an immense asset in any endeavour, and has always been a feature of the hunting field, evoking some of the richest English literary caricature in the pages of Surtees.

This element is as alive as ever: I could introduce you to a surprising number of Surteesian characters still abounding in the modern hunting field. There are humorous contributions in this book, notably from Ulrica Murray Smith and from Charles James.

Mrs. Murray Smith, Joint Master of the Quorn since 1959, is one of the most popular personalities in the sport, and her contributions to *Horse and Hound* have greatly widened the circle of those who warmly appreciate and enjoy her distinctive brand of wit and wisdom.

Charles James is the nom de plume of a Master and

amateur huntsman of considerable experience, being the fortunate possessor of a most amusing pen.

The caring of horses, the choice of clothes, the problems of following hounds; all are subjects of absorbing interest to those who endeavour to follow in the field, and they are covered here with a modern appreciation of the foxhunter's problems.

At the heart of the matter is the science of venery; a science with more than a touch of art in it when an exceptional man is hunting hounds.

I venture to suggest that aside from any other consideration, it has been well worth while to produce a book which has outstanding contributions from three of this century's greatest Masters and huntsmen: the Duke of Beaufort, Sir Peter Farquhar, and Captain Ronnie Wallace.

The Duke of Beaufort has been Master of his own great Hunt since 1924, but he has been "Master" of the entire foxhunting and equestrian scene in a wider sense, setting examples in the conduct of sport for all to admire, to enjoy, and to seek to emulate.

I am greatly indebted to His Grace for writing the Foreword, and for being able to include the verbatim report of a fascinating lecture on handling hounds in the field.

Sir Peter Farquhar has long been one of the most distinguished and influential hound breeders. He was a successful amateur huntsman in the 1930's, and after the war became Joint Master and huntsman of the Portman country in Dorset where he put into effect his views on hound breeding, which had a considerable impact on the conformation and performance of the modern foxhound.

Capt. Ronnie Wallace is that phenomenon, a legend in

his own time. Concluding his remarkable 25 years' Mastership of the Heythrop in 1976, he become Joint Master and huntsman of the Exmoor and continues to produce splendid sport there with undimmed zest and skill. "Hunting with Ronnie" is an unforgettable experience: his brilliance as a huntsman is matched by the forethought and planning which is devoted to the sport beforehand.

During the summer months Ronnie Wallace's expertise as a judge of hounds is a feature of many a Hunt's puppy show, and of course he has often judged at the major hound shows. His article on hound judging, selected for this anthology, crystallises this elusive art.

Contributions from such successful Masters and amateur huntsmen as Dermot Kelly, formerly of the Meynell, Martin Scott of the V.W.H., and Martin Letts of the College Valley, widen the scope of the Companion considerably. There is a typically colourful and informative piece from our unique columnist, Loriner.

I started a regular weekly hunting column, Foxford's Hunting Diary, in 1973, beginning somewhat tentatively with short notes, and later introducing lengthier reports on visits to Hunts. The wonderful encouragement, and considerable hospitality, I received throughout the United Kingdom and Ireland, have made the Diary even more enjoyable and rewarding than I could have guessed.

To ride after hounds in High Leicestershire one week, to tackle the big banks of County Limerick the next, and then perhaps to jump the hedges and drops of Dorset the following week, following some of the best packs of hounds in the world, is a privilege indeed.

No matter what the weather, nor the standard of sport achieved, each visit is always fun. Whether I can maintain the frequency of Hunt visits in future remains to be seen, but it has been a remarkable experience so far. In my busiest season I visited 42 Hunts and rode more than 50 horses.

I have included some of these Foxford reports in an attempt to give some impression of the marvellous variety of foxhunting which still flourishes in the British Isles.

I hope this Companion will enhance your hunting, whether past, present, or future.

MICHAEL CLAYTON

Askett, Buckinghamshire, 1978

Summer

Summertime is a delightful, yet highly important, part of the foxhunting year. It must never be forgotten that a pack of hounds and hunting country need attention throughout a year, and the decisions and actions taken during the non-hunting months are vital.

The summer months are the time when the hound man has a tremendous advantage over the man who merely hunts to ride, hangs up his boots in the spring and more or less forgets about the Chase until the following autumn.

Throughout the summer each Hunt holds its own puppy show, when the young hounds are judged by two visiting hound experts, usually eminent Masters of Foxhounds who have bred and hunted hounds for many years.

The puppy show, like so much else in foxhunting, follows an established ritual which allows for a great deal of sociability between people from all sections of the local rural community.

How should the new Master of Foxhounds embark on organising a puppy show?

Here, with tongue in cheek, is the advice of Arthur James, the nom de plume of a much liked and respected amateur huntsman and M.F.H., currently hunting the North. His substantial frame and sober mien cloak one of the most engaging humorists in the contemporary foxhunting world.

Getting It Right Twixt Muxbury and Loamshire

IT is the unshakeable belief of most hunting people that their M.F.H. spends most of his summer, and his guarantee, in the South of France. The fact that he probably spends his time wobbling from farm to farm poised between a disreputable hat and a rusty bicycle is discounted. Be that as it may, once a year he has to put aside his polaroids and sun tan lotion, tether his bicycle, and produce – Hey Presto! a puppy show.

The primary aim of the puppy show is to thank the puppy walkers. Those wonderful, generous people, who year after year open their doors and their hearts to the greedy lump of trouble and mischief that is a foxhound puppy.

A simple, straightforward, happy idea you might think, but as those worn and grizzled by experience will tell you, nothing related to foxhunting is simple and straightforward. The puppy show is no exception.

Let us consider our young Master, pink with the enthusiasm of his first pack of hounds, into whose soul no iron has yet entered, and see if we can guide him over the obstacle of his first puppy show.

Puppy shows come in assorted shapes and sizes. At one end of the scale might be the Muxbury and Hogsnorton Harriers. This is a splendidly enthusiastic and casual

affair. The puppies come in very assorted forms, but all look very keen.

Indeed were it not for the fact that they are all firmly tethered to their walkers by various leads, couples, and bits of baler cord, they would give practical proof of their keenness by leaving the rather rickety ring, and going three rounds with the kennel cat.

If the young Master is lucky enough to be asked to the Muxbury and Hogsnorton show, he should realize that his sternest test will come after the massive tea, when he will be firmly marched off to the night shift at the Fox and Pullet.

The Fox and Pullet has never heard of licensing hours and if the young Master thinks he will be allowed to keep his promise to his mother of nothing stronger than bitter lemon, he has got another think – and a nasty headache – coming.

The other end of the puppy show scale might be represented by the Loamshire.

Everybody has heard of the Loamshire and their redoubtable Master and huntsman, the Hon. Perceval "Piggy" Plantagenet.

The Loamshire puppy show is an occasion in the foxhunting world and our young Master will do well to try and wangle an invitation. He will be properly impressed by the enormous kennels and stables, built by the "Red Earl" in 1880 in good Victorian workhouse style, where everything that cannot walk is freshly painted.

He will also be impressed by the large and knowledgeable crowd. A solid phalanx of dark suited and bowler hatted Hunt servants on one side of the ring, facing the massed ranks of Masters of Foxhounds, all wearing Herbert Johnson straw hats and knowing expressions.

Two very senior Masters will have the task of sorting out a seemingly unending stream of lovely young hounds, shown in a masterly manner by that doyen of Hunt servants, Ernie Blowhard.

It is all frightfully impressive, but the tea, by some very special caterers, will not be half as good as the Muxbury and Hogsnorton Harriers spread. All this will give our young Master food for thought, and he will probably set his sights somewhere in the middle.

We have assumed that our young Master has some puppies to show. Should he be in any doubt, they will be the ones who knock him down every time he walks the hounds out by galloping the fully stretched chains of the couples into the backs of his knees. As a last resort he should consult his kennel-huntsman.

Next he must find himself some judges. A little caution and forethought is advisable here. It is not a good thing to have your judges come to blows in the ring over their mutual wife. Nor is it good to have judges with such entirely opposing views that they are still judging the doghounds at 9 o'clock at night.

Major Spurde Feele-Boote, who rides 24st. and does not like his hounds to get away from him, will not be a happy nick with "Fizzy" Todhunter, who is 8st. of whipcord and has three blood horses a day to follow his varminty little bitches.

If the young Master wants to make a good first impression, he should be wary of judges who relish telling rather meaty stories at puppy shows. Miss Spruce who is 5ft of whale bone corset and long blue knickers, and has walked four puppies a year for the past 30, might not take kindly to the more way out antics of the actress and the bishop.

Apart from the puppy walkers, the young Master

should invite his neighbouring Masters, who will all want to say how much worse his entry is than their own. Also the neighbouring Hunt servants, so that they can tell each other how badly kept the kennels/hounds are compared with their own.

He should also invite the senior Members of the Hunt, who will spend the whole afternoon either dozing or talking loudly about the wonderful puppy shows the previous Master used to put on, with a rick of champagne and the band of H.M. Royal Marines.

Before the show the young Master should produce a spot of luncheon for the judges and anyone else whom he considers deserving. However caution is advisable. If the young Master has some '47 Claret or some '50 Port, let him keep it for himself.

If he does his guests too well: (a) he will not be able to flog them down to the show before 4 p.m.; (b) most of them will promptly go to sleep when they get there and frighten the puppies with their snoring; and (c) the actress and the bishop will raise their ugly heads, or something worse, during the speeches.

After the judging come the speeches. We have touched on some of the possible snags here, but a good speech by a judge does help the afternoon along. A good judge, who is a good speaker too, is worth taking trouble to find. Some judges will not speak, and some will not stop. The first kind is preferable.

The young Master will be expected to say a few words of thanks to everybody concerned, especially the puppy walkers. He should keep his speech, short, pithy, and in one octave.

If he should want to tell a funny story, I would suggest that he tries it on his kennelman first. Kennelmen are serious people, not much given to the frivolities of life. If the young Master gets a wintry smile, he is on a real winner.

The puppy show tea is a high spot of the afternoon, but it should always be under cover. It is an established custom that it always rains during puppy show teas.

The young Master can, of course, go to great expense and call in a caterer, who will produce a second rate tea at a first-rate price. However, if he is going to make the grade as an M.F.H., he should be able to do some crafty work amongst his female followers (No, No, not that sort of work!).

Many ladies are compulsive cake makers and with a little encouragement the young Master will find himself with a marvellous tea at a minimal cost. He will probably be able to keep himself on chocolate sponge for a month afterwards.

Drinks can be a vexed question. Drink would certainly have flowed at the Loamshire, while at the Muxbury and Hogsnorton everybody bought their own in the Fox and Pullet. It will rather depend on the length of the young Master's pocket.

He can always hope that his kennel-huntsman will ask him in for a drink. This might happen if the kennel-huntsman thinks that his employer is green enough to provide good sport for the visiting Hunt servants.

The only certain advice I can give the young Master is that whatever drink he may produce will disappear like the dew in morning. Therefore I strongly advise concealing enough for a fighting whisky for himself afterwards. He will need it.

All in all, there is quite a lot of thought required in putting on a puppy show. But practice makes perfect, and over the years the young Master will perfect a system.

I have quite a good one. I send my Joint-Master a cable from the South of France and tell him to get on with the arrangements.

ARTHUR JAMES

* * *

For a much more serious look at puppy shows let us visit the most illustrious held during the season: the Duke of Beaufort's at Badminton.

The 10th Duke, known universally by foxhunters and a great many others in the equestrian world as Master, is undoubtedly Foxhunter Number One. His Grace hunted the family pack for 47 years, and has continued in office as senior Joint Master since he ceased to carry the horn in 1967.

The doyen of writers on foxhounds is Daphne Moore, who lives on the Badminton estate, and has been closely involved with the fortunes of the famous Badminton Kennel for many years.

The influence on contemporary hound breeding of the Duke of Beaufort's pack has been immense.

Here Daphne Moore describes the Duke of Beaufort's achievements as a hound breeder, after 50 years of his Mastership, in 1974.

Why Hunting Owes So Much to Badminton

AT this summer's Badminton Puppy Show in June, the Duke of Beaufort saw the result of 50 years' consecutive breeding of his own foxhounds, when the doghound entry was perhaps the best that this famous kennel has yet produced.

He inherited the title – and the kennel – from his father, the 9th Duke, in 1924, and ever since then has bred with infinite care the pack whose forerunners had been in the family for some 200 years. The hounds which came to him on the death of his father were big and strong, as was the fashion in the early century. They were largely by Belvoir sires.

As the Marquess of Worcester the Duke had had plenty of experience in hunting hounds, since from 1920 to 1924 his father had allowed him to hunt a pack of the smaller bitches, with which he showed phenomenal sport, assisted by amateur whippers-in who were his personal friends.

The pack consisted of 14-16 couple, and he can still recall some of those hounds of which he was particularly fond, amongst them Dorothy ('16), whose two sons became stallion hounds when he succeeded to the family pack.

After his accession to the Mastership he gradually set about breeding a lighter-framed, more active type of hound. His first entry, in 1925, was exclusively by home-bred sires; the next year saw the progeny of Berkeley Waggoner ('22), one of which Wagtail ('26) became a notable foxhound and brood bitch, producing two Peterborough Doghound Champions.

The year 1927 saw further produce of Berkeley Waggoner; 1928 proved to be a red-letter year in the annals of the Badminton Kennel. Through that wise and dedicated hound breeder, Mr. "Ikey" Bell, the Duke heard of a dog down in the West Country who was making a name for himself and who might well prove to be a useful outcross sire.

He lost no time in going to see the hound in question and he liked what he saw, with the result that the subsequently famous Tiverton Actor ('22) came to Badminton, being lent by the late Sir Ian Amory for the season 1928–1929.

His was the same male line – to Four Burrow Whipcord ('05) – as that of Berkeley Waggoner ('22), who had already proved his worth. He was a light-coated dog in an era when Belvoir Tan was predominant, and was perhaps the first light-coated sire to have been used at Badminton since the time of the blue-pied Leveller ('10).

He proved to be a remarkable foxhound, flying gates and even fences in his stride; moreover, he was a remarkable sire. His grandsons, Autocrat ('32) and Fencer ('32), were probably the first light-coloured hounds to win championships at Peterborough since Milton Rector ('07) in 1910.

Another notable year was 1932. Not only did the entry include the above mentioned Peterborough champions, it also included four litters by South and West Wilts Godfrey ('28), that outstanding stallion hound bred at the Carlow by the late Mrs. Hall ("the Miss'us") and given unentered to Ikey Bell. Godfrey was an instant and outstanding success at Badminton.

What the F.K.S.B. of that year does not show was the acquisition by the Duke of a little blue badger-pied bitch, Petrel ('32), pure Brecon in blood, who was given to Master (as the Duke of Beaufort is universally known) by Ikey Bell in gratitude for judging the South and West Wilts entry at short notice.

Master was allowed to take his pick, and characteristically – for he is ever broad-minded where hounds are concerned – he chose Petrel, despite her Welsh ancestry and slightly broken coat. She appears in the Errata and Addenda of the 1934 studbook.

Since then her descendants have been "as sands of the sea, which cannot be numbered," and hers is one of the strongest female lines in the kennel today. Moreover, she bred a Peterborough champion in Pelican ('35) who united two precious lines of blood, those of Tiverton Actor and Petrel herself.

The Duke has never been afraid to experiment, and another such trial was made since the war, when he imported a bitch from the United States, Elkridge-Harford Daring ('57). She possessed a wonderful nose and voice, and her slight lack of constitution was atoned for when she was mated with the iron-hard Badminton doghounds. This line is still maintained and greatly valued.

After the 1939-1945 war a new male line was becoming popular, creeping in almost unnoticed at first by the use of South and West Wilts Phoenix ('28). It produced its first Peterborough champion – from the Meynell – in 1949. In the next three years the Duke of Beaufort's Remus and Rector ('47) (two litter brothers), and Ringbolt ('50) were made champions, and all came of this obscure line, that of Glog Nimrod ('04), a pure Welsh sire, used by Sir Edward Curre; the blood being handed down via Brecon Paragon ('23) to South and West Wilts.

Meynell Pageant ('35), bred by Sir Peter Farquhar during his last year at the Meynell, had brought this tail-male to Badminton. Pageant was lent to the Duke during the war and proved a fine foxhound with great nose and voice.

It was an immense stroke of fortune that his influence was experienced during the lean war years, and it has proved to be an enduring one. His was the tail-male of possibly the most renowned and influential sire ever to be bred at Badminton. I refer, of course, to the incomparable Palmer ('59), who founded a lasting dynasty, not only in his own kennel, but in others as well, for he was used in a total of 19 kennels.

His pedigree is filled with the finest blood of the F.K.S.B. and his mating to Woeful ('60) (the alliance of two Peterborough champions of the same year) produced four brood bitches and a stallion hound. This family might be said to be the backbone of the kennel today.

Four Burrow Pleader ('38) is another name which is to be found repeated again and again in present-day pedigrees at Badminton. He was the great great-grandson of Tiverton Actor ('22) and his blood provided a happy nick.

Portman and Heythrop sires (bred by Sir Peter Farquhar and Captain Ronnie Wallace respectively) have contributed greatly to the success of more recent Badminton hounds, Portman Pedlar ('55) being especially noteworthy as the sire of Palmer ('59), whilst Portman Grossman ('52) and Heythrop Craftsman ('62) have both been of great importance. Carlow Striver ('63) and

Tipperary Growler ('64) have exerted immense influence in the past decade.

Some of the Duke's best doghounds of the past 20-odd years have been Distaff ('52), Tetrarch ('52), Dreamer ('53), Woodcock ('55), Dragon ('56), Palmer ('59), Godfrey ('60), Badle and Bellman ('66), Gaffer and Grocer ('68).

He regards the following as having been the most beneficial "outside" sires of his Mastership: Tiverton Actor ('22), South and West Wilts Godfrey ('28), Meynell Pageant ('35), Four Burrow Pleader ('38), Portman Pedlar ('55), Carlow Striver ('63), and Tipperary Growler ('64).

It is almost invidious to single out any of the famous Badminton bitches, but one cannot omit mention of Posy ('63), Palmer's memorable daughter; Peterborough champion and dam of champions, who hunted into her eighth season, still retaining her beautiful outlines at the age of nine. Her line is very strong in the present kennels, and last year's Peterborough Doghound Champion, Pontiff ('70), was bred by her, as well as Beadle ('66), the 1968 winner.

Since he started to breed his own hounds, the Duke has won no fewer than 20 doghound championships at Peterborough and 10 bitch championships; a very remarkable record in just 50 years.

The Duke's most recent experiment with sires from other kennels has been the use of College Valley Bellman ('70), who hunted with the Badminton doghounds with great success last season and has been mated with a number of bitches this year. The progeny of Crawley and Horsham Farley ('70) in the past two years have been extremely prominent at the puppy shows, whilst the first-season hounds have done well in the field.

By judicious breeding during the past half-century the Duke of Beaufort has materially changed the make and shape of his hounds, whilst retaining the stout constitutions for which they are renowned. They have always been bred for work, and fortunate is the pack which obtains hounds from this kennel.

A glance through the pages of the Foxhound Kennel Stud Book shows just how numerous are the packs which have benefitted from the Duke's proverbial generosity. With the infiltration of this blood into smaller kennels, far and wide, we are likely to experience more and more surprises at the major hound shows, when possibly small two-day a week packs will produce hounds, 100 per cent "Badminton" in pedigree, to carry off a coveted silver cup to some comparatively obscure corner of England.

DAPHNE MOORE

*   *   *

Judging hounds is an art, and a craft. Long experience is essential for a senior judge at that holy of holies, Peterborough Royal Foxhound Show, but "hound sense", an innate sympathy and understanding of hounds, is the quality which sets apart the real hound man from the rest.

Captain Ronnie Wallace, Chairman of the Masters of Foxhounds Association, has been acknowledged as a genius with hounds for most of his life. He began by hunting the Eton beagles, and later distinguished himself at the Ludlow and the Cotswold before embarking on one of the great contemporary Masterships: 25 years as Joint Master and huntsman of the Heythrop, which he concluded in 1976, going west to the Exmoor country where he continues to hunt hounds with amazing zest and expertise as Joint Master of the Exmoor Foxhounds with Mr. Jack Hosegood.

Here, Captain Wallace provides a fascinating guide to the

precepts of hound judging on the "flags" (the flagstones, used so that a hound's feet may be seen clearly by the judge; if a hound is judged on grass some defects of the foot may be hidden).

Judging on the Flags

HOUND shows are pleasant summer occasions which give hunting people a chance to get together and discuss their sport. If the right sort of hound goes to the top, then shows make an important contribution to hound breeding. They enable hound breeders to see the best which the foremost kennels are producing, setting a standard for the future. The foxhound is pre-eminently a working animal, but he needs the most suitable conformation to perform his work successfully in the hunting field.

The first impression you get when you see a hound in the ring is most important. This is why you never want to look at hounds on a lead. The second they come into the ring they should be freed from the lead, and this gives the judge an immediate opportunity to see whether each hound has balance, activity and general quality.

If you have a standard in your mind's eye, then you can make up your mind straight away whether it is worth going ahead to consider a hound in detail.

What you are looking for in judging a hound is the conformation most suitable for speed and stamina. In the hunting field it must be able to go the fastest, and the farthest.

The two most vital areas you will consider are the elbow, which is the key to the front department, and the strength of the loin which is the key to the back department.

No fads or fancies, such as colour or eyes, should be

taken into account – except curly sterns which are considered a fault as they are so ugly and hereditary; but sterns should be permitted to curl gently; it is no good expecting them to be like pointers.

The shape of the head itself does not matter much, although of course a hound must have a level mouth; it must not be under-shot, or over- shot. (In the same way, you reject a horse with a parrot mouth.)

Some people like a masculine head on a dog hound, but there are some very good dog hounds with sharp features; it is a good old fashioned appearance.

Ideally the foxhound's neck should be a long one, but it is nowhere near as important as the shoulders. People talk about 'neck and shoulders' as if they were the same thing, but of course they are two different features of conformation.

You might well prefer a hound with a good shoulder and a short neck, but you would not select a winning hound with a bad shoulder and a long neck.

A good length of humerus bone is most important.

The shoulder blades should not appear too wide apart over the back. You should look over the top and the sides of the hound to discern the shoulder movement. There should not be a straight line from the point of the shoulder to the tip of the toes, because with this confrontation there is not sufficient "cushion" when the hound moves its fore-limbs.

The position of the elbow gives you the clue to the quality of the shoulder; ideally the hound's shoulder and fore-leg should move with the true swing of the pendulum.

I like to see a hound step off at the walk, because then you see the length of his stride. There should be enough play for the elbow to move freely, and ideally this movement should be parallel to the body.

If a hound's elbow is stuck out then it is bound to move rather like a "round arm bowler", but in a young hound you can often anticipate that there will be some improvement and "filling-in" in this respect, and you should make due allowance for this.

The worst fault is an elbow which is pinned in underneath. It probably goes with crookedness in front.

You should look to see whether the hound is crooked. Does he turn his toes out? If his elbow is wrong, then he probably moves crookedly. Super straightness of the forelimbs could be a fault because you get a tendency to knuckle over at the knee; it is better slightly back.

Moving straight is more important than the legs actually being totally straight.

The forearm wants to be a strong one, in good proportion to the size of the hound.

The knee needs to have a little bit of elasticity. As I mention above, it is preferable to be slightly back rather than over.

Pasterns should be slightly sloping, rather than straight with the knee, as this all helps to avoid jarring.

You are looking for a sensible foot with the toenails evenly worn. I have seen hounds which remain sound with very slightly spreading feet.

But there are two types one definitely does not like: the very tight feet with no room between the toes for chafing; or puddingy, fleshy feet which are difficult in that they are unlikely to wear well.

A "let down" toe is a fault, for it is a sign of foot weakness.

The foxhound's chest should not be too wide; the bosomy hound is certainly not required. Width bears so much on the movement of the hound. The chest should be sensibly in proportion to the size of the hound, definitely avoiding the other extreme where both legs are "coming out of one hole".

The stamina of the hound is much affected by conformation in this area. So you are looking for plenty of heart room. It is better for the rib bones to be deep rather than round, because the round bodied rib cage pushes the elbow out.

As far as the underline of the body is concerned, I do not mind a hound "running up" a bit, but of course it should not be too narrow gutted.

It is very nice to see a back bone set in two cushions of muscle so that you could roll a billiard ball down it with no difficulty.

One doesn't like these knobbly backs with the backbone sticking right out.

You can have either a straight back, or the arched loins known as "wheel backs". Either of these may be acceptable, but you must have the right equipment at the back to go with them.

The stern should be set on nicely, which means preferably quite high.

With the wheel back, well developed second thighs are particularly important, and the hocks should be set low and wide apart.

With a straight back the hocks may be set under the hound.

What you do not want is a hound with rather weak second thighs, hocks a long way behind, and "cow hocked".

There is another point worth remembering about wheel backs. They used to say that if a hound had a dip behind his shoulder then it must be a bad shoulder. This would be so in the case of a hound with a straight back, but a wheel backed hound is bound to have a slight dip behind the shoulder.

Concentration is vital in hound judging. Retain the standard in your mind's eye, and quickly discard the hounds which don't come near it.

There are probably many hounds to be judged during the day. So don't waste time – get for-orrard!

CAPTAIN RONNIE WALLACE

* * *

Hounds are vital in the Chase of course, but so is the horse if you are to keep near the pack in real foxhunting country.

During the summer months, the hunter showing classes at the major county shows and horse shows, see a considerable gathering of hunting folk at the ringside.

Show hunters are not just kept for show; all are bound to go into the hunting field at some stage in their career. In the show ring their role is to set a standard for breeders and owners, but when their showing days are over they inevitably go hunting regularly without the inhibition of acquiring blemishes which might have prejudiced their career in the ring.

Working hunter classes have grown immensely in popularity in the postwar years, and these provide more opportunity to see hunters performing in the ring as well as on show for the benefit of the judges.

Pamela MacGregor-Morris, Horse and Hound's *authoritative and widely read shows correspondent, here gives a detailed indication of the requirements of a hunter class judge.*

What the Hunter Judge Looks For

THE requirements of the show judge are basically those of any knowledgeable person buying a horse, except that he is not asked to prognosticate on soundness unless a horse is obviously lame.

He looks for a strong, deep, wide horse on short legs, with good limbs and movement, full of quality, standing over ground, and best suited to perform its job in life – staying with hounds over the water-logged winter countryside that is such a far cry from the smooth green sward of the show ring.

In selecting the prototype he will look, too, for additional attributes, which, desirable though they may be, are not essential to the workaday hunter. A really good front, which gives the rider the feeling that he has all the world in front of him; and the vital quality of presence, the majestic bearing that commands his two-legged peers to "Look at me!" Which invests him with the star quality that wins championships.

This much may be seen from the ground. The ultimate test is the ride. Experience will give a fair indication of how a horse may be expected to ride, but appearances can be deceptive and disappointing. Shoulders that appear to be quite good from the floor may prove to be loaded when seated behind them.

The perfectly-balanced horse that is a joy to ride at all paces is best proved from the saddle; as are smoothness of pace, length of stride, and the onward-bound instinct that is an integral part of any hunter worthy of the name.

The judge gets his first view of the class as it enters the ring at a walk. First impressions are important. A good walker is seldom a bad horse, and when weighing up the overall appearance – looking at the horse firstly as a horse rather than as a collection of points, good, bad or indifferent – he will assess symmetry, general proportions, and length of stride.

He will watch the stride again at the trot, for movement that comes from the shoulder rather than the knee, for hind legs that reach well forward under the belly to drive the horse on.

He will not appreciate hocks that trail behind in the last parish, nor be carried away by the exaggerated front action sometimes affected by hacks and ponies. Disliking much knee action, nor will he favour the daisy-cutter, who will stumble in deep or rough going.

Again in the canter he seeks the long, low stride which covers the ground and a smooth, easy way of going. Much of a day's hunting is spent at a canter, and as the hours go by is increasingly necessary.

Finally, the gallop, with the horse ideally, as the dealers have it "lying down" to gallop *ventre à terre*, not going into the ground by reaching for it and gathering it towards him.

Though it is the gallop that wins so many championships, some consider that it is overdone today. There is no point in going faster than hounds run, and at the end of a long hunt it is the horse who goes the shortest way, not the flying machine, who is there at the finish.

While it is essential to show that the horse is able to gallop, which many are not, a short, sharp burst down the long side of the ring can please the judge more than a mad race, with the horses off balance and searching in vain for a fifth leg roung every corner.

Next comes the walk-round, and then the call-in, in tentative order of merit. After this, the ride will confirm or refute his first impressions. Finally, each horse will be led out before him in turn, stripped of its saddle, stood up for minute scrutiny, then walked away and trotted back to see if it moves straight.

Just as the strength of a table is in its legs, so with the horse. Most judges then start with the feet and work upwards.

Few horses with really bad feet get as far as the show ring, probably because they do not stay sound enough to withstand a summer's showing on going that can be hard for weeks; though I have seen the odd colt in the led classes with twisted feet.

Both fore and hind feet should be identical pairs, free from cracks and rings, neither flat and spread nor narrow and boxy. A well developed frog, in contact with the ground to absorb shock, is the best indication of a healthy foot.

These are the engine, and hock formation is paramount, for much depends on it in terms of soundness, and it creates all propulsion and impulsion.

Viewed from the side, a sickle-like formation denotes weakness, predisposing it to curbs and spavins. Yet too straight a hind leg, which is a far more rare phenomenon, is also disposed to strain.

The judge will also hope to find strong, muscular

second thighs above the big, clean hocks. Higher still, he will like good length and slope from the points of the hips to the points of the buttocks, below the high-set tail, when a plumb line should drop vertically through the point of the hocks to the fetlocks.

He will stand behind the horse, pulling the tail aside to ensure that it is not cow-hocked, with the points touching, nor the reverse.

The fore-leg starts with the pasterns. Both back and front, they should be sloping and of medium length. Too short, they will give a bumpy ride; they, too, are shock-absorbers. Longer, they give a springy ride, but extreme length is a weakness, which can cause the fetlock joint to touch the ground.

The joints themselves should be hard and flat rather than round and puffy, showing a lot of work which may take the form of windgalls, though not, one would hope, in the show horse. The tendons running into them must likewise be hard, standing out like whipcord.

Conformation which puts tendons at risk is known as being back at the knee, which should be convex when viewed from the side, large and flat from the front. The forearms above them, like the second thigh, should be strong and muscular. Higher still, the elbow should stand freely away from the body, not tied in.

The more bone, provided it is flat and flinty, the more weight the horse will carry, depth and substance being equal. It is measured below the knee, and no self-respecting hunter should have less than eight inches – nine in a big horse is preferable.

Judges do not, at this juncture, take out a tape measure. For most, a glance will suffice, though some may span it briefly with their hand, feeling for splints at the same time.

The hunter should be wide through the chest, not tall and narrow, and deep through the girth for good heart room.

Ideally, shoulders should be narrow on top, and as flat as possible. Shoulders with breadth on top of the wither, being wide apart, are not attractive aesthetically and are not likely to aid the horse's action; they tend to look lumpy, and are known as loaded shoulders.

A horse lacking in "front" is, of course, going to be placed well down the line. It means the horse has upright shoulder blades, scapulas, which make an abrupt meeting of shoulder and neck.

The neck should be strong, of medium length, with a convex topline. The way in which it goes into the shoulders bears upon the symmetry on which correct head carriage is dependent. The angle at which the head is set on governs respiration, through the degree of natural flexion.

The rib cage should be rounded and well sprung and the back short. The horse that is well ribbed up, with no pronounced gap between his last rib and the point of his hip, will have greater stamina.

From the saddle, the judge will look for well-defined withers, strong muscular loins behind the saddle, strong and wide quarters and a well-set-on tail on the top of his back, after a muscular croup.

The head comes last of all in terms of conformation, yet whatever fixation the judge may have in terms of hind legs or shoulders, he is almost bound to look at it first. For in one way it is the least important factor, and in others the most important, all else being equal, in that here and here only the soul of the horse is made manifest; at least, the character.

However excellent the conformation, the horse with a

coarse, common head and a bulge between the eyes is unlikely to be generous and brave, setting his other qualities at naught.

The judge will look for a finely-chiselled, quality head with large, intelligent eyes, a kind expression and, ideally, that questing look that is best described as "always listening for hounds". A certain plainness of head is desirable, adding to his workmanlike appearance, for a hunter should never be pretty.

To sum up, the judge is seeking a strong, well-made horse, deep and on a short leg, with his knees and hocks near the ground, built to carry weight through deep going, to gallop and jump over any country and to withstand long hours out of the stable.

Different judges have different priorities and, as the perfect horse (like the perfect human being) has yet to be foaled, they all have to compromise in the search for their *beau ideal*.

Yet they will not go far wrong if they look, in the words of Whyte-Melville, for:

A head like a snake, and a skin like a mouse,
An eye like a woman, bright, gentle and brown,
With loins and a back that would carry a house,
And quarters to lift him smack over a town!

PAMELA MACGREGOR-MORRIS

* * *

Foxhunting, as a dynamic, living sport, is far from being the never changing, traditional pastime which is suggested by the outward trappings of red coats, stirrup cups, and hunting horns.

In this century the foxhound itself has seen dramatic changes in conformation and type, bred to cope with the enormous challenge of finding and hunting a fox in the modern countryside which has so many hazards and distractions unknown to our grandfathers.

Lt.-Col. Sir Peter Farquhar is one of the most distinguished and admired of contemporary hound breeders and judges. His Mastership of the Portman Hunt in Dorset since the war saw the introduction of some of the most influential of modern breeding lines.

Here, Sir Peter, explains the difference between the "old" foxhound and the hound of today.

Why They Changed the Modern Foxhound

I THINK there would be little doubt, that if any huntsman of olden days could see the conditions under which the foxhound has to operate today, he would say it would be impossible for hounds to hunt a fox at all – let alone to catch him.

But, as we know, he would be wrong simply because that wonderful animal the foxhound, as always, has risen to the occasion and adapted himself to changed conditions. So I think it would be of interest to look back to the various periods, and changing conditions of hunting, from which the present-day foxhound has evolved.

Some 250 years ago, before the Enclosure Acts, our countryside consisted solely of open areas and woodlands. Hounds mostly hunted deep at that time and the whole emphasis in hunting was on the hound – the art of venery. The followers rode horses or cobs, which were usually unclipped, simply as a conveyance to watch hounds work.

I think that the hounds of that period were heavy-tongued, rather slow and ponderous, and they would work up to their quarry through the overnight "drag", the resulting hunt usually being a somewhat long, drawn-out affair.

Incidentally we learn from contemporary pictures that their hounds were mostly light-coloured and many of them had curly sterns.

People nowadays ask where all the modern light colour in hounds comes from. The answer is that hounds were *originally* light-coloured and tan-coloured packs such as the Belvoir and Brocklesby were achieved by dint of selective breeding. Directly you mate light-coloured hounds back into these lines the off-spring will revert to their natural colour again.

The curly stern is now the only "fashion" left in foxhound breeding. We think it unsightly and, quite rightly, try to eliminate it; yet it is not really a fault – indeed nine times out of ten it is a sign of a strong back!

The fox in those early days was regarded as vermin and was mostly dug out and killed with the aid of terriers. In parts of the West Country when a fox's earth was

discovered the church bells would be rung and the whole population of the village would turn out to help dig out the poor creatures.

Then came the Enclosure Acts, which were enacted in the latter half of the 18th century and the early part of the 19th century. Pastures were fenced with thorn, timber, banks and stone walls and the whole aspect of hunting changed. The "ride" became the major interest to most followers, and blood horses which could gallop and jump were the order of the day. The whole tempo of the Chase had to alter and hounds were required to be much speedier and, what is more, to keep it up all day.

We read, that when the famous Hugo Meynell took the Quorn in 1753, he had to breed his hounds with great pace as otherwise they got jumped upon by the thrusters who hunted with him. His example was followed by others such as Osbaldeston and Peter Beckford, and later by those two greatest of hound breeders, Lord Henry Bentinck and Lord Willoughby de Broke. And it was in 1762 that the 5th Duke of Beaufort changed from stag to foxhunting.

In the process hounds undoubtedly became much lighter-tongued; indeed one reads in a contemporary poem describing the behaviour of hounds during a very fast hunt:

Mute as a dream his pursuers were racing
For silence you know is the criterion of pace.

This did not matter all that much in those days, as fences were well-kept and there was no wire, so Hunt servants and followers could ride field to field with hounds. But it would not do nowadays – by the time you had got off to open a wired-up gate, and ridden round three sides of a 60-acre wheatfield, hounds would be lost unless they were running with a great cry. And there is nothing more undignified for a huntsman than to be traipsing round the countryside asking all and sundry if they have seen his hounds.

The 19th century, of course, was the golden era of foxhunting and the hounds of that period were probably as near to perfection as possible for the job they were called upon to do. There was no wire; cattle were wintered in yards and sheep mostly folded so the fields were "clean"; there were no artificial manures; roads were gravelled and there were no cars or tractors to pump petrol or diesel fumes into hounds noses, and to "head" the fox on every possible occasion.

However, towards the end of this century and up to the 1914-18 War, there came a very sad period in the history of the foxhound. Their breeding got into the hands of a few influential Masters who did not hunt their own hounds, but bred for fashion and the show ring. They created what was later to be known as the "Peterborough type". They wanted a hound to be very big, very wide through the chest, which of course put the elbows out, and to have tremendous bone. Above all, he had to be plumb straight, which involved a short, rigid pastern, which nature intended to be supple so as to act as a shock absorber; with knuckling over knees and tight cat-feet all the stress came on the front two pads, the other three being off the ground.

Such hounds were nothing more nor less than cripples; they could not gallop nor had they much inclination to hunt. The unfortunate Hunt servants had to do the hounds' work for them, which is why galloping about all over the countryside (interpreted as brilliant casts) became the normal practice in fashionable countries.

A few English packs, notably perhaps the Heythrop,

Berkeley and Brocklesby, resisted this fashion, but of course their breeding policy became very limited and difficult.

But there were none of these inhibitions in the Fell countries, nor in Wales.

Soon after the turn of the century there emerged a most remarkable man – Mr. Isaac Bell – who, in my opinion, has had a far greater influence on hound breeding during this century then any other man.

He was remarkable in many ways – not least because he was an American citizen, without any hunting background, and was brought up by a widowed mother in Paris, where mounted on one of his mother's carriage horses, he astonished the natives by galloping round the Champs Elysées, blowing a hunting horn, whilst hunting an imaginary pack of hounds.

From his earliest childhood he thought and dreamt of nothing but foxhunting; he read everything that had ever been written about hounds and hunting and made a comprehensive study of hound pedigrees. Luckily his mother sent him to England to be educated and, at Harrow, he made many foxhunting friends.

As soon as possible he set himself up in a hunting box in Leicestershire, but quickly became disenchanted with the performance of the hounds with which he hunted. So in 1903 he moved to Ireland and took the Galway Blazers; five years later he moved to Kilkenny, where he began to experiment with the Welsh cross, and bred a fine pack of hounds.

After the 1914-18 War a few of us younger Masters – hunting our own hounds – found ourselves not very happy with the type of hound that then prevailed; too big, not active enough, lacking drive and intelligence, and short of both nose and tongue. By great good fortune

Ikey Bell had returned from Ireland and taken the South and West Wilts country; and with his help and advice we started going to Wales, where we found four great hound breeders, all of whom had bred outstanding packs by crossing the best of the old English lines with their native Welsh hounds.

They were Sir Edward Curre of Itton, Mr. Jack Evans, Master of the Brecon, Lord Coventry at Carmarthen and Mr. David Davies who hunted his own private pack.

Again by great good fortune, their hounds were entered in the Foxhound Kennel Stud Book which enabled us to use them (as well as numerous top-class stallion hounds from the South and West Wilts) without being completely ostracized; although many of the "old guard" believed that we were ruining foxhound and said so – loud and clear!

Our justification lies in the fact that in almost every foxhound kennel today there are countless lines back to Brecon Paragon ('23), Carmarthenshire Nimrod ('24), Mr. David Davies's Banker ('24) and several different lines back to Curre which, together with Kilkenny Gory ('21) and Tiverton Actor ('22), revitalized the English foxhound.

Between the wars was, I think, a sort of mini-golden era for foxhunting. The standard of hounds improved tremendously. Because farming was, in the main, unprofitable we were genuinely able to help farmers by buying their hay, straw and oats, and with hedge-laying competitions, etc., wire was not difficult to get down and replace in the spring.

We had the advantage of a limited amount of modern transport and telephone communication, the big estates were still intact and taxation was comparatively low and horses were plentiful and not too expensive. I count myself very fortunate indeed to have had the privilege of hunting a pack of hounds throughout most of this period.

Then another war, after which the foxhound was faced with a tremendous challenge. On the credit side, I was delighted to find that the sometimes rather bitter Welsh-cross controversy was dead. Post-war Masters just wanted to breed the type of hound most suited to showing sport and catching foxes in their particular countries. And catching foxes, which had previously only mattered much to hounds and huntsman, now became a valid justification for foxhunting.

Also, and most important of all, because farming had now become a profitable and essential industry, farmers were able to take their proper place in the hunting field – mounted on a horse – instead of watching from the sidelines, on foot, as so many had to do in the past. On the debit side, however, the difficulties were enormous.

Farming practices had undergone a radical change, as a result of which almost every other field was "foiled". This vital question of "clean" and "foiled" ground is possibly not fully appreciated by the average person who goes hunting, but every modern huntsman will have experienced, only too often, that hopeless feeling on a bad scenting day when he looks ahead and can see only field after field filled with cattle, sheep and tractors. Also, the question of damage to either stock or crops loomed large in the minds of every Master and huntsman.

The large estates were increasingly split up, resulting in numerous shooting syndicates. Woodlands that used to be hollow underneath, now consisted of acre upon acre of impenetrable brambles, since the high timber had mostly been cut during the war.

"Anti's" appeared on the scene and tried their best to

bewilder hounds and huntsman, traffic-laden main roads and motorways added to the problems, and ever since the war we have lived under continual threat of legislation to stop hunting. With regard to the latter, it is interesting to note that there is really nothing new in this world.

I have always been vastly intrigued by the fact that as long ago as the middle of the last century, Bromley Davenport, in his immortal poem Lowesby Hall (a brilliant parody on Tennyson's Loxby Hall) included the following verse:

Brother Thrusters! Brother Funkers! you may well look rather blue,
For the future that's impending is a queerish one for you.
For I looked into its pages, and I read the Book of Fate,
And saw Foxhunting abolished by an order from the State.

Well, this prophet proved wrong and I have no doubt that our present opponents will fare no better.

So then the foxhound of today must have the ability to deal with all these new difficulties and, in my opinion, he is proving conclusively that he is well able to do so.

What then is the secret of his success?

First of all he must have the ability to keep close to his fox; if he once gets far behind he stands little chance of coming up with him again. To achieve this he must have the conformation to gallop effortlessly, taking the minimum amount of energy out of himself, thus leaving the maximum amount for the mental work involved in hunting and catching the fox.

The mental effort is so important, as a hound must think and react very quickly. He needs tremendous acceleration – straight into top gear if only for a few yards – so as to keep saving precious seconds – and "four-wheel brakes" so as to turn short with his fox.

And it is essential that, if hounds have checked and unsuccessfully made their own cast, they should return to where they last owned the line. If they have drifted on, the huntsman, when he has to take a hand, will be basing his cast on a wrong assumption.

Of course, they must have superlative noses and a heavy tongue: and these two requisites, I believe, have especially gained from outcrosses to Wales.

In 1955 the Foxhound Kennel Stud Book was opened, which has allowed breeders, if they so wished, to find an outcross from packs such as the College Valley, the Fell or the pure Welsh hounds. It is to the benefit of fox-hunting that several discerning Masters are taking advantage of this opportunity, in order to ensure that their options remain open for the future.

People sometimes tell me that they think the modern foxhound is too fast, but it is not the pace at which they can gallop that matters – it is the pace at which they hunt. Any old pack of hounds will beat horses, under present-day conditions, on a screaming scent.

But such days are few and far between, and it is the fast,

intelligent, hard-driving packs of hounds which show sport, and catch foxes, day in and day out, throughout the season. And long may they continue to do so.

LT.-COL. SIR PETER FARQUHAR

* * *

Sir Peter Farquhar's views are controversial. They provoked some fascinating correspondence in Horse and Hound *which provides more than a clue to one of the fundamental differences of opinion in the foxhunting world.*

Defending the "Old-fashioned Foxhound"

SIR, – I am surprised and saddened by the remarks in an article about the old-fashioned foxhound and by the unjust criticisms of those who bred and hunted that noble animal. In my opinion those judgments are totally untrue.

Comparisons are odious, we are told; but when I see some of today's prize winners I see *them* as the real "cripples" – not their old-fashioned predecessors. Too often, the present-day hound is crooked, back at the knee, with feet like an Alsatian and hocks back in the next parish.

It was always understood that the points of a hound were those of a horse – and a horse that wins up and down the country, not the kind that some present-day Masters and judges ride, and expect their staff to ride and hunt hounds on.

I've seen 'em, and it is obvious that their owners know

very little about horses, and cannot tell a good ride from a bad one or they would never buy them. Most of the old-fashioned hounds are straight and may stand over rather than back, with their hocks in under them.

Their cat-like feet will stand up to the wear and tear a damn sight better than the flat-footed, back at the knee specimens we see so much of today. (This also goes for the human race!)

I have been in Hunt service nearly 50 years, beginning as stable lad and becoming successively second whip, first whip and kennel-huntsman before serving as huntsman for 13 years.

For goodness sake, Masters and judges, come away from these Greyhound-Alsatian types that are so fashionable today. Hunting is hunting, not coursing.

Believe me, the type of hounds the old Masters and huntsmen bred should not be allowed to die out. The long hunts we had speak for themselves, and our hounds would last for six or seven seasons. They had stamina and their wonderful feet would bring them home.

Your contributor's description of the Peterborough type simply is not true. They were *not* wide through the chest, big and out at elbow and knuckled over on short pasterns. To say that they could not gallop and had not much inclination to hunt is totally false, and I am surprised to read such a mis-representation.

One of our longest journeys from kennel to meet was 15 miles – several were between 10 and 12. There was no lorrying in those days! Trot on, hunt into the dark, and trot back.

You present-day Masters know nothing about it, and if you do not change your minds about conformation, legs and feet, our packs will surely be the worse for it.

The majority of runs today are of short duration. The

old "Peterborough type" would be so disgusted they would go home and tell the hot bitches they hadn't missed much.

OLD TIME HUNT SERVANT

In Defence of the Modern Hound

SIR, – "Old Time Hunt Servant's" forthright defence of the old Peterborough type of foxhound is less than fair to Sir Peter Farquhar's excellent article.

Sir Peter was far less sweeping in his condemnation of the old type of hound than is alleged by his critic.

I suspect that, as in so many aspects of breeding policy, there is a degree of justification on both sides in comparing the methods of som old foxhounds, and the modern hound.

Yet no matter how much "Old Time Hunt Servant" may huff and puff, it cannot be denied that the breeding initiatives taken by Ikey Bell, Sir Peter Farquhar and others wrought considerable overall improvements in the foxhound – in terms of performance.

It simply is not good enough to condemn modern hunting, and allege that it makes far less demands on the hound than the conditions prevailing earlier in the century when the Peterborough type was so popular.

No one denies that the quality of riding countries has generally deteriorated, but the demands on hounds in *catching* foxes are far greater. To hunt successfully in the modern countryside, with all its variety of foil, barbed wire, busy roads and other distractions, the modern hound must have a superlative nose, and above all, must hunt accurately and very quickly.

The success of the modern foxhound in overcoming

current difficulties manifestly justifies the outcrosses introduced earlier this century.

I would concede, however, that the main problem in most forms of animal breeding is human nature: nearly everyone tends to "jump on the bandwagon" and follow the popular trend.

It is an excellent thing that the "improved modern foxhound" was resisted in certain kennels, such as the Belvoir and the Limerick, and similarly it will be a pity if there are not some kennels who resist the current introduction of new Welsh lines.

These may well be excellent, and Sir Newton Rycroft is to be congratulated on his pioneering work in the New Forest, but it will hardly be necessary to see woolly hounds sprouting in every kennel throughout the land.

But breeding must be a dynamic process; new lines must be found in the long run, and we are fortunate that so much has been achieved in ensuring that the modern foxhound continues to do his job so well, and remains so immeasurably superior to the non-working domestic dog which has, in the main, been totally ruined by commercial breeders following fashion ruthlessly solely to make money.

NEW TIME HUNT SERVANT

Why We Developed Our Type of Hound

SIR, – Much has been said and written since you published Sir Peter Farquhar's very interesting article.

It may, however, have been unfortunate that you, sir, gave it the title "Why they changed the Modern Foxhound," for the implication was that the type of hound Sir Peter produced was modern and all else out of date; hence the "needle" that has crept into the correspondence.

Written by Sir Peter the title should have undoubtedly been: "Why we went to Wales!" or "Why we developed our type of hound."

Mr. Isaac Bell, Sir Peter and Captain Ronnie Wallace produced a type of hound which is today hunting in many, perhaps most, countries.

They knew what they were doing, why they were doing it, and they were brilliantly successful. It may well be more than coincidence that their three principal countries, the South & West Wilts, the Portman, and the Heythrop, have more than a passing similarity.

I do not think that one of them has ever claimed that the answer they came up with was the complete and only possible answer.

If they had the followers of the Wynnstay, the Dumfriesshire and the College Valley, among others, would deny the claim; for in each of these three countries a totally different type of hound has been developed which shows excellent sport in its own country.

Sir Peter in his article made reference to the change in agricultural conditions.

There are, however, two other major changes which make comparison between Foxhunting and hounds today and 40 years ago largely irrelevant. The first of these is the changes that have taken place with regard to the fox.

Mr. Claude Whitley was quoted in your paper as saying that the greatest change in his Mastership of the South Devon was the decline in the wildness of the fox. Add to this their undoubted increase in numbers in many, if not all areas, and you have the basis for a major alteration in sport.

If you go on to consider the results of myxamatosis – a major change in diet, and an increased density of cover or habitat – you find you are hunting a very different animal.

It is one that is more numerous, less fit, has a more limited knowledge of country, is less shy and has denser cover in which to live. It is perhaps remarkable that comparison can be made at all.

I may be wrong but I think that the second major change is the attitude to the sport of a majority of huntsmen. The balance between fox-control and "showing sport" has always been a nice point. But I believe that today more importance is placed on the tally than was formerly the case. The number of foxes, the requirements of the farming population, the difficulties of crossing a country, all these help to tilt this balance.

The long points of former days prove nothing except that foxes were wilder and more adventurous, traffic not so bad – a larger tally may prove nothing but that they are more numerous, or their huntsman more bloodthirsty.

Different conditions bring diferent results – these results do not prove that the hound is better or worse than his predecessors. It has been truly said that comparison is odious.

I am sure only of one thing and that is that the well-bred foxhound is a very wonderful animal whether he is English – Welsh – Fell – American or Kerry Beagle, or a mixture of two or more.

By "well-bred" I mean carefully bred, with the requirements of his country in the mind of the breeder whose study is of bloodlines and qualities not fashion or show.

He is a wonderful animal provided his huntsman respects him, tells him no lies, and allows him to do his job, hunt the fox.

This was as true in the past as it is today – no generation with immunity, for history repeats itself; and today's fashion may be tomorrow's fault. However, in one respect today's hound-breeders do have a great advantage over their predecessors – the appearance of the Epivax innoculation at least removes those ghastly twins distemper and jaundice from the horizon, so that the "well-bred" modern foxhound, of whatever type, should at least survive!

JOHN WILLIAMS
Much Fawley, Hereford

* * *

The main focus of hound judging during the summer months is Peterborough Royal Foxhound Show. The Prince of Wales accepted the Presidency of the Show in 1978, an immensely popular presidency, since Prince Charles is a particularly keen hunting man and has made many friends in visiting Hunts all over Britain.

In 1975 Princess Anne was President of the Show, and Dermot Kelly wrote a fascinating description of the unique atmosphere of this great annual institution, held on the Alwalton showground, near Peterborough, during the annual East of England agricultural and horse show.

Dermot Kelly was one of the most successful Masters and amateur huntsmen in the Midlands, being in office at the Meynell before and after its amalgamation with the South Staffordshire. He is a keen hound breeder, and is noted for his pungent comments expressed without fear or favour on and off the hunting field, but leavened with a sense of humour and great enthusiasm for the sport.

Why Peterborough Is Unique

WHAT an institution Peterborough Royal Foxhound Show is – and truly royal this year with Princess Anne attending as the President next Wednesday.

Her Royal Highness and Capt. Mark Phillips have proved themselves in the hunting field as true foxhunters. In addition, the Prince of Wales has more recently taken to foxhunting, following in the steps of their ancestors; surely the best thing to happen to foxhunting for many years.

Let nobody doubt that this year's President is a knowledgeable foxhunter. Last summer she judged some unusual hounds at a puppy show, and did the job very well indeed.

Showing hounds at Peterborough, or for that matter elsewhere, is a serious game, but it is an amusing summer game which *shows the standard of hound to be reached for*, and is no substitute for foxhunting.

Some people say that it is undesirable to show hounds, in that it encourages Masters to breed from a prizewinner whether it is a good hunter or not.

Any owner of a prizewinning hound that is *not* good in its work and who encourages its use is doing a grave disservice to foxhunting. Equally, any M.F.H. who uses a stallion hound knowing that it is not top class in its work needs his head examining.

Luckily for breeders of foxhounds, most of the main and consistent prize-winning packs at Peterborough are also high up amongst the leading packs famous for their sport and the number of foxes they account for.

Perhaps this tells its own tale, for if a hound is good in its conformation, it should be able to hunt more efficiently and with less effort, and thus with this economy of effort be able to devote more of its time to developing "fox-sense," which is the most vital characteristic of a top class hound.

Of course there are exceptions to this rule; of individual ugly hounds being brilliant in their work, but I have noticed that these hounds, although they may be brilliant themselves, tend not to run up at top pace into their fifth or subsequent seasons, and are ultimately less valuable to a huntsman than the brilliant hound with good conformation who has greater longevity.

Another important factor is that ugly hounds will probably pass on many of their worst characteristics to their progeny, and then you have a hard job in eradicating the worst conformation faults in future generations.

Sometimes M.F.Hs and other hunting people say that they couldn't care less what their hounds look like as long as they hunt, and that their hounds are as good as any in the British Isles, etc, etc.

Well that is all right so far as it goes, but one sometimes wonders with what they are comparing them. Class hounds, like class horses or class anything else, must in the end beat the non- class ones all ends up.

If on account of one's weight or pocket one has to hunt common horses, well so be it, but there is no need, except through choice or ignorance to hunt common hounds; it can only be a handicap and the only thing to benefit is the fox.

Some kennels sometimes have a famous hunting strain

who are great fox catchers, and are a bit comical to look at. Obviously such a strain wants treasuring. Generally if you look at their conformation objectively there is not too much wrong with it.

At the Meynell we had our D line who were brilliant but a bit comical to look at. When we eventually produced a show hound from this line the b........ thing wouldn't hunt at all – which slightly destroys my argument!

Judging at Peterborough can be an awe-inspiring business, with the ring surrounded by all the experts and would be experts, who no doubt think they know very much more than the judge. They may well be right too!

Luckily it is not possible to judge hounds from the ringside, as you have to be able to stand over them properly in the ring to be effective. And anyway when all is said and done, it is the judge's opinion on the day which counts.

Some Hunt servants are masters of the showing game. If their hounds have a fault, they are quite rightly all out to conceal it from the judges. The judges can make this more difficult for them, if they insist on the hounds being off the couples straight away when they come into the ring to give their show.

The judges will also be able to notice a hound's faults when the hound is relaxing when it is back on the couples. No Hunt servant can keep his hounds alert and up to the biscuit all the time, so the judge needs eyes in the back of his head!

The two couple class is often a difficult one to judge, but often there are three good ones in the entry and one less good which the expert showman will keep well covered up; again it is much more difficult for him when the hounds are giving their show loose.

What an honour it is to judge at any puppy show or hound show, but of course the ultimate honour is to judge at Peterborough. If you thought you knew what you were doing before you started, by the end of the judging you may well be only too aware how little you knew.

It is all taken very seriously, and it has been known for certain famous M.F.H's to make their displeasure known if their hounds have been placed incorrectly.

It is sometimes wise for the judges to take avoiding action after the judging is over to avoid a confrontation until tempers have cooled!

One must never take oneself too seriously judging. I thought I was very important when I was asked to judge at Honiton one year. I was staying with a well known foxhunting lady who lives in the West Country, but hunts in the Midlands.

As I was leaving her house to go to the show, I said to her "I hope I'll see you later at the show." She replied "You certainly won't. All those b......... hounds get in *my* way more than enough in the winter without wasting my time going to see them in the summer".

I was forced to see what she meant sometimes when she hunted with me subsequently!

I remember another time when I was due to judge at Clonmel in Ireland and I was staying with a famous M.F.H. It became obvious that we were going to get to the show rather late, so I said to him "I think we had better try to speed up a bit."

He replied "I'm going as slow as I can as my hounds left the kennels late, and the b......... can't start the judging until you get there!"

But more seriously, what a day it will be next week, some of the finest hounds in the land being judged in front of their President. The whole ring will be a kaleidoscope of colour, surrounded by a smartly turned out audience; there to show and express their interest in that unique animal THE FOXHOUND.

DERMOT KELLY

* * *

Daphne Moore here provides more historical background to Peterborough, and looks at the other major hound shows: the South of England at Ardingly; the Welsh at Builth Wells; the North of England at Harrogate; and the West of England at Honiton.

Looking Ahead to the Hound Shows

THE hunting season is ended for many. Sooner than it seems possible, the fixture cards bear the words: *To Finish The Season*, and our thoughts turn to the summer shows, those enjoyable gatherings which help so successfully to pass the foxhunters' so-called "idle summer".

Peterborough, of course, admits of no comparison. There is but one Peterborough. Nevertheless, the satellite shows are each, in their own way, excellent and the hounds shown nowadays are usually of a high standard.

Each show has its own particular distinctive personality. Peterborough has all the *elegance* in the world; bowler-hatted Masters of Foxhounds in well-cut Savile Row suits are accompanied by their ladies, dressed as for a garden party, with fashionable hats and charming dresses. The inevitable tightly-rolled umbrellas carried by the men are almost part of the igsignia of Peterborough.

It is a great place for meeting friends, for renewing acquaintances, for hound-talk and hunting-talk; while, of course, the hounds, their presentation, their judging, their points, their merits and de-merits, are all-absorbing.

It is always a gay and colourful scene; the red Hunt coats, white breeches and well-polished boots may be an anomaly in July, but they add greatly to the pageantry. The stiff collars, umbrellas and bowler hats may be old-fashioned to the "mods" of 1974 – but which of us would have it otherwise?

During that intensely hot Peterborough of 1969, when the temperatures soared into the 90s, even those to whom tropical heat is almost worse than death scarcely noticed it, for it was one of the highest-class shows for many years, and the hounds and their judging held all our attention.

Nearly a century has passed since the first Peterborough Show, held in 1878. The site was then at Boroughbury, where it remained until 1886. After that the showground was at Millfield, and eventually it found its resting-place in 1911 at Eastfield.

This popular ground survived two world wars; it was honoured by a number of Royal visitors, from King Edward VII (while Prince of Wales) to our present Queen and the Queen Mother.

There is no doubt that it saw a great metamorphosis in the make and shape of the foxhound exhibited upon its sacred flags. The hounds which won championships in the early part of this century were built on very different lines from those which were winning in the '50s and '60s.

The post-war champions have, for the most part, been very far removed from the massive, over-knuckling, pigeon-toed animals which delighted the judges 50 years ago. If one contrasts pictures of the two types it is hard to believe that *both* were bred with a view to catching foxes!

The lovely quality, active foxhounds, which graced the Eastfield ground in its latter years were made for speed and stamina alike, and were surely more danger to the fox population than their weighty predecessors.

In 1965 the last show was held at Eastfield before moving to a new area outside the city of Peterborough, at Alwalton. The Duke of Beaufort was president of the show that year, and, as he so rightly said, the year of 1965 marked the end of a tradition that increased in popularity over nearly a century.

"It is sad to think," he wrote, "that we shall never again meet our friends on this acre of ground that has known so many triumphs and disappointments."

That, however, was nearly a decade ago. "Royal Peterborough" (it was given the Royal title by permission of King George V in 1934) has shaken itself and settled down happily at last in its new surroundings.

Tension, drama and excitement have been enacted here as at the old ground. Indeed, in the very first year at Alwalton the Earl Fitzwilliam Champion Cup for the best bitch in the show was won for Ireland by the lovely Tipperary Grizzle '64 – the first time this cup ever left the country.

It was a most popular victory, however, and was greeted with an exuberance very rare at Peterborough. Cheers, clapping and shouts of applause lasted for minutes, and were only matched by the enthusiasm which welcomed the similar triumph of Eridge Freedom '60 on the old showground in 1964. This was an immense victory for Ireland, and for the "Tipps" on their first visit to Peterborough.

Then only last year, came an unexpected drama, again in the bitch championship, when West Kent Payment '72 was given the award against formidable opposition. It was nearly a quarter of a century since this pack was represented at Peterborough.

In 1970 the Warwickshire won the champion cup, given by the Duke of Beaufort, for the best doghound in all classes with Partner '68. In Peterborough's early days the Warwickshire were frequent winners; but they had not won a championship since 1909, with Trickster, 1908, and great was the rejoicing among their supporters.

The Duke of Beaufort's and the Heythrop are, of course, consistent winners, and every year the green coat-sleeves of their respective huntsman and kennel-huntsman are covered with prize-winners' rosettes.

How well-deserved these victories are! The proverbial "Badminton backs," the superb quality and perfect conformation of the hounds representing these two kennels are too wellknown to require description.

The Duke of Beaufort's have won 21 champion cups since the war; whilst the Heythrop (who never showed at Peterborough until 1955) have a total of 14.

One of the major changes at today's foxhound shows

LUNCH TIME

in comparison with those of our fathers' and grandfathers' day is the prevalence of light-coloured hounds. In most kennels during the fashion of "Belvoir Tan," light-coated whelps were ruthlessly weeded out.

But in the 1930s, due principally to the use of Tiverton Actor '22 at Badminton and Sir Edward Curre's blood in a number of kennels, light-coated hounds began to be shown at Peterborough and even to win championships.

Gradually, the tide having turned at last, Belvoir Tan became less as white, lemon-and-white, hare-pie and badger-pie increased.

In the very strong two couples bitch class at Peterborough in 1969, when the ring was thronged with a galaxy of beauty numbering no less than 60 hounds at the same time, almost all were light-coated. At the start of the century this scene could not have been imagined, much less become reality.

The artistry of the huntsmen or kennel-huntsmen responsible for showing the hounds is, nowadays, of a very high standard and it is fascinating to see the various tactics which they adopt to keep their charges alert and looking their best. *Suspense* is the keynote, and the hounds should always be kept guessing, and their attention never allowed to flag.

In chronological order, the subsidiary shows are: Ardingly, Builth Wells, Harrogate and Honiton.

Ardingly (the South of England Show), is now the permanent showground for what was formerly Aldershot, briefly Kingsclere, but since 1968 has found its lasting home in Sussex. Large entries and expert judges have helped to make a great success of this show.

The Welsh Hound Show, held at Builth, is a well-organized and intensely interesting affair; the only recognized hound show at which one can see the Welsh foxhound in its native setting. And not only Welsh, but some high-class English hounds, and beagles, too, judged simultaneously in adjoining rings.

Harrogate takes place the week before Peterborough, and frequently some of the same hounds are shown at both, which provides added interest. This is the show for the North-country man; the Peterborough of the north, no less!

At Honiton, it is the turn of the West-country, and what a warm-hearted, friendly show it is, with a flavour all of its own. It is also often a show of many surprises; champions have been toppled here and quite often unexpected decisions made.

I wonder what 1974 will bring in the way of new champions? What Peterborough will have up her voluminous sleeve? Maybe some hitherto unknown kennel will achieve a meteoric rise to fame.

To the student of foxhound breeding, one item of outstanding importance would be the emergence in the doghound championship, or other doghound prize-winners, of a new male line, a much-required and desirable factor to revitalize the modern foxhound. It remains to be seen whether fresh tails-male will become established in the Foxhound Kennel Stud Book since the amendment to Rule 28 in 1955 – but only *four* established male lines are all too few.

DAPHNE MOORE

* * *

Whilst the public appearances of hounds at shows are important, the work in the kennel and the hunting country during the summer months is the most vital of all in ensuring sport in the winter months ahead. Dermot Kelly deals with the question which may occasionally have occurred to the Hunt subscriber who only sees his M.F.H. in a red coat.

What Does a Master Do in the Summer?

MANY hunting people, having finished hunting themselves during March with much regret, but not wanting to partake or hear about the sport until November, often wonder what on earth the Master does with himself during these months.

No doubt some of them inagine that he immediately takes off for foreign places and spends a substantial part of the guarantee!

The Master himself is probably quite relieved when the end of the season has arrived. He may well have hunted on about 100 days and is a trifle stale; probably also he hasn't many sound horses left.

The farmers, particularly if it has been a wet season, have had enough of him.

Also his urge to see the fox caught has probably diminished, as he will know of quite a few litters about. So it is with only slight regret that he blows home for the last time.

More than likely he will not have been away from his country hardly at all since the beginning of the cub-hunting, so he may well take the opportunity to have a break somewhere; with or most likely without the guarantee! In any case this will undoubtedly have been spent, with some of his own money as well, on running his country.

What is he to do about the horses? He may well have a top-class stud, but they are getting older, and there are one or two showing a bit of wear and tear. If he keeps them on, eventually they will have lost most of their value and it will almost certainly cost him a small fortune to replace them.

On the other hand if he sends them all up to Leicester Sales, he will find it a hard job to replace them altogether, let alone the strain on his nerves riding a fresh lot that he and his Hunt staff do not know at the start of the new season.

Probably he will compromise, and send some of the older horses with one or two of the star turns to help sell the others. The star turns can, after all, have a very high reserve put on them!

What is he to do about that ghastly pile of bills, which he has been putting off paying? Well, there is only one answer – pay them!

It is now that he realizes, with a sickening feeling in the pit of his stomach, what it has all cost, and goodness knows what it will cost for the next season. By now he is probably in the depths of depression, and cursing himself for saying that he would go on for another season!

And it will only take a row with his wife, or Joint-Master, or Hunt chairman, or most likely the Hunt secretary to make him finally take to the bottle.

Probably he has an ominously long list of farmers to see, who have been upset in some way during the season, and whom he had promised to see *again* during the spring or early summer. Luckily, memories are short and nature is a wonderful healer, so he will probably be pleasantly surprised as to the reception he gets from the farmer, and with a bit of luck you won't be able to see where the Hunt had been on the grass, or where some unmentionable fools had jumped into the corn!

By April the last of the young hounds will have come in from walk, and maybe it looks like being a good entry – maybe there even looks to be a Peterborough winner amongst them – all one's geese tend to look like swans at this time of year! Anyway, it cheers our Master up no end, and he actually begins to look forward again to the new season.

He arranges for the whelps to go out to walk, and probably goes round the puppy walkers himself doing the puppies' injections, as that not only saves money but also enables him to see the most long-suffering and nicest group of people that he will ever meet.

He has his own puppy show to organize, the judges to invite, the marquee and tea to order, and prizes to be bought. Certainly it will be the highlight of the summer, and apart from anything else it ensures that the kennels, stables and premises are given a really good spring clean, so that they are at their smartest and best for the puppy walkers, whose day it is.

Our Master will probably want to go to the major

hound shows and if he is lucky he may be invited to judge at other Masters' puppy shows. Whatever else changes in this world, puppy shows mercifully remain the same over the length and breadth of the land.

At the hound shows, he will see the standard to be reached for, and at both will meet other like-minded people, and he may find a stallion hound to use in the future.

Also during the spring and summer there will be working parties to organize, to lay coverts, cut rides and generally try to improve the coverts and woods. In addition the Hunt's damage man will be putting in new hunting gates, bridges and, where there is no alternative, tiger traps and jumping places, and maintaining the existing ones – all these activities will be under the Master's direction.

Hound exercise starts towards the end of June, for which stable staff have to be engaged, and the cub-hunters got up from grass. The hay, straws and oats have to be obtained for the ensuing season.

The Master, if hunting his hounds, must get them fit, handy and steady on sheep, hens, cattle and cur dogs. It is not often acknowledged what a feat this is.

Just imagine taking up to 100 of whatever breed your own pet dog is for a walk across the countryside, and imagine what would happen – the mind boggles at the thought.

Cubhunting in most countries gets going when enough corn is cut, generally at the beginning of September. I often think cubhunting is a bad name. Non-hunting people imagine that you are pursuing a small, rather lovable furry animal, and do not realize that the cubs have matured into fully-grown young foxes, which need an expert to tell apart from an old fox.

I think autumn foxhunting would be a more accurate and appropriate description.

Many hunting people do not understand cubhunting, and I suppose never will. It is the Master's private hunting in order to educate foxes and hounds alike, and it is also the time when the fox population is most effectively controlled.

Officially, anybody wishing to go out cubhunting, whether on a horse or on foot, should ask the Master's permission. In effect, the Master will most likely be only too glad to have anybody's assistance, whether they have observed this courtesy or not.

Certainly the foot people, who are generally far more knowledgeable about foxhunting than the mounted field, come into their own and take a leading part in the proceedings. The more tiresome members of the mounted followers, who only want to gallop and jump or gossip, are much better employed at a hunter trial or similar activity.

By now all the horses will be up from grass, and our Master may well reflect that he has had a busy summer. In addition to all the above, he will have attended most of his Supporters' Club activities and some Pony Club ones, as well as attending numerous other activities in his country.

That first morning's cubhunting will be imminent; early in the morning with the dew on the ground and the day just breaking, that marvellous moment when the old hounds open to their first fox, and the young hounds leave his horse's side to go to the glorious cry – surely the best music in the world.

Then all the problems of modern day foxhunting disappear in a flash, and any Master, whether hunting his hounds or not, will realize what a very lucky man he is, and he will reflect that he would not change places with anybody in the world.

DERMOT KELLY

* * *

Summer hunting's most active ingredient is hound exercise. Here, Foxford describes a hound exercise ride with Captain Ronnie Wallace on Exmoor.

There's So Much More to Hound Exercise than "Taking the Dog for a Walk"

It is often said that the sport in the winter months is made during "summer hunting." Many foxhunters will nod sagely at this remark but hardly know what it really means.

Part of the summer task for the Master is to ensure that the country is in "good order". The wise Master will have made sure that he has had plenty of opportunities during the summer months to meet socially as many landowners and farmers as possible in his country, especially newcomers, and he will have a pretty good idea what is happening in and around the major coverts in his country long before cubhunting commences.

It is, of course, the quality and performance of hounds which will make or mar the season's sport ahead. The care of brood bitches and their whelps, finding puppy walkers for young hounds, and a satisfactory summer routine for the older hounds in kennel, are all important. Yet one of the vital aspects of summer work for the huntsman, which is seldom seen or understood even by those who have ridden to hounds for many years, is the mounted hound exercise which immediately precedes cubhunting.

I was once asked by a foreign publication if I could contribute an article on "the training of the foxhound." The overseas editor, in his letter, clearly thought that a foxhound was trained much the same as a police dog or a gun dog to perform a specific task. The fact is, of course, that the training of a hound in a pack is a far more subtle business, much of the training being achieved by the older hounds.

The psychology and group behaviour of a pack of hounds is fascinating indeed, and I am surprised that some erudite chap has not yet chosen it for his thesis at University. One of the most interesting television programmes I have ever seen illustrated the behaviour of a pack of wild dogs in East Africa; their ability to hunt as a team, and their domestic social behaviour, where nature ensured that the fittest survived, sometimes cruelly at the expense of the lives of the weakest members of the pack.

In a much modified form, of course, the behaviour of a pack of hounds inevitably has something in common with customs of wilder brethren, with the vital distinction that the pack's teamwork is totally subject to the discipline of human domination.

Apart from the obvious economic advantages to the Hunt, the importance of puppy walking is that it puts a young hound closely in touch with human influence at a formative stage in its development, sharpening its intelligence and making it more responsive to human command.

Yet much remains to be done when the young foxhound returns to the pack and is about to be entered for the job for which it has been bred for the past 200 years at least, with a degree of skill and selection outmatching any other hunting dog in the world.

Therefore, I was fascinated the other day to be able to accompany a highly experienced amateur huntsman who was taking his hounds out for exercise only a few weeks before cubhunting. We assembled at 7 a.m. at the kennels; the Master, a Joint-Master, two whippers-in and myself. Hound exercise conjures up a cosy, easy-going prospect. It was to be a far more arduous and interesting morning than I had expected.

Light rain was falling as we mounted, and we walked out of the kennels amid a veritable carpet of hounds, for we were taking 39½ couple, about 40 per cent of them unentered. When you consider that a huntsman usually takes about 15 to 18 couple out on a hunting day, the size of our pack out at hound exercise can be more easily imagined.

One young bitch hound was coupled with a short length of chain, from a collar, to the collar of a large and sagacious-looking doghound.

"She's always stopping to pick up rubbish that one," said the whipper-in laconically.

Much of the country was grass, moorland, with some

thick woodland as well. Soon we were off the road and the huntsman jogged across a field, but in the next field he broke into a hand canter and hounds streamed all around him, a marvellous sight, with the whippers-in riding out on the flank and, I noticed, not making overt attempts to keep hounds "on" to the huntsman all the time.

The pack was allowed considerable freedom in the open, but the older, entered hounds, kept as close to the huntsman's horse as possible, and most of the unentered hounds followed their example.

There were occasionally a few exceptions. I looked round and saw one hound standing half a field back, gazing uncertainly after the retreating sterns of her friends, but for some reason unwilling to follow.

"Don't look back," shouted the huntsman. "Let her make her own mind up." It was just like dealing with a recalcitrant child who hangs back, when the elders are walking ahead, on an outing. Eventually the young hound lingering behind did catch up, and clearly the pressure of conforming with the behaviour and movements of the rest of the pack was the dominant factor on these occasions.

Soon we entered a wood and rode along narrow paths. Here, there was obviously acute danger of a fox getting up and a mass hunt getting under way all too quickly. The whippers-in kept hounds together, and reproved the occasional older hound who wandered off the main path to sniff enquiringly at thickets. Soon we were through the wood without any trouble.

Afterwards the Master told me: "There was slight risk in going through such a place with so many hounds, and if they had got away, even temporarily, it would have done the pack no good at all. On the other hand, it was well worth the risk, because going through such a place in a disciplined way together does the young hounds a great deal of good."

In the next open field some of the older hounds certainly behaved as if a fox had moved on just before we got there, but they were quickly put on to the main body of the pack, and we continued without any trouble.

The next stage of hound exercise was the most interesting, and instructive of all.

Hounds were taken through a field containing a large flock of sheep. The huntsman cantered along the side of a field well away from the flock, with hounds all round him, but he was keeping a sharp eye on the hounds on his flank. Just one hound took a little interest in the sheep, and veered off in their direction, merely looking at them inquisitively, yet continuing to go in the same direction as the rest of the pack.

That was enough! Immediately the huntsman pulled up and said, "that one," pointing to the hound concerned. The whipper-in jumped off his horse straight away, ran up to the hound, seized it by the stern and gave it a drubbing on either side of the ribs with the whip.

The hound rolled on his back and shrieked. He was not being hurt physically very much at all, but his feelings were indeed ruffled; the indignity of the whole thing, right in front of the rest of the pack, was clearly what was upsetting him most of all. The huntsman, remaining on his horse, kept growling at the hound and calling his name, and it was fascinating to observe the reactions of the other hounds in the pack. Older hounds looked like elderly aunts who have just heard a niece swear during a picnic, and the young hounds looked aghast, horrified at the treatment meted out to one of their fellows. The whipper-in remounted and the exercise was repeated a number of times near sheep.

"Hounds must be as steady as a rock with sheep and all other forms of riot, such as deer or hare, must be similarly discouraged firmly," said the huntsman later.

"Just one hound can cause untold trouble, and you must find out which hound is likely to be the trouble-maker. It can have a chance or two during hound exercise, but I would not give such a hound even one chance during cubhunting. Any nonsense then, and the hound must go out of the pack straight away."

Soon we were out on open moorland, and this time hounds were confronted by black-faced sheep which lie in the heather and spring up in front of hounds, smelling very similar to a deer. Hounds were taken right through a flock of sheep grazing out on the moor, and I saw some get up and actually bump into the hounds, yet every hound, whether unentered or a veteran, studiously ignored the sheep and continued on its way with all the seriousness of a city gent being accosted by a street urchin whilst on the way to the office.

During the morning we stopped at several farm-houses. Farmers, and sometimes their wives and children too, came to the gate and admired the throng of hounds standing patiently around the huntsman's horse.

"Yes, of course we shall look forward to seeing you here during the season," they said. And various useful pieces of information were passed about the whereabouts of litters of cubs, and the best routes across their land. Goodwill? As we sat in a farmyard drinking a glass of milk – with something stronger in it – there was no need to be reminded that foxhunting is still a major part of country life and exists only with the co-operation and participation of country people.

It was nearly one o'clock when we eventually returned to the kennels – five hours of hound exercise, in which the pack had certainly been exercised but, just as important, had extended its education.

"Just poking about in gateways while I talk to people is very good for the hounds, quite apart from the reminders about sheep," said the Master with a smile. As hounds returned to their lodges, I had a feeling there was going to be much new material for "thought and discussion" among the young hounds in kennels that night . . . and all of it would be in the interests of sport in the season ahead.

FOXFORD

Autumn

Autumn is the time when young hounds are introduced to the sport through cubhunting. They are put into the coverts to cull the foxes. Most of the young hound's education is gained from his older brothers and sisters in the pack.

For the huntsman it is a vital period of the hunting year, when he may make a pack which will work together effectively later in the season. In some countries the coverts are "heldup", although not rigorously. Mounted and foot followers stand around each covert and attempt to deter foxes from running into the open. Many will do so, despite these "holding up" activities, but hounds will hunt and kill foxes mainly inside the covert at this time of the year.

Meets are arranged in the early hours when the dew is still on the grass, and scent is likely to be better than later in the day when autumn sunshine so often blazes down.

Horse and Hound*'s celebrated weekly columnist Loriner sets the scene for cubhunting.*

Song of September

"EVERYONE suddenly burst out singing." It is appropriate that it was Siegfried Sassoon who wrote that, because it was Siegfried Sassoon who wrote *The Memoirs of a Foxhunting Man* and it is foxhunting that has inspired me to start this article with that quotation, though it was not foxhunting that originally inspired it.

Yes, foxhunting is with us again – just. This year, with the appalling weather in August it seemed as though, in our part of the country at any rate, cubhunting would never get started.

Eventually, however, it did, thanks to a large wood from which it is difficult enough to evict foxes at the height of the season and from which cubs are most unlikely to leave, leading hounds into isolated fields of corn still standing.

For plenty of fields outstanding there still are, alas. And unless the weather picks up, as surely it must soon, it is not going to be easy to keep going; and not easy, therefore, to get round the country in time for the opening meet.

Nevertheless, we have made a start, and that is something, though it was by no means the romantic scene that one would have liked: no sun glinting through the mist, cobwebs hanging magically along the hedgerows, the fields a carpet of dew.

It was not like that at all. It was damp, half drizzling, lowering clouds; the mud squelching like November, puddles in the gutter; everything drab, dreary, depressing.

But for many there was magic enough: just the sight of the hounds, waving their sterns in eager anticipation, their eyes never leaving the figures of their huntsman – sitting patiently, happily on his cubhunter – a useful cob lent to him by a farmer friend – his coat stained and dark, his cap torn, with the peak irregular.

On the fringe the whipper-in on something little more than a pony, flicking his whip to keep the young ones from wandering.

Yes, for many there was magic in the picture absent from the English countryside for five long months and more; a magic reflected in the little band of faithful foot-followers for whom the sight of the hounds each Saturday is the week's highlight.

Nor is it only Saturdays, for many of those up to greet the hounds at 7 o'clock showed by their carriage and their lined faces that their working days were over. For them it is the hounds as often as possible.

Some have their cars or scooters, many follow on

bicycle; a few still rely on their feet, and it is for such that cubhunting provides the best of foxhunting, for hounds do not cover so much country.

The little crowd swells every minute. One or two arrive mounted, their hunters looking fat and ungainly, except, of course, for the children, who incidentally far out-number the adults. Their ponies are, for the most part, positively sylph-like after a summer holiday of gymkhanas, Pony Club camps, shows, sponsored rides and the like.

But those on foot easily out-number the mounted, and will do so for several weeks, the bad weather having discouraged people from getting in their hunters – which in due course they might regret, for it is unlikely that the opening meet will be delayed whether or not the country has been properly cubhunted. The best part of the season, the weeks before Christmas when holdups are unlikely, is far too short in any case.

A few minutes past seven and a move is made. Politely the huntsman asks various mounted people to go to a vantage point. "Give him a turn if he should pop out" – a not very likely proposition, which means a not very interesting assignment for those asked to co-operate; not that they are likely to complain, knowing, hopefully, that during cubhunting they are the guests of the Master and expected to be co-operative.

A note on the horn and hounds move towards the wood, followed by the little army of enthusiasts. The whipper-in opens the gate and the older hounds, needing no encouragement, dive into the covert. The young ones, less certain, hesitate, pausing on the ride looking up at their huntsman.

"Leu-in, there! Leu in!" He rides down the muddy track, not yet harassing the young hounds, as yet a little

bewildered. They follow him, uncertain. Occasionally one follows an older hound in; another sits down to contemplate the matter.

Suddenly a hound speaks, then another; in a moment the old hounds, as if they had never missed a day since March, are united in a chorus.

The huntsman cheers them on and sounds his horn. A number of the young hounds on the ride dive instinctively into the covert to join the music, forcing their way through the thicket, struggling to get to the others.

The chorus moves down the side of the ride. Then, not 10 yards in front of the huntsman, a cub pops out on to the ride. A little startled, it hesitates, one foot poised in the

air, then, glancing furtively at the huntsman, it hops across the ride and disappears into the undergrowth the other side.

The leading hounds are not far behind, and in a matter of seconds are streaming across the ride. First one, then another of the young hounds are compelled, by instinct, breeding, excitement to join the rest of the pack, encouraged by the huntsman, now doubling his horn and making the whole woodland ring to his fine, falsetto voice.

Tally-ho over! The cub is over the next ride. Another tally-ho over farther on suggests that there is more than one afoot, a litter perhaps. There are, as a rule, at least two litters in this great stronghold. A faint tally-ho back up at the top suggests that one old one has tried to sneak away.

A roar from a gang of foot-followers at the cross-roads where the two main rides meet informs the huntsman of yet another cub – but divides the pack.

For the next 20 minutes two separate choruses can be heard, punctuated by holloas, tally-ho overs and various other raucous sounds that pass for enthusiastic information to the huntsman. But topping all is the huntsman's dedicated, experienced voice and the thrilling note of his horn.

Tally-ho over! Another! And so on until "That's enough for this morning."

A brace of cubs has been accounted for; the young hounds have begun to learn what it's all about. We are cubhunting again and . . . "Everyone suddenly burst out singing," as Siegfried Sassoon did more than half a century ago, as his ancestors and our ancestors did one, two, three centuries ago.

LORINER

* * *

Martin Scott is a keen Master of Foxhounds and amateur huntsman. He was a great success in the Tiverton country and then joined the V.W.H. in these roles in 1977. He describes what the start of a season means to him.

Cubhunting

When Autumn is flaunting his banner of pride
For glory that summer has fled,
Arrayed in the robes of his royalty, dyed
In tawny and orange and red;
When oak is yet rife with the vigour of life,
Though the acorns are dropping below,
Through the bramble and brake shall the echoes awake,
To the ring of a clear Tally-Ho!

G. J. WHYTE-MELVILLE

"CUBHUNTING" not cubbing, I remember my sister correcting me long ago, as we were struggling to pull on our jodhpurs at 4 a.m. before rushing downstairs to boiled eggs and toast and then hacking to the meet.

The difference for me between now and then is vast, for in those days I had no responsibility (except to try to turn the odd cub back and remain on my pony without doing any mischief to anyone or anything – and failing in both duties). Little did I realise the vast amount of work involved in organizing just one day's hunting, let alone a season.

Cubhunting is one of the most enjoyable times for a huntsman for he can concentrate fully on educating his young hounds and hunting the fox without having to show sport to a large mounted field. The monotonous yet necessary hound exercise will be over, and hunting takes its place.

The excitement before the first morning is hard to describe; I know I always find it hard to sleep before the start of the season. The hounds also seem to know when the season is about to start, and it is a delight to hear them singing the night before the first morning.

I find it a real pleasure to see the hounds one has bred entering, and this season's entry is better than ever.

What a wonderful autumn we have had, some of the early morning sights have been a feast for the eyes. From our kennels we can see the sun rising over the distant Blackdown Hills, and how beautiful this view has been this season. It may have been too dry for some people, and after such a glorious summer a lot of our farmers are short of hay. As most motorway drivers will have noticed, straw has been brought down to the West Country from East Anglia in vast quantities to help offset the likely food shortage.

The difference between last season and this is extreme, for last season you will remember the terrible time when a mass of corn was not cut at all, and on most days cubhunting we returned home soaked to the skin.

This year it has been much better and all the harvest has been gathered in, although not very good yields have been had. The ground is hard and dry and the few showers we have had so far have made little difference. Hunting has been hot for hounds and horses; yet dry, making it more enjoyable for the followers.

On most occasions scent has been better outside covert than in, and it has been necessary to let the cubs go a lot earlier than usual. I believe in taking every advantage there is for hounds, and an early morning start is more than beneficial, especially with a good dew and before the sun gets really hot.

Last year in my article some people may have thought that I had over-emphasized the importance of "cry". And this year they will be saying what about "nose".

As well as shape full well he knows,
To kill their Fox they must have nose.

. . . as Jorrocks said to himself when hunting his hounds on The Cat and Custard Pot day. However, he did go on to say "that to kill their Fox they must press 'im, at some period o' the chase."

Hounds with good noses have been invaluable this season so far, and most kennels have one or two lines with extra good noses. We have a bitch named Panda ('73) who is a great road hunter and all her family have been renowned for their noses.

She goes back to Old Berkshire Bashful ('58), who produced a mass of good noses for that pack, and she goes back to Portman Maxim ('31), an old favourite of my father's who was bred by Sir E. Curre.

Lord Willoughby de Broke, in his book *Hunting the Fox*, wrote that the primary object to cubhunting is to teach the young hounds to hunt, and in addition to complete the education of last year's entry. There are various ways of doing this; Loriner wrote quite recently in *Horse and Hound* about two different schools of thought concerning cubhunting.

There are those in favour of hunting the big woodlands, so teaching young hounds to find and make them go to the cry of the older hounds. Then there are those who prefer to hold-up when smaller coverts are visited and young hounds really get amongst the cubs and certainly learn what it is all about.

I believe in both methods and try to arrange the meets accordingly, so that following a "holding-up day," when hounds may have caught a lot of foxes and may have been handled a bit too much, the next time they go out they are left almost completely alone and have more of a woodland-type day.

I had gathered throughout the summer that there were many more litters about than usual, and therefore I thought it would be necessary to put in some extra days cubhunting. Having a certain amount of corn in our country an earlier start than normal was impossible to forecast.

With our hardworking staff already doing more than their fair share of work, as well as lack of horse power, an extra morning a week was out of the question. So I decided to try some evening cubhunting on foot, while continuing to go out regularly three mornings a week.

The advantages of this were that it would enable us to get round a few more of the coverts, and the young hounds would get more hunting to start with. (I do not like to take out too many young hounds together, for if there are too many of them they are unlikely to learn so much, and more likely to get into trouble.)

Hopefully, scent should improve with the temperature dropping as the evening goes on and dew may begin to form. It would not be too hot for hounds and would give more people a chance to come out hunting, for the necessary early mornings are a bit too early for some!

Evening cubhunting was only practicable up to the end of September because of the nights drawing in. Darkness always came too quickly for me, and the thought of losing hounds on an old fox was worrying. Luckily the one time hounds hunted an old one away scent was not too good and we were able to stop them eventually.

Careful selection of the right covert was important, and although a great deal of care was taken two certain finds were blank, and the alternative places nearby were not really suitable for evening cubhunting.

To sum up, hounds were out on 32 days and caught 40½ brace (22½ above ground). The great majority of these were caught in September, when the dry yet settled weather made scenting conditions better than October, when the occasional rain storm was followed by dry, easterly winds which made scenting conditions bad.

Although the evenings were not always successful (when is hunting ever completely successful?), I think the gret enthusiasm and support for evening hunting made it thoroughly worth while, and it will certainly be considered again. With the mass of foxes about, everything looks set for a really good season. Good hunting!

MARTIN SCOTT

* * *

Arthur James takes a more light-hearted look at cubhunting, but there are many truths in his examination of the rewards, and the ordeal, which cubhunting may present to the huntsman.

"Leu in! We're Cubhunting at Long Last"

THE first morning's cubhunting: if the thought of it does not make your turgid summer blood bubble a little, and send a little tingle down your spine, then, bless you, you will never be a foxhunter.

It looks like an early cubhunting this droughty year. As I write this I know that some packs have already started. From my study window I can see combines at work – even our Hill country is a good month forward.

The summer seems to have flown, and it hardly feels any time since the horn went into the case for the last time in season 1975-76.

The last day of the season is always a little sad, but I think that most huntsmen would admit to a sneaking feeling of relief. It is a long season and however good it has been a certain staleness creeps in towards the end.

But, of course, as soon as one season ends the next begins. The summer is a quieter time and most of us let out our belts a notch or two, but there is plenty to be done. Charity and fox catching begin at home.

It is amazing how many hunting people seem to think that all work stops in the summer.

"Nothing to do now, I suppose," they say. I sometimes think that they really believe that the hounds are wrapped up in grease proof paper and put away in boxes for the summer.

I know one Master who took unto himself a "Joint," a

cheerful Yeoman of substance, with a great reputation as a foxhunter. At the end of the season my friend was told that the Yeoman expected the kennel staff to be made available for work on his farm. "After all they have nothing else to do in the summer."

Better pens than mine have written about "summer hunting" and kennel routine. Just an added word of caution. Farmers are hospitable people, but their hospitality takes many forms. My advice is stick to tea or a modest whisky, if you are lucky enough to be offered it, beware of home made cider or wine. These can result in anything from involuntary colonic lavage to cerise elephants. You have been warned.

Another feature of the summer is bicycle exercise. The kennel bicycle is worthy of note. They are ill-conditioned, sullen creatures who have come down in the world. If they get you down, they will savage you. If you stay mounted they will emasculate you.

Why do we suppose huntsmen are able to make all those strange high-pitched noises? The kennel bicycle's great delight is to entangle your whip in a wheel, stop dead, and drop you right in the path of an enormous cauliflower lorry from Bagnoles-de-l'Orne.

Then comes hound exercise proper. Out come the cobs, the old bowler hats, and the ancient plum-coloured coats.

I do not enjoy hound exercise. It is boring. Mind you it has its moments, like the other morning up on the Moors. The sun is warm, the air like Dom Perignon. On one side the deep, shadowy coombs twist away up into the high hills. On the other the land slopes away to the patchwork quilt of the Vale and the blue loom of distant hills perhaps 30 miles away.

We are fortunate in having great scope for exercise but

some countries are restricted perforce. Even the prettiest village palls after the 29th visit.

Hound exercise is a necessary chore, but a chore none the less.

I was dining with an eminent Master once and he was waxing lyrical over the delights of hound exercise, the snail on the thorn, the dew on the grass, and so forth. Eventually overcoming my respect, both for his port and his eminence, I suggested that, even so, it palled a bit after six weeks. He looked at me, quite astonished. "My dear old boy," he said, "I only go once a year."

Everything comes to an end. The standing corn gradually disappears and every one you meet on the road, or in the four ale bar of the Squire and Strumpet, asks when you are going to make a start. Quite suddenly the first morning's cubhunting is upon you.

Cubhunting is the Master's private and personal time, and there are probably as many private and personal theories as to how it should be conducted as there are Masters.

Some cannot start too soon and some put it off as long as possible. Some like to start in small coverts and some in large. Some like to catch cubs and some to exercise their hounds.

A man I know once took a certain pack. He was a varminty chap and had a good cubhunting. He was summoned by the chairman just before the opening meet and informed that he had already caught his quota of foxes for the full season, and would he please see to it that his hounds caught no more! Well everyone to their own ideas.

I like an early start. The great Lord Willoughby de Broke wrote: "*Cubhunting should begin the very moment the state of the harvest will allow, and should be pursued relentlessly, no matter how hard the ground may be.*" I subscribe to that. I feel that those who intend to wait for softer going this year, may well have rather a short cubhunting.

I am not too fussy about the size of the covert for starting. I think the two necessary conditions are that one should be able to drop on a litter straight away and that one should be able to get about the covert well enough to keep an eye on things.

I have mixed feelings about holding-up. For me it very much depends on circumstances and the human element. People are very much better at turning foxes when you do not want them headed, than when you do.

I hate noisy cubhunting. I went cubhunting with a real circus once. The huntsman spent the morning galloping from one end of the covert to the other, shrieking and hooting. Hounds very sensibly decided that it was far too noisy for them to hunt so they sat on the ride and scratched themselves in the sun.

Lord Willoughby de Broke again: "*It cannot be too often repeated that the primary object of cubhunting is to teach young hounds to hunt, and in addition to complete the education of the last year's entry.*" So let them get on with it. It is a great temptation sometimes to think you know better than the hounds.

You seldom do. Anyway I doubt that they would let you get into the Foxhound Kennel Stud Book.

I can remember a great variety of first mornings in all conditions from desert to deluge. There have been first mornings in forests and little fox coverts, in withy beds and hedgerows, on the high moors and the sea marshes.

They have been good, bad and indifferent, but they have all had that special magic quality.

The night before you put out the old patched boots

and the faded cap. You go to bed but not really to sleep. There is a tight knot in your stomach. You have three alarm clocks set, but it's a guinea to a gooseberry you wake before them.

You get up and struggle into your clothes in a combination of excitement and early morning misery. Your stock tie rebels and the button hook has gone for a walk. You force down a cup of tea, food is unthinkable.

It is still dark when you arrive at the stables. Alert heads with pricked ears look out from the brightly-lit boxes. Hounds have been singing all night. They always know.

Very little is said but there is an all-pervading air of excitement. There are a few hardy souls at the Kennels and there will be more at vantage points around the straggling covert on the hill. A light autumn mist and a snap in the air – a real cubhunting morning.

Hounds come pouring out, a dim tumbling mass in the early dawn. Then away up the lane, the shoes striking sparks on the stones.

The field gate is opened and for a moment you pause. Hounds are bunched trembling round your horse. Things start to take shape in the creeping, grey light.

"Leu in!" and hounds are gone, fanning out as they race to the covertside. The puppies race around squeaking and gallop back to look for you.

For a moment there is silence, then a whimper, another, a deep challenge, and then a crash of music and you are launched on the start of another cubhunting.

There will, I hope, be many great and exciting moments for us all in the coming season, but for me nothing has quite the same tingling anticipation, or excitement, as the moment you find the first fox on the first morning's cubhunting.

ARTHUR JAMES

* * *

The hunting man and woman have a major task in the autumn: getting their horses fit to follow hounds in the full ardour of the Chase later.

Much patient slow exercise is necessary for the hunter brought up from grass. Other essential attention is described here by our veterinary correspondent, C. J. Vogel M.R.C.V.S.

Golden Rules for Hunters

"OLD habits die hard" – or so the saying goes. This certainly applies to the way in which some riders prepare their horses for the hunting season. A hundred years ago the first step in this process was to get the horse up from grass, and to purge it with a horse ball.

We still get the occasional call at the end of the summer for a "purge" or "ball" for this purpose, although a better understanding of what horsemen sought to achieve would show how outdated this practice is. A purge so irritated the gut lining that scouring was induced (sometimes never to be stopped).

This served two main purposes; one was to remove by the debilitating effect of the scouring some of the fat put on whilst grazing, and the other was mechanically to remove some of the worms by sheer force of flow, there being no specific anthelmintics available for the purpose.

Dosing with a modern anthelmintic is still the first stage in preparing a horse for the hunting season ahead, but other aspects must also receive careful attention.

When you first get your horse up from grass, it is a very good opportunity to have a long, hard look at its bodily condition. This applies especially to the "old favourite." If you are in any doubt as to whether such a horse can stand another season's hunting, seek veterinary advice.

It often appears that bony conditions such as navicular disease have progressed during the summer at grass and may be causing pain which treatment could relieve. Butazolidin has had a bad "Press" this year, but it is a valuable drug which can make the difference between using a horse for another year or not.

Warbles have been rather a problem this year, and an inspection of the back may reveal their presence. Small lumps will probably only need the skin hardening, e.g. with surgical spirit, in order to prevent the saddle chafing this area. Where heat and inflammation are present there may be a larva inside which needs removing.

Some people neglect their horse's feet whilst they are turned out at grass. This is a false economy as the cracking which often occurs in over-grown horn may involve the whole thickness of the wall, and cause lameness by pinching the sentitive laminae of the feet.

It is essential to start the hunting season with good feet, and the farrier should be consulted before the exercise programme is under way. After all, the horse's feet are literally the foundations on which the whole season will be carried.

This preliminary stage prior to the exercise programme is also the time for a routine veterinary visit. I find that owners have great trouble in remembering when their horses have had any routine vaccinations. If you make it a rule to have these prior to every hunting season, you will always be up to date, and will save yourself worry later on.

I recommend routine vaccination against both tetanus and equine influenza. It may be carried out either separately, or perhaps more conveniently, in a combined form. Horses are very susceptible to tetanus, a paralysing nervous disease which is often fatal in unvaccinated horses, and because the infection establishes itself most readily in small penetrating wounds, such as often occur out hunting, it is advisable that all hunters, and indeed all other horses, should be protected.

Vaccination does not give life long protection, and needs regular boosting if its nearly 100 per cent effectiveness is to be maintained. Having a regular booster vaccination eliminates the difficult problem of whether to call the vet out on a late winter's afternoon to see a small wound which would only need dressing if it were not for the danger of tetanus.

Vaccination against equine influenza is less essential because influenza is a sporadically occurring disease, and only rearely causes death. Nevertheless it is better to be prepared rather than to have to seek protection during an outbreak.

Vaccination at such a time will not be effective until the course is completed by the second injection after a period of a month. In the combined form the extra cost involved for protection against equine influenza is very modest.

During this routine veterinary inspection the teeth can be checked. Many people do not realize that horses teeth differ radically from ours due to their adaptation for grazing. The cheek teeth or molars have flat surfaces which are used for grinding food. These surfaces, however, are set at an angle with the result that the upper teeth are longer on the outside, and shorter on the inner surface, and the lower teeth are the opposite to this.

During the grinding action sharp points are often formed at the edges which can rub on the sensitive membranes of the mouth and tongue. The end result of

such uneven wear may be that the horse does not chew properly, in which case "hard" food especially will be inefficiently digested; or it may cause problems with the bit.

Neither of these conditions is desirable in a horse which should be performing well at peak fitness. If the veterinary surgeon does find evidence of uneven wear, he will rasp the teeth to remove the sharp points. With its teeth in good shape the horse is ready to face the change-over from grass to concentrate food.

This must be a very gradual change-over to allow the digestive tract to adapt, otherwise colic may occur. High energy feed does not, of itself, make a fit horse. Feeds such as oats and horse cubes only provide the fuel for the horse's muscles, and these muscles will not be able to utilize the fuel unless they have been exercised properly.

Getting a horse fit for hunting requires an ever increasing amount of slow work, coupled with a gradual increase in the amount of feed provided. Fast work should be avoided until the horse is fit enough to have a good gallop, and still be ready for more. If you are prepared to spend sufficient time on road work, etc., your horse's muscles and tendons will be properly fit and less likely to succumb to strain.

Just as it is false economy not to service a expensive motor car regularly, it is false economy not to prepare your horse physically for the efforts you will require. Prevention is better than cure, and I feel sure you will find your effort pays dividends in the long hunting season ahead.

C. J. VOGEL

* * *

During the autumn cubhunting, the foxhunter will wear "ratcatcher" dress. He will change into full fig for the opening meet, on or near November 1st. What to wear? How much does it cost? These are questions which have been of consuming interest to foxhunters for generations.

Foxford here attempts to give some advice on a subject fraught with hazards.

The Rising Cost of Sartorial Splendour

"No sir, we couldn't possibly guarantee having it ready by November 1," they assured me in a certain London tailors when I asked them at the end of September to refurbish a red Hunt coat.

I gathered the pressure of such business was "much the same as usual at this time of the year," but I could not help wondering if more people are having coats repaired and "revived" rather than buying new ones.

Some inquiries in London revealed that if you can get hunting kit at "the old prices" it is probably well worth doing so, since the new stock coming in is seeing some astronomic increases.

One shop which sells off-the-peg red Hunt coats at about £65 informed me the next batch will cost "well over £100." Tailor made coats at about £85 at another shop, will now cost at least £120, and of course you *can* pay more.

We already know what increasing leather prices have done to the cost of tack. The best handmade boots *can* be bought for £180 a pair, I hear, but there is a waiting list. What a shame!

I heard £37.50 quoted as the price of a new silk hat, but again you *can* pay more; bowlers may be bought at £12.45 and velvet caps at £6.45.

The quality of the hunting cloths you wear is, of course, entirely up to you. Unless they are riding side-saddle the ladies are fortunate in being able to kit themselves out smartly for generally lower prices than are available for the male plumage.

The prices I quote above are, of course, at the top of the market and there is a much wider price range in boots and breeches for both men and women. Modern stretch breeches, from my discreet observations, usually fit better than some of the old ready made styles; indeed, sometimes the fit is disconcertingly all too perfect!

It is fortunate that good hunting kit does last extraordinarily well, if properly looked after, and it is seldom necessary to renew more than one major item at a time.

For those who may be contemplating changing their form of hunting dress, or donning "full fig" for the first time this season, it will not do any harm to restate what *is* correct in the hunting field whether what you wear is tailor made, off-the-peg, or handed down from Uncle Bertie.

MEN: a red coat is normally never worn unless the wearer is entitled to sport a Hunt button; with it should be worn: a top hat, white breeches, with top boots and white boot garters, a white stock (or more correctly, it is called a hunting tie), and white gloves. Gentlemen's Hunt coats come basically in two styles: swallow-tailed or skirted, the former being generally more suited to the slim chap who rides Thoroughbred horses rather fast.

With a black coat, a man may wear a silk hat and a white stock; he may wear white breeches which should be accompanied by top boots; or buff breeches with plain black boots, or top boots with shiny patent leather tops.

Spurs, a short necked blunt pair, should be worn with all boots.

A hunting whip (*not* crop) with a long lash and thong, is correct; a thin cutting whip is sometimes carried instead for equestrian reasons which are unfathomable.

"Ratcatcher" dress is worn during cubhunting or during the season when it is especially convenient to do so. It comprises: a tweed hacking jacket; tan or fawn breeches, gloves, and long boots, black, or brown as an alternative when cubhunting.

Velvet caps should only be worn by Masters, former Masters, Hunt staff, and farmers. Those ribbons dangling at the back should be removed, except by Masters and Hunt staff.

WOMEN: a bowler hat, dark blue coat, fawn or buff breeches, a white stock, and plain black boots with spurs are *correct*. Yes, I am well aware that many of you prefer velvet caps and white stretch breeches, but do choose a black cap and sew the ribbons inside. Incidentally, plain stock pins are *much* more correct and smarter than those prominently adorned with lucky horseshoes and hunting horns.

"Ratcatcher" dress for ladies is, of course, much the same as for men, and certainly should *not* include jodhpurs.

CHILDREN: velvet caps, ribbonless; tweed hacking jackets and jodhpurs if you must, but preferably boots for comfort and safety. (Have you ever banged your ankle on a gate post?)

No one can blame you if you conform broadly to the above styles while economising with rubber boots, or nylon top hats, but surely it cannot be anything but beneficial for hunting if your kit starts each hunting day *neat and clean*.

To me the essentials in hunting are concerned with a pack of hounds hunting their quarry effectively in its own environment. This element of hunting must be preserved, whatever economies may be forced elsewhere.

But while we continue to endeavour to pay Masters and packs of hounds the compliment of wearing hunting dress while following them, we might as well try to get it right. (By the way, whatever you wear, always take some safety pins. A fall may reveal even more than a mere gap in your horsemanship!)

FOXFORD

* * *

Sartorial problems are also observed by Loriner, who gives more detailed up-to-date advice. As he points out, a hunting stock is more correctly called a hunting tie.

Tipsy Toppers and Sloppy Stocks

RECENTLY, I understand, the Masters of Foxhounds Association conceived the excellent idea of inviting Hunt chairmen to a conference. The attendance, I gather, was most encouraging and Capt. Ronnie Wallace, chairman of the M.F.H.A., was most helpful.

Amongst many matters discussed was turnout. Great emphasis, I am told, was laid on the importance of Hunt followers being correctly and tidily turned out – an interesting point and an opinion which I could not possibly share more warmly.

I have to confess, however, that as I scan through the pages of *Horse and Hound* I am tempted to wonder whether everybody thinks it as important as the M.F.H.A. do

I have before in this column complained of the way so many people wear their top hats, so that they look more like tipsy revellers of Edwardian times rather than foxhunters of today. This, I suppose, is partly due to the fact that people today are not so used to wearing top hats as our forefathers were 60 years ago.

Surely, however, allowing for that lack of familiarity with the headwear, a top hat should never be worn on the back of the head or at a rakish angle.

Hat guards are, I understand, often considered slightly non-U. Come off it, I say; a neat cord attaching the hat to the collar of the coat is surely 10 times better than a hat that keeps blowing off.

It is bad enough to lose a hat in a fall, considering the fearsome cost; but to lose and damage one through it falling off in the wind, just because it is considered not done to wear a hat guard, is ridiculous.

I must say I have a sneaking regard for those who have braved the fury of the traditionalists by saying that they believe that nowadays everyone should wear a hunting cap, which is obviously safer and less expensive. It may come about, as I gather the original silk hat is no longer being made. Anyway, as long as it is made, let's wear it properly.

I am more concerned about the stock, or hunting tie, which fewer and fewer people seem to be able to tie correctly, with the result that people come out looking as if they had wrapped a towel round their neck, or with the ends flying out, as is so often, alas, the case with the show jumpers.

It always used to be said that you could tell a gentleman by his neckwear and his shoes – a little reactionary, perhaps, but it does make for rather unflattering suggestions pertaining to a modern-day hunting field.

It may be that they no longer issue a little diagram with a stock showing one how to tie it when one buys one – as they used to with bow ties. A pity.

One should not, I suppose, complain of ill-fitting coats. Thanks to the quite prohibitive cost people are reluctant to buy new ones, being only too thankful to accept a second-hand one – one that was originally made for someone of a totally different shape. Alternatively, despite the fact that one has grown larger or shrunk, one can cling to an old coat that may well not only look somewhat ancient, but either only fits where it touches or is bursting at the seams. The same, of course, could be said of breeches and boots.

Who can be blamed for buying breeches off the peg, which may or may not give the wearer a good thigh? Who can be blamed for resorting to rubber boots, which can now admittedly look highly polished, though tops present a problem?

In this day and age one does not want to be too critical. The problems – first of cost, secondly of cleaning – are too great.

Nevertheless, and here I agree wholeheartedly with the M.F.H.A.'s chairman, one can at least look neat and tidy – and clean.

I am convinced, too, that the survival of hunting in its present traditional form does up to a point depend on it – up to quite a considerable point.

From the point of view of the general public, to see a really well-turned-out field is an inspiration, something to admire. After all, it is something that is completely unique in the somewhat drab days in which we live: men and women dressed up in colourful Victorian gear – coloured coats, top hats, high-polished boots.

To see a large number of people looking a shambles is simply to make them a laughing stock, a mockery. No one can respect them, and therefore they cannot expect to have the support of the public.

I do not believe that it really costs any more to be properly turned out. It is nice, of course, to have a splendid new cut-away coat, sleek thigh-fitting breeches, smart mahogany tops. But it is not essential.

As long as one's coat and breeches are clean, the hat worn at a proper angle, the stock tied neatly and the boots clean – at least at the meet – one can get by.

There are, however, details, and it is details that are most telling.

So often a smart coat is spoilt by dirty buttons. So often

a good pair of boots is spoilt by the garters being all anyhow, with the buckles somewhere round the back instead of against the buttons.

So often the straps of spurs are so loose that it is a miracle that the spurs are held on. Not infrequently spurs are upside down – or even not a proper pair. And whatever the sentimentalists may say, spurs are part of hunting costume; that they can be so blunt as to be virtually ineffective is beside the point.

What else? Oh, yes, the hunting whip. I will not deny that in a recently published picture it looked all wrong to see a smartly turned out gent, scarlet and top hat, carrying a racing whip. Yet how practical is the thonged crop? For many it makes quite a fistful. Few, I regret to say, know how properly to crack a whip these days.

Yet it has always been part of hunting costume, and it still has a use in that it can help to keep hounds from getting too close to one's horse.

On the other hand it is far easier just to give one's horse a smack down the shoulder with a stick if it appears to be stopping, than to pick up one's hunting whip and wallop it down the ribs.

No doubt this is the reason why one sees so many more sticks out hunting these days, but, although it does appear to be a much more practical weapon, I have to admit that I feel it out of place with a top hat – though I am quite prepared to accept it with less formal wear.

The M.F.H.A. did a service in bringing this matter up at their conference. Recently I expressed a hope that the Pony Club would do all that it could to help children being properly instructed in hunting knowledge and hunting behaviour.

One hopes now that Hunt chairmen will remind their Masters that it is they, the Masters, who are responsible for the turnout of their field. Not only can they set a good example themselves – which, alas, is not always the case – but they are entitled to complain at the poor turnout of their field, individually or collectively.

All of which may sound a but stuffy, until one remembers that the future of hunting could depend on it.

LORINER

* * *

The last word on hunting dress should go to a lady. No-one is better qualified to comment than Ulrica Murray Smith, Joint Master of the Quorn since 1959, and one of the most popular figures in the Shires and throughout the hunting world.

Mrs. Murray Smith's articles in Horse and Hound *have been one of the most popular features in our hunting pages in recent years. Her memories, her perceptive comments, are laced with her distinctive wit and common sense.*

For Those Seeking Style in the Hunting Field

To start at the top – HATS. I do not feel that I can go into all the controversy of who should or should not wear hunting caps; but they certainly look very nice. Ladies are very occasionally to be seen astride wearing veils with their hunting caps, but I have noticed that this habit is peculiar to peeresses. Perhaps their faces need more protection due to their blue blood?

Top hats are extremely elegant, but they are also very expensive. They should look sleek and shiny, and I believe ought to be cleaned with beer. Certain characteristics are shown by the angle at which people wear their hats.

Obvious dash was portrayed by Admiral Beatty and King Edward VIII (then Prince of Wales). Rather later in time, I remember Sir Rupert Hardy, a Colonel in the Life Guards, telling a young Blues Officer (who was later to become an M.F.H. and today hunts his own hounds) not to wear his hat on the back of his head, and look such an oaf.

The young officer replied "handsome is as handsome does Colonel," and rode away with his hat still on the back of his head.

Hat guards are not, and never have been, worn in the Shires. They were considered possible for provincial wear, presumably the idea being that in the provinces you jump, push, or creep through, whereas in Leicestershire you always sail over the top. (Well, in theory, that is what you do.)

Hunt servants wear very neat, smart, flat ties – and I do not know why more people do not copy them. Ties (not called stocks for some reason) should never be loose and floppy, or give the idea that the neck is swathed in bandages.

Ronnie Marmont ties a beautiful starched hunting tie, and when he rode in a Hunt team at the big shows, always insisted on tying his team mates' ties for them.

One poor young lady from the Meynell had to be rushed to the ambulance tent because he had tied her tie so tight that she was purple in the face and practically strangled. We all know *Il faut suffrir pour être belle*, but it is essential to breathe.

I wear a very unorthodox arrangement as neck wear, copied from Sir George Earle, who was always impeccably turned out. The base is a clergyman's collar, which is especially made for me at an ecclesiastical outfitters, 1 in. higher and several sizes smaller than a standard clergyman's.

I imagine that they picture me as a rather pedantic and very scrawny curate. A plain gold pin is preferable to one adorned with horse shoes, diamonds, or in fact anything fancy.

Several safety pins are a necessity.

For some reason show jumpers seldom seem to wear pins in their ties. I often wonder why these courageous men have such mortal fear of what damage a small safety pin could do to their manly bosoms.

COATS: Gentlemen who are tall and slim look terrific in swallow tails; those who are short and dumpy, not quite so good. Scarlet, in my opinion, is much the smartest colour. (Though if you want to show hounds green is more effective.)

But for the wearer of scarlet it can be embarrassing to find himself in the middle of a wheat field, or similar predicament, when he may wish he looked rather more nondescript.

On the other hand it has its advantages. Jonathan Inglesant was riding along a few seasons ago when he espied a dash of scarlet two fields away. He hastened to investigate and found Leigh Boulter lying unconscious – had Leigh been in rat-catcher he might be there still!

Ladies astride should wear what I call black, and the tailors call grey, coats; personally I think that they look smarter with two buttons at the back. I am dead against women wearing scarlet coats, because they end up either looking like the "Tallyho Band" or wizened little men; neither alternative being particularly desirable in the hunting field. Anyway, it is impossible to get a lipstick to match!

Show jumping is rather different, especially indoors, as it has a theatrical atmosphere. Years ago when the side-saddle was predominant, and hunting caps taboo for the fair sex (with a few exceptions who produced phoney doctor's certificates to say that they had cracked their skulls), ladies riding astride in bowler hats, black coats and boots, with beige breeches, were said to look like second horsemen – a race now extinct.

So some females wore blue coats with breeches to match, looking like chauffeurs instead.

Breeches: I was dreading getting to them, because I do think stretch nylon white breeches look wrong, they are too "bright" white, like the advertisements for washing powder. But they are a quarter the price and far more comfortable, and I have to admit many of us wear them.

Lord Knutsford said to me some years ago that he could not understand why ladies north of the Thames all wore tights instead of breeches – I would hazard a guess that it has got south of the Thames by now! But just think how funny those first world war balloon breeches, as worn by James Bellamy in "Upstairs, Downstairs," look now.

Leathers are no longer obtainable, and the only person who comes to mind who still wears them is Sir John Miller. And that, coupled with the fact that he likes to ride a tall grey horse, makes it extremely difficult for him ever to say "Oh no, that was not me!"

Boots: You must have a good leg for them, but that is really up to God, or possibly heredity, and there is not much you can do about it. I am told that plastic surgeons in the States will take a slice off your bottom for some exorbitant sum, so perhaps they would remove the calf of your leg, but I honestly doubt if it is worth it.

Boot Garters should always be worn and put between the third and fourth button, where they are apt to disappear below your boot top.

Spurs should be worn, and worn the right way up.

Hunting whips should be carried in preference to cutting whips, unless you are riding a very bad horse – which one hopes, for your sake as well as the poor fence menders, that you are not.

A quite new element of doubt has crept in as regards our followers in this present day and age. Which sex are they? If you get close enough I would say that the male shaves, wereas the female does not.

On the other hand the female wears a hair net and the male does not. When I asked my Joint-Master Fred Barker what sex a certain rider was, he only said that he could not see how it could possibly matter to me.

There is always the nightmare, especially if you go away to hunt, of what piece of essential clothing you have forgotten. I mutter to myself, "hat, whip, gloves," every time I leave the house, but I am at least already dressed.

If I am staying away, I wake up in a cold sweat wondering if I have packed my shirt or some other important item.

Colonel Rid Myddelton has driven back to Wales at crack of dawn more than once to fetch his coat, and various characters have appeared at the meet in full regalia with a cloth cap.

Major Gar Barker was staying with his son Fred one year for our opening meet, and he found that he had forgotten his coat, so a helicopter came dashing up from Wiltshire with it. But then we do things in style with the Quorn!

I think, however, the best episode of this kind was

when Jack Littleworth forgot his teeth, and so was quite unable to blow his horn – a distinct disadvantage for a huntsman. He had to have Michael Farrin, then whipping-in, ride beside him to blow the horn for him.

ULRICA MURRAY SMITH

* * *

Cubhunting is the period when the art of hunting hounds may often be observed in more leisurely circumstances than later in the season.

The foxhunter who gains most from his sport watches hounds and the huntsman intently throughout a day's hunting. Much may be learnt in this way, but there are many aspects of hunting hounds which can only be experienced through long years of carrying the horn.

Sir Peter Farquhar here describes the huntsman's role and methods.

On the 'Art' of Hunting Hounds

I HAVE been asked to write about the art of hunting a pack of foxhounds, which I have agreed to try to do with much trepidation, knowing only too well how little qualified I am to expound my views on such a profound subject.

There are so many different aspects of the Chase – so many different types of huntsmen and of hunting countries – which make it impossible, and indeed undesirable, for anyone to try to lay down any form of rules.

To start with, is the hunting of a pack of hounds an art or just an occupation? One certain thing is that huntsmen are born not made. Unless you have a natural flair for controlling a hound you will never make a successful huntsman.

There has to be a link, which I always term an "invisible thread," between a huntsman and his hounds, and the thicker and more unbreakable this is, the greater will be his success. Watching any great huntsman I get the impression that this "thread" almost takes on the proportions of a rope – man and hounds seem tied to each other.

When one sees certain people who are totally incapable of controlling one small dog ("come here at once, Fido, and do as I tell you, you naughty dog," and Fido takes not the slightest notice), or some shooting people whose dogs, if not anchored, will chase anything in sight, it is probably reasonable to label a man capable of handling 25 couple of hounds, by remote control, as an artist at his job.

But having been born lucky with the ability to handle hounds, further success will only achieved through dedication, application, long hours and hard work; old fashioned virtues, maybe, but ones that have been our strength through the centuries and, alas, are so sadly lacking in some other walks of life today.

Huntsmen have always varied very considerably in their methods. At one extreme there is the huntsman who likes to try to hunt the fox himself, with a minmum amount of aid from his hounds. This type, for a variety of reasons, is a rarity these days, if not extinct.

At the other extreme is the man whose sole interest is to breed and train a pack of hounds to hunt and catch their quarry unaided, so far as possible, and only takes a hand himself as a last resort; if he has to do so more than very occasionally, he regards it as an admission of failure on his own part.

And then there is the question of what type of country he is hunting. In a grass country, with a large field of well-mounted followers, he has got to "keep the tambourine a'rolling" to a certain extent, especially with short-running foxes or on a bad scenting day. If he does not satisfy the customers he will be out of a job.

In a less fashionable or a woodland or hill country, there will be less need, and less opportunity, to handle his hounds. But in any case the important thing is to leave them alone as much as possible – the more you help them, the more they will expect to be helped, and the less effort they will make to persevere on their own.

As a young officer cadet at Sandhurst, I well remember the great emphasis that was laid on the five principles of war as a basis for any military action; and I believe that these principles form an equally sound basis for the organization of a day's hunting.

First, OBJECT. To find foxes, hunt them in proper style, and account for them satisfactorily; and, in so doing, to provide the maximum amount of enjoyment for one's followers.

Second, APPRECIATION OF THE SITUATION. This must take in every relevant factor: wind, weather, fox supply, shooting arrangements, farming interests, earthstopping, and many other things.

Third, RECONNAISSANCE. Some famous general was reputed to have said that time spent on reconnaissance was time never wasted. How right he was, and especially during cubhunting is this of vital importance. How stupid one looks if one arrives at a covert only to find there is an uncut field of corn adjoining it, or later in the season, drawing one's best covert blank, only to find out afterwards that all the foxes were in some kale two or three fields away that you did not know about.

One wants to find any new earths which have been opened up, gates that have become grown over and won't open, and in a big woodland, in which quarter the foxes are lying, what the rides are like, and so on.

Fourth, INFORMATION. As to the whereabouts of foxes from landlords, farmers, keepers, earthstoppers, roadmen, woodmen, and any other interested people. Only now is one in a position to make a PLAN, on the soundness of which the success, or otherwise, of a day's hunting depends.

When one comes to think about it, the huntsman's year is divided into three parts – summer exercise, cub-hunting and the regular season.

During summer exercise hounds have to be got hard and fit but, equally important, the young hounds have to be taught discipline and good manners, and the older hounds given a refresher course on how to behave properly.

The huntsman's problem is to strike the right balance between keeping his hounds tightly bunched in – a whipper-in front and another behind – and giving them too much liberty. In the former case they will learn little or nothing and there will bound to be trouble later on when they find themselves unattended when hunting starts.

On the other hand if they are allowed to get into trouble – chasing a cat or a cur-dog – the damage may take a long time to repair (I mean damage to their good behaviour, not to the cat, although that may prove troublesome also!)

Much will depend on the weather – on a hot, sunny morning hounds will be much less on their toes and looking for mischief than on a wet, cold, or windy day.

The important thing is that the huntsman and his whipper-in must be always paying attention and *anticipating*. It is comparatively easy to stop trouble before it starts, but very difficult if one is a second or two too late.

Before cubhunting starts it is necessary that hounds should be stripped of any superfluous flesh. As well as being hard and fit, they need to be lean if they are going to catch foxes in thick, stuffy coverts, on hot mornings in August and September.

Some people, when they see a pack of hounds properly "stripped out" for cubhunting, will shake their heads and say: "If they look like this now, what are they going to be like by Christmas."

In fact this is not applicable because, unlike horses, you can take flesh off a dog, or put it on again, within a few days.

We then come to cubhunting. To me, the first morning's cubhunting was always the most exciting day of the year and one hardly slept a wink the night before.

Leaving kennels in the half-light, the old hounds with their sterns going in a somewhat solemn and purposeful manner, their eyes gleaming with eagerness and delight, knowing that at last the boredom of summer was over and they were going hunting again. What a wonderful feeling it always was, and I am sure always will be.

I suppose the main objectives during cubhunting are the education of one's young hounds and young foxes, and ensurance that there is a proper balance in the fox supply throughout one's country for the coming season.

How, then, should one set about it.

The first thing that comes to mind is the question of "holding up" in countries with small enough coverts to make this possible. Expediency must obviously dictate any decision over this to a very large extent, but I firmly believe that – all else being equal – it is a mistake to hold up tightly more than is necessary.

My reasons for thinking this are threefold. First, so far as young foxes are conccerned, one's aim should surely be to encourage them to leave covert as quickly as they can, and learn that their best chance of survival lies through putting as great a distance as possible between themselves and the hounds.

These will be the foxes who provide good hunts later on. By rigid "holding up" what will probably happen is that the weaker cubs and vixens will hide themselves, or creep into a small hole, whilst the stronger ones keep going until they are eventually caught.

I always like the story of the lady who was taken out cubhunting for the first time in her life and when asked if she had enjoyed it, replied: "Yes I did, but I was terribly sorry for that poor man, Charlie, whom everyone would keep shouting at!"

Second, I cannot believe it can be good training for hounds, just as they are nicely settled on the line of a cub, to be continually stopped and turned back into covert accompanied, as it usually is, by much shouting and whip-cracking.

Up go their heads, their concentration is lost, and everything has to start all over again and very likely on a different fox. They can also learn bad habits. By racing round the outside of a small covert they often get a look at a fox, and perhaps catch him or, at any rate, "nick in" in front, and thus become confirmed skirters.

Third, I believe it is important not just to hunt each covert, but also to stir up the local neighbourhood around each one. Foxes are generally bred in rabbit holes and hedgerows outside, and will probably use several of these during the summer months.

If one does not find these places during cubhunting, and make arrangements to have them stopped during regular hunting, foxes will tend to lie to ground in them – and good coverts, perhaps, will be drawn blank.

Ideally, I believe, one should "hold up" for a short while until any old foxes and one or two determined cubs are out of the way (one does not want a five-mile point over a blind country in September) and then let hounds go away with whatever cub they are hunting.

If it is a big litter, one can return to the covert and repeat the operation. In such circumstances the use of whistles can be very helpful in order to convey information to the huntsman (who is probably inside the covert) as to what is happening outside it.

But, later on in the season, don't let whistles altogether take the place of the traditional method of signalling that a good fox has gone away. There is nothing that can replace a blood-curdling holloa, which sends tingles down the spine and gives at any rate temporary courage to the old or fainthearted.

Personally, I have always liked to do as much early cubhunting as possible in woodlands where hounds can concentrate on hunting without help or interference. Every fox killed fair and square under these conditions is worth 10 easy ones.

It is during cubhunting, too, that the huntsman has to deal with the question of "riot." I do not believe it is a good thing to try to teach young hounds what "game" (as opposed to domestic animals or park deer) that they may *not* hunt, until you have taught them what they *should* hunt.

Regarding hares it is comparatively easy and what I have always liked to do, on the way home after a good morning when they have killed a fox or two, is to wander about amongst hares on some friendly farmer's stubble fields.

If it has come out hot so much the better – I remember an old huntsman once telling me that the best second whipper-in one can possibly have is a good hot sun.

With deer it is more difficult as they live in woodlands in which the rides are not always as well kept as they used to be. Luckily hounds hunt a deer with quite a different "cry" from when hunting a fox, which means that the huntsman can spot it at once and, with luck, can stop them with his voice and horn before they really get going.

In this case the horn should be blown with a long drawn-out discordant note which means "stop doing whatever it is you are doing, and come back here."

It also serves to warn his whipper-in and other intelligent helpers that he wants hounds stopped. A sensible huntsman will make as much use as possible of his old hounds to help him train his young entry, in the same way as shepherds do when teaching their puppies.

It always amused me to watch the technique of the older hounds when a young offender was rated back to the pack. With hackles up, they crowd round him growling and cursing, and I am sure that whatever it is that they say to him has much more effect than the ministrations of any whipper-in.

With all riot, if the old hounds are steady, there is no great problem; if they are not, there will be trouble all through the season and a lot of good hunts will be spoilt until such time as the trouble is rectified.

And so to the regular season, during which good sport will depend very largely on the success or otherwise of the huntsman's training of his hounds during the summer and autumn.

I think I had better steady up and just deal with a few specific points which will, or may, arise during a day's hunting.

First of all I think a huntsman should make every effort

to unbox his hounds a few miles short of the meet. This gives them a chance to get the petrol fumes out of their noses, to "tune in" to the prevailing scenting conditions of the day, and to empty themselves.

In most countries one has to use hound-vans these days owing to the dangerous traffic on the roads, but I am sure that hounds used to be much steadier, and make much more sense, in the days when we were able to hack on 10 or 12 miles to the meet.

Next, how best should a huntsman attempt to "draw" his coverts? As a general rule upwind and, particularly in large woodlands, it pays dividends to go out of his way if necessary in order to get the right way of the wind.

He should give his hounds plenty of time and encourage them to quest into the thick stuff, which they will only do if they are quite certain that he will not then move hurriedly on, or gallop off to a distant holloa, leaving them stranded in the middle of an impenetrable jungle of thorn or briar.

On the other hand, in small or bare coverts, it may sometimes be advisable to "draw" down the wind, and, perhaps, touch your horn two or three times, so that the fox can get on his legs before hounds find him and so avoid getting "chopped."

On rare occasions when a well-known old dog-fox, who has provided good hunts in the past, is known to inhabit a thick covert in company with lesser colleagues, one may hold up one's hounds at the upwind end of the covert and stand there blowing one's horn for a few minutes.

The chances are that the good fox will leave in a hurry, whereupon you can slip your hounds quickly round the outside of the covert and get a flying start with him. There is nothing more maddening than to hear a good

fox holloaed away and one cannot get one's hounds because they are running hard with a cub or vixen inside covert.

Incidentally, the wind plays a vastly more important role in hunting, and indeed in shooting and fishing too, than most people give it credit for. If a fox runs up the wind, then all is plain sailing and he will have to hurry in order to reach refuge in the earth for which he is probably making.

But, preferably, foxes run downwind, at any rate until they reach strange country and then they may start to circle towards their home.

But in a real gale of wind they will mostly run across it,

which produces an interesting and puzzling situation for the huntsman until he cottons on to what is hapening. In fact hounds are running perhaps 100 yards or more downwind of where the fox actually went because his scent is drifting rapidly with the wind.

If the fox, for one reason or another, veers up closer into the wind his scent suddenly fails to carry as far as the point at which hounds are running, with the result that they throw up, perhaps in the middle of a field, for apparently no reason, as if the fox has just disappeared into the ground or been wafted into the air by some friendly helicopter.

All the huntsman has to do is to hold them up into the wind until they hit it off and go racing away again. Under these conditions, especially in very open country, I remember several occasions when this process has had to be continually repeated.

Let us revert, however, to the point when hounds have successfully drawn a covert and found perhaps more than one fox and are running in two or three lots. Obviously the huntsman wants to get his hounds away with the first fox that leaves because this is probably the fox who will provide the best hunt.

He should do everything possible to achieve this but must resist the temptation of going away with only half the pack, and hoping his whipper-in will be able to "stop" and collect the remainder and bring them on.

The vital thing between huntsman and hounds is that each should trust each other implicitly and feel complete confidence that neither will play a fast ball on the other. More than anything else hounds hate to be deserted and left behind through no fault of their own and doghounds particularly resent such treatment and will cease to co-operate.

Even with a pack of hounds that is absolutely trustworthy it is sometimes difficult for a huntsman to retain faith in hounds against seemingly concrete evidence that they are wrong. Many is the time that I have been told by would-be helpful motorcar followers, or slightly more scornful mounted ones, that my hounds were hunting a hare, or more than one, which were evident for all to see.

In fact what has actually happened is that the fox had gone by before the informant arrived, and the hares were running the same line behind him. On these occasions some hounds may seem to be a bit hesitant but trust them and a few fields farther on, where the hare has turned aside, they will all drive on together again with renewed confidence and vigour.

Hounds hunting the line of a fox, particularly on a poor scent or at the end of a hunt when he is tiring and running short, requires an intense amount of concentration which, once broken, is very hard to recapture.

Thus it is of vital importance that the field should not press on them too closely and, if the huntsman has to help, he should do so very quietly and just "nudge" them along. If he hurries them and gets their heads up, the fox will generally escape him.

Ninety-nine times out of 100, when hounds check and are left alone and given time, they will either hit it off for themselves, or, failing this, convey to the watching huntsman the direction in which they know their fox has gone.

Hounds definitely have a sort of sixth sense – fox sense I call it – and in certain hounds this is developed to a tremendous degree, which of course is worth untold gold to a discerning huntsman. I have been lucky enough to have had several such hounds during my lifetime but one in particular – Portman Pedlar ('55) – stands out by himself.

When hounds had tried and failed to recover the line, he would often leave the pack and literally "push off" into the blue. All one had to do was to pick up the rest of the pack and follow him as quickly as one could because he didn't waste much time.

He would go for perhaps as much as half a mile or more before hitting off the line and telling one so in no uncertain way; he had a great voice.

One season I lent him to my friend the Duke of Beaufort and, on his very first day out, hounds checked on the runway of a disused aerodrome. After a minute or two, Major Gundry suddenly heard a hound hunting right on beyond the aerodrome, and, of course it was Pedlar; he subsequently sired the Duke's famous dog Palmer ('59).

There will be times, of course, when a huntsman has to make a cast of his own contrivance, particularly when the fox has run a road. On these occasions, there are a few things I have found helpful. Before setting off in the direction in which you and your hounds think the fox has gone, make a quick, short cast in the opposite direction.

An insurance policy, in fact, and you can then set off on your chosen route with comparative confidence. Otherwise, if you fail to hit it off for some distance you start to have a nasty feeling at the back of your mind that you are wrong and the fox has run the road, or whatever it was, the other way. You may even be tempted to go back and if you do so and that fails, it is then too late to do anything more about it.

Another thing to bear in mind is that most foxes – other than travellers – tend to run in a circle. It is therefore helpful to take note, as early as possible, as to whether you are hunting a right-handed or left-handed fox, because he will probably continue to turn in the same direction all through. Even if, for some reason or another, he is pushed off his course in the opposite direction, he will probably regain it at a later stage.

In conclusion, may I re-emphasize the importance – to my way of thinking – that a huntsman should trust his hounds, give them time and leave them alone as much as possible, even though he may be criticized as slow and incompetent by ignorant followers.

I was once paid what I consider the greatest compliment of my life, which I was told about years later by a friend who was hunting with my hounds on a particular day when two "toffs" – as he called them – were also out:

At the end of the day he found himself hacking home with them and their conversation went as follows – "Well that, I think, was just about as good a day's hunting as one could possibly have."

"Quite agree, three cracking hunts over a grand country, and all three foxes killed in the open. What more could you want?"

"What did you think of this young amateur huntsman they've got?"

"Absolutely useless, I thought. Never saw him do a thing all day."

"Nor did I, and come to think about it, I don't think I even heard him blow his horn."

"Probably doesn't know how to, poor chap."

I am fully aware that everything I have written is elementary to all exerienced huntsmen, some of whom will probably disagree over certain points. But I hope that it might provide food for thought for young huntsmen just starting their careers, and for the many followers of a pack of foxhounds who are genuinely interested in venery and the science of foxhunting.

LT.-COL. SIR PETER FARQUHAR

* * *

So far we have given little of the space in our Foxhunting Companion to the gentleman who occupies the centre of the stage on any foxhunting day: Charles James himself.

Foxford wrote the following study of the fox and the modern huntsman, relying largely on an interview with Captain Ronnie Wallace.

The Fox and the Huntsman

WITH very real enthusiasm and admiration in his voice, an experienced professional huntsman said to me recently: "The fox is a wonderful little animal. I never stop learning more about him."

"The fox is the animal I like the best – next to the hound of course."

It was R.S. Surtees, through his immortal hunting grocer, Jorrocks, who best explained the hunting man's ambivalence towards the quarry:

> "Oh, how that beautiful word, Fox, gladdens my 'eart, and warms the declinin' embers of my age. The 'oss and the 'ound were made for each other, and nature threw in the Fox as a connectin' link between the two."
>
> "He's perfect symmetry, and my affection for him is a perfect paradox. In the summer I loves him with all hardour or affection, not an 'air of his beautiful 'ead would I hurt; the sight of him is more glorious nor the Lord Mayor's show!
>
> "But when the h'autumn comes – when the browin' copse and cracklin' stubble proclaim the farmer's fears are past, then, dash my vig, 'ow i glories in pursuing him to destruction . . .
>
> "And yet," added Mr. Jorrocks thoughtfully, "it aren't that I loves the fox less, but that I loves the 'ound more . . ."

The sentiments of Jorrocks can still be translated into practical terms. For it is in a hunting country that the fox is culled and kept at an acceptable level, but his habitat is preserved by the Hunt, he is hunted according to a strict code of conduct, and a close season is rigidly observed.

I have been discussing the fox recently with Capt. Ronnie Wallace, chairman of the Masters of Foxhounds Association, and one of the most distinguished of contemporary amateur huntsmen, now completing his 25th season as Joint-Master and huntsman of the Heythrop.

FOXFORD: How would you sum up the modern huntsman's attitude to the fox?

CAPT. WALLACE: As country people we do not claim to exterminate the fox. The fox has got a perfect right to be in the district, but we do reckon to control the fox more or less to the satisfaction of the countryside.

And if you get a chap who is evil minded, and out to destroy every fox in the country which he controls, he is undoubtedly destroying other things as well.

He is bound to do so by his methods. If he uses poison, which is more or less illegal, he is bound to kill valuable wild birds and domestic animals, with snares he is bound to kill badgers; and with cyanide gas in earths he is bound to kill badgers as well.

Altogether, that is not a healthy way of keeping the countryside for all. The alternative to hunting tends to be either anarchy, or organized slaughter.

FOXFORD: Has the modern fox population changed a great deal?

CAPT. WALLACE: The post-war fox population has remained overall much the same. The fox is a most resilient animal, and if you get a "black" area, where he is being exterminated, immediately that extermination policy ceases the foxes will appear again in the first year.

FOXFORD: I get the impression from reading old hunting diaries that foxes were much less plentiful in the last century than nowadays?

CAPT. WALLACE. I think that is right. The big increase was in Edwardian England, and between the wars. To some extent in pre-war England, and certainly since the war, the larger areas of kale and various green crops made additional harbours for foxes.

FOXFORD: What are the qualities of the fox which have impressed you the most?

CAPT. WALLACE: His intelligence and his agility are among the most remarkable of his attributes. Running the roads, and on the tops of walls, are intelligent things to do if you are being pursued by a pack of hounds, and foxes certainly do both. I have heard instances of foxes submerging themselves in ponds, with just their noses above the water.

FOXFORD: But, of course, during any hunt the dice is always heavily loaded in the fox's favour?

CAPT. WALLACE: Heavens, yes, unless someone does a silly thing which heads the fox, and perhaps demoralizes it. The so-called Hunt saboteurs do not realize how likely they are to precipitate a fox's death by their antics.

FOXFORD: When it comes to hunting the fox, some people have evolved wonderfully elaborate theories about scent, which is after all the key to catching him. Do you think there really is such a thing as a workable theory on scent?

CAPT. WALLACE: No, I don't think so. So much depends on the way that dice rolls: how you find your fox, whether he is a true-running fox; the time of day you find him; the sort of fields he goes away on; whether the hounds get a chance to settle.

FOXFORD: Presumably an important factor is that one fox carries a good deal more scent than another?

CAPT. WALLACE: Undoubtedly, and the fox is good at turning – and getting turned.

FOXFORD: Is this current season a poor scenting one mainly because the barometer is so unsteady?

CAPT. WALLACE: Yes, it is because the barometer has

been up and down, and I also think we are in particular difficulties over the very big areas of corn which have been planted lately.

The winter wheat is always a problem in a hunting country, but at least by this time of year it is green and you think hounds will run across it. Well, now it's brown and nobody can tell whether it's planted or not, and I suppose the fertilizer is still very close to the top. Therefore, you get hounds barely settled, and then hitting one of these large areas of "neutral ground" and it breaks the continuity at the moment when you rather hope to get warmed up.

Also, the grass fields after the sun had parched them, and then the stock grazed heavily this autumn, are very "dirty" this winter.

I can't see it being a great scenting season now; I may be quite confounded, and for the remainder of January hounds will run like mad, but I don't see it.

I have always thought that the foxhound has got to be capable of hunting on a day of the age in which he lives, and hounds do adapt themselves to some quite tricky conditions.

But I have seen scent almost worse this season in November than I ever remember.

FOXFORD: Do you often get to recognize an individual fox which hounds have hunted?

CAPT. WALLACE: We had a bobtailed fox in this country, and I knew him for 14 years. He was found dead in a farmyard eventually.

You get instances of very good hunts from certain coverts, and it is often thought to be the same fox, but I think sometimes it is the same litter, because you can have a very good run, kill the fox, and yet later you can have almost exactly the same run again from that covert.

FOXFORD: Do you think there are more suburban foxes nowadays?

CAPT. WALLACE: People always say so, but I think what has increased is the area of suburbia, and the food available. It is not true to say there weren't many suburban foxes before the war; there were a lot.

Foxes living in urban and suburban areas tend to be physically much worse in condition than those living in the countryside, and I was not surprised to see this confirmed by a recent research project.

FOXFORD: It is sometimes said that deer are not so wild nowadays as they used to be. Do you think this applies to foxes also?

CAPT. WALLACE: I think foxes are absolutely wild still, and I think they are exactly the same animal in their capacity, and stamina. The only thing is that they undoubtedly take more rousing, and this is because nowadays they live in such a noisy countryside. They are much more accustomed to noise.

If the fox moved nowadays every time he heard a suspicious noise he would be on the move day and night. On a good scenting day this can handicap the fox a little bit because hounds may start right at him quickly. On the other hand, the conditions in most hunting countries nowadays – with the exception of the hill countries – are not suitable for holding scent; you are lucky if you get a holding scent because of modern farming methods.

My own belief is that foxes still do run pretty well, and it is often in the mind of the huntsman that the fox has turned because there are more cars about and so on, but very often the hunted fox has gone on.

Captain Ronnie Wallace at a cubhunting meet of the Heythrop, of which he was Joint-Master and Huntsman for twenty-five years. He is now Joint Master of the Exmoor Foxhounds.

Of course, you do get short running foxes, but I am certain foxes are aware of motor cars and except where there is also a solid wall of shouting people, they don't turn on roads for motor cars.

FOXFORD: Do you find they run the roads more than they used to?

CAPT. WALLACE: They always did, and in fact in the old days they probably ran the roads much more because they were quieter. The minor roads were not even tarmacked, with the result that you had your "road hunting hounds" much more frequently. You hear much less about road hunting hounds now than even 10 years ago, simply because whichever road you hit nowadays you are lucky if you don't encounter a car.

FOXFORD: One of the oldest conflicts in the countryside among field sportsmen is, of course, the preservation of foxes in shooting coverts, and the access of hounds to such coverts during the shooting season. How do you view this problem nowadays?

CAPT. WALLACE: When it comes to the question of fox control, I have had very good support from the chairman of the Game Conservancy, and from the Director of WAGBI, who are very inclined to be as helpful as possible.

FOXFORD: What are the practical problems which may arise for a Hunt in a shooting area?

CAPT. WALLACE: From a Master's point of view, it is extremely difficult when one person says you can bring the hounds one week, and the neighbouring property says on no account can you come that particular week.

Hunting is not a sport that can be conducted on a very local basis.

The wild fox is an integral part of a foxhunting country. When one sees the efforts of some amateurs who rear pheasants successfully on an amateur basis, and where foxes are numerous, it is a little difficult to see why some gamekeepers cannot provide a proper show of foxes on hunting days.

FOXFORD: Of course, there are many exceptions to this?

CAPT. WALLACE: I would like to emphasize that I for one, and many other Masters of Hounds, know splendid gamekeepers who regard it in the old fashioned way as their job to show game on shooting days, and foxes on hunting days. That should be their objective, and the failure of either is not to be contemplated. But, of course, it is up to the Hunt to co-operate fully with shooting interests. I would point out that Rule 15 of the M.F.H.A. reads as follows:

"Masters should make arrangements with shooting owners and tenants about drawing their coverts, and the possibility of hounds running through. One sport should on no account be allowed to spoil another."

If one approaches any conflict of interest in that spirit, one cannot go too far wrong.

In these difficult days, access to the countryside for the public is an important issue. Hunting *is* access, and in contrast shooting has to some extent to be kept private. I feel that from that point of view, shooting interests cannot afford to be selfish.

FOXFORD: You have, of course, achieved quite a lot with your fox/pheasant project in helping the dialogue between hunting and shooting interests. I believe the Hunt drew shooting coverts on a Wednesday, and they were shot successfully three days later?

CAPT. WALLACE: It showed what can be done. At the original site for the experiment, Batsford Park in the

Heythrop country, year after year the shooting is very good, and at the same time the foxes turn up in optimum numbers.

They have a very experienced gamekeeper who is quite happy with that arrangement. He says it does involve a good deal of hard work, but that is the story of gamekeeping, and that is the story of being a Hunt servant.

I do not say that a three-day gap between hunting and shooting in one covert is normally quite long enough, but we proved that it could be done. Hounds go to Batsford one week, and they shoot there the next week regularly.

FOXFORD: It absolutely explodes the idea that you cannot have hounds drawing shooting coverts until after Christmas?

CAPT. WALLACE: Absolutely. People say it cannot be done on very small areas. One can understand a chap who is rearing a cageful of pheasants on, say, 200 acres being tempted to say no to a visit from hounds, but surely the hounds are not going to spend all day on his 200 acres. The fact that they draw elsewhere, and possibly run through his coverts, either has no effect on the pheasants' movements, or it is just as likely to put his pheasants back off his neighbours' land on to his, as the reverse. Pheasants are great at wandering off on their own anyway.

FOXFORD: Presumably it is particularly difficult to maintain good hunting/shooting relationships nowadays in some areas where syndicate shoots are on the increase? In some cases the syndicates may compromise people who do not live in the countryside, and are not always sympathetic to the needs of other field sports?

CAPT. WALLACE: Yes, but I am tremendously against the commercialization of sport. In the long run we shall be in dead trouble over this. Game as a crop is a most dangerous concept if pursued to the ultimate.

It is wrong to make sport into a commercially-orientated proposition. If you get sport on that basis then there is a tendency for people to demand their "money's worth." That is wrong; there should be no such thing as "money's worth" because this destroys the whole spirit of sport.

Of course, those who organize sport should leave no stone unturned to see that it is as good as possible, but it should not be run simply on a financial basis. That is a continental, foreign way of giving sport, whereby, for example, you pay so much and you are allowed to shoot so much. This is exactly what our sport isn't, and exactly why other people want to come here and join us. Tourism is one of the ways by which this country endeavours to solve its balance of payments problem, and field sports, conducted on a well-tried system, are in a position to make a considerable contribution to this.

FOXFORD

* * *

Now for a scientist's view of the fox. David W. Macdonald was the subject of a widely acclaimed B.B.C. Television programme "The Night of the Fox". As an Oxford University research zoologist he has been studying the life of the fox, and describes his efforts to explore the patterns of fox behaviour.

The Fox and the Zoologist

OVER 2000 years ago the Greek Achilochus divided all animals into one of two categories, typified by the fox and the hedgehog. The former versatile, opportunistic and resourceful, the latter inflexible and staid. Achilochus's classification was perceptive, preconceiving the modern ecologist's division of species into either generalists or "specialists".

Further, it is fitting that the fox should be chosen to epitomize the generalists, since the same species (Vulpes vulpes) that abounds throughout the British Isles is so versatile in its behaviour that it can be found throughout the northern hemisphere, adapting to almost every major habitat type from Arctic tundra to desert.

Although the fox's tremendous capacity to adapt has clearly been appreciated for centuries, its nocturnal habits have obscured the details of its behaviour so that only recently has knowledge of the species begun to struggle free from generations of improvized myth and legend.

During the past four years I have managed, by combining modern equipment with traditional fieldcraft, to overcome some of the difficulties of seeing in the dark, and hence to probe the private life of the fox.

In order to study their movements I have captured wild foxes and fitted each with a miniature radio-transmitter, suspended from a collar which can be attached to the animal's neck in the manner of a St. Bernard wearing a brandy cask.

Each fox's transmitter emits bleeps that I can detect on a receiver. With a directionally sensitive antenna each fox's position can be pinpointed and by following the "bleep" from dusk to dawn I can record the details of fox night life.

To explore the versatility that had so impressed the ancient Greek I have studied the movements of foxes in contrasting habitats, including agricultural and suburban land in Oxfordshire, the fells of Cumbria and, farther afield, mountainous areas of Italy and deserts of Israel.

The differences in the average size of radio-fox home-ranges between these varied habitats is enormous. For instance, in one area of rural suburbia, characterized by large gardens, orchards and deciduous woodland bordering on agricultural land, I have found ranges as small as 30 hectares (approximately 70 acres) in area. Contrast this with the fell-top where the figure exceeds 1000 hectares (2500 acres).

But to know what area the fox is travelling, or even to know where it is at any given moment, is really only very basic information. The crucial question is what it is doing in each place. Using infra-red binoculars which enable one to see, while remaining unseen, on the darkest night, I have followed my radio-foxes on foot.

Stealthily stalking the bleeps and always, of course, using the wind, it can take hours to gather only a few minutes' direct observation of undisturbed fox behaviour. But with each successive observation over months and years another fragment is added to the jigsaw puzzle.

For example, to consider the extreme figures for home-range size quoted above: in the area where ranges are tiny the foxes devote much of their hunting to the pursuit of earthworms.

Earthworms surface on moist, mild nights and so can, as every angler knows, be caught by those with the knack. These foxes also eat plenty of fruit, when it is in season, and the ground beneath one apple tree can provide sufficent "hunting" for more than one night's feasting.

In contrast the fell fox takes many rabbits, sometimes travelling fast across stretches of barren moor between neighbouring warrens. In each different study area the local foxes thrive on completely different prey species, each of which requiring different capture techniques. All this certainly endorses Achilochus's decision to characterize flexibility by the fox.

So far I have mentioned how far individual foxes may travel but have said nothing of how these foxes relate to each other. Fox social life can clearly be better studied where it is not disrupted by some external force and hence, in practical terms, in an area where men do not interfere with it.

This requirement is most nearly met in my rural/suburban study area. There the foxes are arranged into family groups which defend joint territories from neighbouring groups.

Members of one group intermix freely with each other within the confines of their shared territorial border, but attack any neighbours that trespass. These groups only contain one dog-fox but may include five or six vixens.

When, in the past, people have described the fox in terms of the anti-social Mr. Tod or Enid Blyton's stories I believe that they have been misled by the fact that foxes invariably hunt alone.

Indeed, little advantage would accrue to foxes hunting co-operatively in packs, since their common prey are easily small enough to be handled and eaten by only one fox. In this the fox contrasts with wolves, hyenas and hunting dogs, which frequently hunt prey considerably larger than themselves and which can only be overcome with the combined strength of the entire pack.

However, despite being solitary hunters, it is apparent from the group structure disclosed by my observations that foxes lead a highly complicated social life.

So far I have only described the relatively stable social system of foxes resident within clearly defined territories. Another section of the fox population behaves rather differently. These are the animals that are not territory holders; many are males and they are particularly in evidence in winter, when it seems that young dogs leave or are expelled from the territory of their birth.

These animals cover relatively enormous distances compared to the travels of residents. In the area where resident territories were small an itinerant dog-fox might traverse several complete resident territories in a couple of hours. These foxes are hard to follow on foot, but the few glimpses I have had of them strongly suggest that they are attacked and chased by any residents that they encounter.

These itinerant dog-foxes seem particularly susceptible to mis-adventure: many gamekeepers notice a disproportionate number of males caught in their snares during winter. This might be explained if travellers are more trap-prone than residents, perhaps because of unfamiliarity with the locality.

I have known several radio-tagged dog-foxes to converge on one radio vixen that was probably on heat, but I have had little opportunity to observe the outcome of such gatherings, nor to follow the eventual process of territory establishment of these itinerant dogs, since their unpredictable movements and the limited battery life of my radios make them hard to keep track of.

In fact there are many tantalizing details of fox behaviour that remain out of reach, in spite of sophisticated equipment, because of the difficulty in keeping one fox in view for long periods. An example would be any attempt to study the role of scent marking in the maintenance of territory borders, an investigation that would easily be thwarted by the possibility that the fox was marking during the moments when it was obscured from view.

To overcome this type of problem I use tame, hand-reared foxes. While these captive foxes are tame they are not pets. They are reared in a way that approximates as closely as possible to the natural situation. From the age of eight weeks they walk where they wish through the countryside, pulling me behind on a long leash.

They do as they please and I simply follow and watch as an inescapable shadow. As adults these foxes are as scared of people as are their wild cousins, but they retain their trust in my wife and I. So we can walk with them through the fields, observing the minutiae of their behaviour without risk of interruption.

To continue with the example of scent marking. By mapping the location of every place where the tame vixens urinate it is possible to "see" a smell picture of the landscape. A detailed pattern emerges: an adult vixen may urine mark over 150 times during a couple of hours. Many of her marks will be on conspicuous objects, like molehills or treestumps, that she will have marked previously. One tussock of grass was marked 70 times in three months!

Such detailed knowledge of behaviours like urine marking (and others like food preference, maternal behaviour and caching) could not have been achieved working on wild foxes alone. Yet one must always be cautious that ideas derived from study of the captive foxes are applicable in the wild and so every idea is cross-checked in both situations.

Hopefully these techniques will continue to yield results, for there are many more unanswered questions. One encouraging feature of long-term studies like mine is that when I catch a new fox now it is probable that I will already have information on its parents, perhaps even its grandparents and other relatives.

The course of such long-term relationships may hold the key to understanding the form and function of fox social organization. Such an understanding is crucial if we are to cope objectively with fox management problems ranging from agricultural losses to rabies epidemiology.

DAVID W. MACDONALD

Winter

November 1st is the key date for the start of the foxhunting season proper. Hunts begin their fixtures at 11 a.m. in the last week in October, or the first week in November.

From now on, the real excitements of the season are expected. Often, November is a disappointing month: redolent with mists or fog, with bad scenting conditions for hounds, and with foxes disinclined to run far. January and February are usually the months which provide the longest and fastest runs.

Yet the opening meet has a special magic. Here Loriner opens the door on a new season.

The Magic of the Opening Meet

WHAT'S in a name? Thursday it was cubhunting, Saturday is the opening meet – and there's all the difference in the world.

It is worth analysing. As October progresses and there is less holding up, more letting hounds go, sport is obviously more akin to hunting proper; often in the old days, when one was able to start cubhunting earlier and, therefore, was more easily able to get round the country, one had some first-class hunts in October, the country seeming, for some reason, to have been less blind.

It was probably because in those days one had earlier frosts than one seems to have today, when, except in an exceptional year like last year, the seasons all seem very much alike; the winter is less severe, the summer less hot. The result was that one could set off across country much more confidently than one can in October these days.

By and large, however, cubhunting is a gentle, leisurely sport. It is all much less formal, usually much less organized. People take it less seriously, sometimes turning up as much as an hour or even more after the appointed time. (Perhaps people today are less early risers than in the old days.)

Though, hopefully, there is plenty of activity in covert, with plenty of cry and plenty of music from the horn, yet cubhunting can be described as a quiet time – compared with hunting proper that is. This is because autumn is basically a quiet time, a time of fading and dying – and October is surely the personification of autumn. "Season of mists," and mists are deadening.

All this results in an absence of hustle and bustle. People have time to think, chat, school their horses a little. There are fewer pressures which is why so many people enjoy their cubhunting as much as or even more than their hunting. A run is a bonus.

Most people go out cubhunting – if they go at all, other than of necessity to get their horse fit – just to stand around, listen to the lovely sounds produced by the huntsman and hounds, get an exciting look at Charlie, revel in the countryside with its colours, its sweeping vistas, even its pearly skies.

But with the opening meet it all changes: suddenly there is pageantry; suddenly there is sport.

It is the knowledge of these things that gets everyone so teed up. Are the horses fit? Is the hunting kit ready? Is the box or the Land-Rover and trailer in good order with enough petrol or diesel?

After some seven months of it all lying dormant, suddenly it is with us again. The rush and bother getting ready to leave for the meet on time; the polishing of boots and buttons, the sorting out of tack, the cleaning of tack and preparation of horses.

For 24 hours before the opening meet all in the stables is bustle. Everyone is in a hurry, yet trying in their hurry not to forget something vital.

"Where are my gloves?"

"Did I ever have a new lash put on my whip?"

"Did I replace that broken spur strap or garter?"

"What happened to the glove with a hole in it?"

"Where did I leave my stock-pin?"

In seven months all sorts of things can disappear, or at the best get mislaid; even something as vital as one's hunting cap. A hole in a boot has never been mended, a button never sewn on, a veil – and there are plenty who still wear them – has been torn and not replaced.

Eventually, almost at the 11th hour very often, everything is ready and a start is made.

Why is it that everyone else at the meet looks so much more prepared, so much less harassed than one does oneself? The picture is one of elegance, style, experience. If there are others who have lost things and had to make do they seem to have hidden themselves away; or perhaps these things just do not show themselves; or perhaps others just have not the time or inclination to notice one's own shortcomings.

In cubhunting it just did not matter – though, perhaps, it should have done, but at the opening meet – !

Everyone seems delighted to see each other, greeting each other like old friends though they were all at the Master's cocktail party last week or at the cross-country event on Sunday.

It is the excitement, something that is shared: a common experience of anticipation and relief – relief that hunting proper has started once again with five full months ahead of us.

At last the order is given to move off. The great cavalcade led by the hounds and Hunt staff sets off in the direction of the first draw.

A small number of "outsiders" discreetly make their

way past the hounds and hurry on to the covert lest Charlie should slip away, hearing the hoofs of the horses jogging down the lane before the field has arrived. It can happen so easily, especially when the opening meet chatter is often louder than the clop-clop-clop of the horses' hoofs.

The Master holds the field well back as the hounds are put into the covert. For a few moments there is silence and a wave of anxiety sweeps through the field. Suddenly everyone is listening.

Then, at first hesitant, a hound speaks; a pause, then another, and another; soon it is a chorus, swelling and fading as hounds move up and down the covert.

Then, at last, the sound that we have all been waiting for. The whipper-in's holloa at the end of the covert. Within seconds we hear the music of the huntsman's horn, the ever thrilling "gone-away" – never more so than on this day of days.

There is a surge forward, needing firm restraint from the Master, then away we go, and it's every man for himself – the first hunt of the new season, as thrilling as the first hunt of last season, or the season before that, or 20 years ago.

The first hunt of the new season. It is as different from cubhunting as chalk from cheese. Every foxhunter knows that there is magic in that name given to the first day of a new season, the opening meet. It is the name surely that is so unfailingly – and magically – evocative.

LORINER

* * *

Starting a new season successfully depends on organisation as much as any other factor. Captain Ronnie Wallace here takes stock at the start of the season, as Chairman of the Masters of Foxhounds Association.

Foxhunting Organisation

FOXHUNTING starts the season in good heart. It faces problems; it has always faced problems. Yet many people are thoroughly enjoying the sport, and a wonderful variety of hunting is still available throughout the length and breadth of Britain, and our neighbour, Ireland.

The fast increasing costs of hunting, pressures on the countryside, and the problems of accommodating the growing numbers of those who wish to hunt, will all have to be faced in the 1970s.

But before turning to these less comfortable aspects of the Chase, it is worth reflecting on the quality of sport available nowadays.

It has been an excellent cubhunting season. It seems to be an annual event nowadays for dry weather and hard going to persist in the autumn. Last year I would say it was as difficult a cubhunting season as we have ever experienced.

This year I think hounds have run with tremendous verve and cry, and I have heard from several people that they have had similar experience with their packs.

Personally, I have been terribly pleased because I think I have had the best young entry I have ever had in my life. As a number of other people have said the same thing, I do not suppose this is a particularly exceptional experience this year.

Victor McCalmont, Master and huntsman of the Kilkenny, wrote to tell me the other day he did not ever remember a better scenting cubhunting.

It is one of foxhunting's strengths that so many people still gain so much of their pleasure from watching hounds, and taking an interest in their work.

Yet there have always been a thousand different reasons why people go hunting, and this still appertains. I am glad to say the joy of the Chase, jumping the fences, and cutting the others down, is still possible in some countries.

The prospects for the season are therefore pretty good. Wheat prices have gone to some farmers' heads, and there is going to be an awful lot of winter wheat in some countries. But this does not really matter in the long run; we have had this sort of problem before.

The important thing is that the relationship between the farmers and hunting people is, in general, excellent. Fortunately, they are so often the same people anyway!

The farmers have very much to offer us; we have something to offer them, for we are all in the same boat. Those who are interested in the countryside in the end have got to keep together. This applies to all who enjoy and use the countryside, including ramblers.

Turning to some of the problems I referred to above, there is no doubt that the growing popularity of the sport is very much to be welcomed, but it causes some headaches as well.

The difficulty is that we want as many people as possible to hunt, but it is a question of increasing numbers of followers making up formidable mounted fields.

It is much easier nowadays for people to travel longer distances to go hunting. I believe the time has come for people who go hunting on horses to be contributors to

the welfare of the local countryside, and the sport in the country where they wish to hunt.

There may be people who have big estates in one part of the countryside, and want to hunt in another. In my opinion, in most cases, they must transfer or extend their interests to the area where they want to hunt.

If they are not landowners then they must put something "in the pool" in some other way.

Apart from financial support, which is vital nowadays, such hunting people can help in so many ways: walking hound puppies for example; taking a hand in affording the Hunt a practical relationship with local shooting interests; and in assisting the Hunt's public relations generally.

There are a host of other ways in which hunting people can give time and money to assist their sport, and the countryside in which it takes place.

Finance is a particularly acute problem in running a Hunt, owing to current inflation. This may accentuate the problem of young Masters taking over packs for the first time, or it could help to solve it.

What is wanted nowadays is a Master of Hounds who is prepared to be a "managing director" to run a country. At the same time, such a man or woman has got to have the traditional authority of a Master. That is how hunting runs most successfully.

The present monetary inflation, worrying as it is, has perhaps pinpointed the problem. I do not believe Hunts will any longer be able to get Masterships which have open-ended agreements concerning the finance provided by the Master.

It may be possible to appoint a Master or Joint-Masters who will put up a certain sum towards the cost of running the country, but the country will have to find the rest.

But at the same time, the Master must still be treated as the authority. It is no good putting him in as "senior office-boy"; the Hunt just will not run like that.

Connected with this, is the important relationship between the Master and the Hunt servants. They are employed by the Master, which is a very good thing.

Sometimes there is a suggestion nowadays that the Hunt servant should really be employed by the country or the committee, because this gives him security of tenure and more general security.

I strongly disagree with this. In the long run, I do not think this is in the interests of the Hunt servant.

As in any human enterprise, the popularity of the person "in the limelight" tends to wax and wane.

At one moment the Hunt servant may be regarded in the country as a wonderful fellow; later he has suddenly acquired a reputation for being deaf, blind or simply idiotic.

If the Master employs him, he can ride the storm; if he is employed by the Hunt things can be much more difficult. The proper relationship between the Hunt servant and Master is then lost.

No one is more interested than myself in the welfare of the Hunt servant, and I strongly recommend that the old system prevails.

Another problem which may possibly arise is in a case where a Master wishes to dispense with the services of a Hunt servant.

If there is any doubt as to who exactly is employing the man, there may be a tendency for some in the country to say: "Oh well, if he's getting rid of old so-and-so, then we'll get rid of the Master too".

This can far too easily be the cause of a Hunt dispute, and in my opinion, it is an extremely unhealthy situation. It can be completely avoided by the Master being the sole employer of Hunt servants.

Looking at the broad picture of hunting in Britain now, there appears to be some slowing down in the tendency towards amalgamation of neighbouring packs.

I am quite keen on certain amalgamations, but they are not by any means easy to achieve satisfactorily in all cases. Sometimes amalgamations do not make sense on sheer geographical grounds, since they may be too divided by towns and other urbanization to be workable, a situation perhaps most frequently encountered in south-east England.

Yet I still feel it is a pity that if you have a good Hunt establishment – Masters, officials and supporters – that there should not be enough ground for them to hunt on two, three or four days a week.

In some of these cases amalgamation may still be the answer, purely in the interests of sport. On the other hand, I am not in favour of "wholesale amalgamations" in future; there have been some very successful ones in recent years, but they need good people at the top to make them work.

It has been suggested that one solution to ease hunting's economic problems is for two packs to hunt separately in different countries, but to use the same kennels and cut their running costs.

This could work well, and has done so in one case in the North.

Sending out two separate packs from one kennel on the same day poses quite a lot of organizational difficulties, especially if you are trying to cut costs by using fewer staff than you would have in two separate kennels.

Yet such a system is certainly perfectly legitimate, has the advantage of retaining two countries with their own identities, and each retaining its annual point-to-point fixture. Personally, however, I would not wish to preside over such an establishment!

Well, all the writing there ever was will not show good sport, nor catch foxes. So let's hope we are all in for another memorable season.

CAPTAIN RONNIE WALLACE

* * *

Ivor Herbert Meets Lt.-Col. Cyril Heber Percy

FOR 22 of the remarkably contrasted 72 years of his life, Cyril Heber Percy was an M.F.H., hunting hounds, and in two long stints – 10 years with the Cotswold before the war; 12 years with the Cottesmore after it.

"The Cotswold hunted five days a week and I never missed one day in the 10 years. By the season's end I rather longed to get my boots off and go ferreting!"

At the start of his time with the Cottesmore, I was surfacing nearby on the fringe of foxhunting. Tales of the Colonel's prowess, craft and cunning came winging across the border. But he was the reverse of the square-built, scarlet-faced hunting Colonel. He was slim, tall and with a strangely aesthetic, rather romantic face.

One of his officers in the 1st Battalion Welsh Guards told me: "If he slept at all during the campaign, it was with his eyes half-open, like an animal. He'd get up suddenly in the middle of the night and prowl around, sort of sniffing for the enemy, and then wake us all up: "The Germans are coming!" "And," concluded the officer, a quiet, reliable man now high in the City, "they nearly always were."

I put this to the Colonel in his Chilterns cottage where he busies himself with local politics and gardening – "I like the *feel* of soil" (rubbing long fingers together) "I love the feel of *earth*. But I can't tell you the Latin names of many things."

He is constantly occupied, too, with passing migrations of his 11 grandchildren and step-grandchildren. (Both he and his wife have been several times married). "Ten granddaughters – nothing but a bitch pack – and one dog pup!" He demonstrates the swimming pool. "This is why they come. They don't want to see *us*!"

He has long, wispy, grey hair, horn-rimmed glasses now, and a sensitive, donnish look. But his moustache (another contradiction in his rural – artistic, active but contemplative, aristocratic but rustic character) is still clipped as neat as the best pre-war Brigade of Guards subaltern's.

He wears brown corduroy working trousers, but an elegant bottle-green corduroy coat, with a matching foulard silk scarf knotted around his neck.

He laughs (a very high voice) about the war story, but cannot totally deny it. "I've been a poacher all my life." He poached recklessly as a young officer before the war, once escaping capture by keepers only by slipping like Peter Rabbit out of his jacket and losing his nets. "Very foolhardy thing to do. We'd have been slung out of the army immediately, of course." He and his brothers were as wild as the hawks they admired.

He served as a regular for nearly eight years before the war, then asked his commanding officer for six months' leave to hunt a pack of hounds. He was refused. "Army *or* hunting," said his colonel. Hunting won. Only the war interrupted what might have been 30 years as a Master carrying the horn.

So his poaching life, and the fieldcraft which he had learned in such disciplined detail as a boy, stood him in legendary stead throughout the war. "I might just *feel*, d'you see, a German patrol could be coming and perhaps double the sentries. I had a wonderful man as my soldier-servant – Guardsman Berryman. He'd been a poacher before the war and became a gamekeeper after it. He always carried a .22 rifle: I was never short of rabbit or pigeon-pie during the campaign."

The Colonel lived as a child in great state with three brothers on his parents' huge place on the Welsh border: enormous staff, fierce father, "The Squire," a 'keeper, Holding, of deep infallibility in nature's ways, the family standard run up at sunrise and down at dusk on the tower of the Hall . . . .

He wrote beautifully about this now vanished life which he encompasses in "*Us Four*," the third of the books he produced when he finished his hunting career.

Why no more? I have kept urging him.

"I can only write about what I know." Deceptive simplicity, sounding like modesty, but containing the ultimate truth of literature, sometimes forgotten by paid hacks.

And Cyril Heber Percy is stones ahead of a talented amateur. Top professional writers like Henry Williamson and Howard Spring, top sporting journalists like J. K. Stanford and Brian Vesey-Fitzgerald, publicly praised his books: "*Hym*," the story of a famous fox, "*While Others Sleep*" (a poacher's story) and "*Us Four*," about the family in the golden days.

One brother, Alan, likened in an obituary to Rupert of Hentzau, was killed in the National Hunt 'Chase at Cheltenham. Another, Algy, a famour gardener, a perfectionist who inherited the Hall, died at only 56. The youngest, Robert, was in Intelligence in Arabia. "Why?" Cyril demanded. "The Arabs," said Robert, "like polite people . . . !"

Cyril Heber Percy thinks of writing something like "*Wind in the Willows*." "I love it. I read it every year. But I *can't* do it" (kneading his hands in frustration), "I only know about foxes, badgers, rats and mice and natural history."

"But there you are," I say.

He missed hunting terribly when he gave up the Cottesmore. "I ran when hounds spoke. When I heard them I'd run and run, gasping, cursing my cigarettes. Oh, the cry of hounds. . . how one misses it."

He came down to farm in the Chilterns. "It was a fox reserve," he says proudly. "The South Oxfordshire never drew it blank." A young step-son once found a fox in a hen-house. "Quick, Colonel! Bring a gun!"

"Nonsense. Bring a knife." Colonel Heber Percy released his beloved fox and put some wounded chickens out of pain.

He loved most of all about his hunting years – "the excitement of hounds. I didn't mind so much about the horses." (Though he had ridden successfully in races and went like smoke across country.) "I loved the earth-stopping, the bolting of foxes with the terriers."

"And what I loved as a Master was that you *know* everyone. You can walk everywhere. You can knock at anyone's door in the country, and ask 'Can I come in?' "

"It was a lovely life. You were always out in the open. Of *course*, there is glamour in hunting a pack of hounds in Leicestershire. But you had to be more professional; not bringing out a cigarette, not dining out any evening during the season except Saturdays, only going out for Sunday lunch."

"You can't be a Master and hunt hounds unless you 'summer hunt'. It's so important to go round the out-lying farmers. (The ones near the kennels see you all the time.) So we'd send out the cubhunting ponies overnight to the far corners of the country and the hounds would come on in the van. In the summer the farmers have their relations staying with them, and they'd all come down and welcome you and make a great effort."

"Especially from after the war, *you are the farmers' guests*. It's up to *them* whether you hunt or not."

I talk about George Barker getting and keeping all the Quorn farmers involved during the war when I hunted there as a boy. The Colonel nods eagerly. "And Herbert Norman was the same with the Cottesmore. The farmers loved him. He'd have someting to say to every single one of them."

"Before the war it was so easy. There were big estates.

They all had agents. You met a bit of wire in the summer and rang the agent: 'Could you possibly get it down before the opening meet?' Down it came."

"Most estates had clauses in their tenants' leases banning wire and providing timber in its place. Each area had its own carpenter and blacksmith. Dove-tailed oak post-and-rails . . . . Lovely!"

"And before the war so many of the animals were penned in winter, that nearly all the fields were empty. So 200 people making whacking great holes in the fences wasn't a difficulty."

"I think Masters today deserve a halo. The difficulties are so enormous. *Everything* to do with hunting is more difficult."

"And yet the great thing is that so many farmers have now become the squires and are taking their parts in the countryside like the old squires did. You go to county shows: there's a silver cup given by Mr. Jones, a farmer. That's why I think hunting is stronger now than ever before."

"Look! A Hunt gives up a bit of country. What happens? Next minute someone will start a bobbery pack like the miners in Wales. People love hunting."

"The biggest danger to hunting is this: there are too many people out who are strangers to the country. *Who are not known*. And they don't know the name of the face they're chucking mud up into, going through a gateway."

"They don't know the name of the sporting farmer who may cry out: 'That's my wheat. You can cross it. But spread out!' So that they can't thank him by name."

In the war Colonel Cyril Heber Percy, D.S.O., M.C., was shot at Falaise, straight through one shoulder over the ridge of his backbone and right through to his other shoulder. "I saw the fellow in a window. I didn't move quite fast enough." (Laughing.) "The bullet was only a titchy little thing when they cut it out!"

He had taken command three or four days after they landed in Normandy, when both his commanding officer and second-in-command were wounded. Bar the Falaise bullet incident, the Colonel remained in command throughout the campaign. The war gobbled up six foxhunting years, but he quite clearly loved certain elements of it.

When he stopped hunting he wrote his books and, aged over 60, learned to fly and got his pilot's licence. "Frightened myself far more than jumping any five-bar gate!"

Was there anything else in life Cyril Heber Percy would have liked to have done? He thought for a very long time in the study of his cottage in the Chilterns. Then he said, "Yes. I'd have liked to have done some pig-sticking. People who've done both say it's even more exciting than foxhunting. *Because you're your own hound.*"

IVOR HERBERT

* * *

Throughout the season, the key factor in producing sport is scent. Cold, wet weather seems to produce the best scent, but there are no reliable rules. I have seen hounds run very hard on hot, dusty days when I would have sworn there would be no scent.

Certainly, a steady barometer seems to assist scenting conditions, and this may be one reason why November is often so difficult for hounds and huntsmen, since the weather is frequently so changeable then.

The mysteries of scent continue to ensure that one of

hunting's glories is its uncertainty. Each day is a ride into the unknown; an adventure on horseback.

Henry Tegner here contributes some thoughts on the heart of a mystery.

A Soliloquy on Scent

A GREAT friend of mine, the late Dick Straker of Angerton who was an M.F.H., was given a curious device entitled a scentometer by his wife as a Christmas present. This gadget consisted of a barometer, a thermometer, a wind-gauge and a weather-gauge.

A master pointer, or indicator, variously controlled by these several instruments, showed, on a graduated scale, the prospects of scent for the day. It was a very expensive gift but it showed a remarkably poor profit.

The immortal Peter Beckford, who wrote *Thoughts on Hunting*, has quite a lot to say about scent but opens his remarks on the subject with a reference to an earlier authority, William Somerville, who produced a very long poem which he entitled *The Chase*. Beckford, in quoting Somerville, has written that when hunted an animal:

Thro the net-work of the skin perspires;
Leaves a long-steaming-trail behind; which by
The cooler air condens'd, remains, unless
By some rude storm dispers'd, or rarefied.

There is a lot more about scent in Somerville's poem, such as his point that "*To every shrub the warm effluvia clings and hangs on the grass, impregnating earth and sky.*"

All excellent stuff, obviously composed from the personal experiences of a practical hunting man. Beckford, in discussing scent, has surely pressed the right button when he says:

I believe it is very difficult to ascertain exactly what scent is: I have known it alter very often in the same day. I believe, however, that it depends chiefly on two things – "the condition the ground is in, and the temperature of the air".

Beckford, after this generalization, proceeds to discuss various credos and instances, conditions when scent is likely to hold and when it does not appear to exist at all. For example, he says that it hardly ever lies with a north or an east wind, whilst a southerly wind without rain and a westerly wind that is not rough are favourable conditions.

Most hunting people know well enough the old adage that on real windy days you might as well stay at home as hounds will not be able to hunt, or if trees and bushes are sodden that their dripping will fall upon the trail of a hunted animal.

Again, when cobwebs hang on the bushes scent will be pronounced by its absence. There are lots more legends and, it must be faced, myths, too, about the prospects of scent and scenting conditions. But how often are these old beliefs exploded, as when cobwebs have draped the bushes one has experienced a cracking good hunt.

Some meteorological conditions nevertheless seem to be pretty accurate portents of the likelihood of a roaring scent or no scent at all. The advent of snow somehow never fails to favour scent whilst a gale usually kills it.

As opposed to Somerville's delightful definition of scent, it is worth noting a much more recent description, namely that of the eminent naturalist and prominent conservationist, Richard Fitter. Fitter in his very useful *Dictionary of British Natural History* (1967) defines scent thus: "the physical basis of the sense of smell consists in minute droplets of volatile oil given off by certain animals and plants, which carry better in a moist than in a dry atmosphere."

Well, there it is. We now have the situation that whereas Beckford maintains that when bushes and boughs drip there will be no scent, Fitter gives it that moist conditions boost it!

Beckford describes a real hot scent as being *breast-high*, that is the effluvia of the hunted animal lies about the height of a hound's breast or shoulder. Nowadays, on a real good scenting day, one more often hears the expression a "roaring" scent or a "screaming" one – both terms applying to the lovely cry of hounds when hunting a hot line.

To the human nose animals and various running birds smell differently and presumably this also applies to the canine nose. Over the past 50 years during which I have been concerned and fascinated with this problem of scent in the pursuit of the stag, fox, hare and otter with hounds, and the finding of game with game dogs, I have used my own nose to try and determine how the quarry smells.

The conclusions I find curious. All dead specimens were sniffed just after death and whilst still warm. The results are that a fox stinks, giving off a pungent, acrid odour; a roedeer has a distinct pungency of its own; a hare is almost odourless; so, too, are birds like pheasants, partridges and grouse; and yet all these species appear to emanate both a very attractive and alluring effluvium to the canine nose.

In one element, at least, scent can behave in an even more peculiar manner than it does on land – and that is in water. It has been stated by many famous Masters of the Chase that the hunting of the otter is the highest form of venerie, because man uses a terrestial beast to hunt an aquatic one in its own element.

Certainly the scent of an otter can lie for an extraordinary long time. The otter huntsman says for many hours, if not days. Once the quarry is water-borne, does the air carry the hunted's odour or does the water? Whichever it is, and it may be a combination of both, scent can, and does, behave in a most peculiar way.

I have a scentometer of my own. She is of the canine variety, a little Australian Terrier with the appropriate kennel name of Waltzing Mathilda. Mattie's nose is well nigh infallible. She prefers her game in this order: hare, cock pheasant, roe-deer, cat, rat, and then the rest.

When I want to predict what scent is likely to be on a particular day I go with her on her first run out in the morning. She nearly always picks up the drag of some marauding night cat. How quickly she runs the line tells me whether scent will make hounds "scream" that day or cause them to remain comparatively silent.

Beckford points out that different land and different soils carry scent in different ways. This is certainly true; cold plough does not hold well whilst yellow grasslands and heather often provide a breast-high scent. This may be because the vegetation retains for a time the odour of the departed quarry.

I suppose the soil specialist, earth analyst or sedimentologist, with his intricate scientific skill, could say why certain soils hold whilst others don't. Furthermore, in this age of computers one would have thought that someone would have computerised scent and scenting conditions.

My friend's scentometer appears to have been some form of early scent-computer, although admittedly not a very efficient one. Scent, fortunately, appears to be one of those intriguing phenomena of nature which has, so far, successfully defied this maniac-technological age of micro-analysis and computers.

HENRY TEGNER

* * *

Despite the postwar opportunities in industry, agriculture and elsewhere the profession of huntsman continues to attract splendid young men. Here, Loriner writes a timely Christmas reminder of the true worth of such men.

The Men Who Should Top Every Christmas Box List

As I write this there are quite a number of strikes of one sort or another. As you read this the likelihood is that there will still, regrettably, be a number of strikes.

But I know of one group of people who will not be on strike, despite the fact that, if it is true that the average pay for manual workers in this country is something between £70 and £80, then most of them are earning something that is little more than half that figure.

Admittedly there are perks: accommodation, rent free and rate free, as a rule; possibly a car; certainly something towards the heat and light and possibly towards kit as well.

But their hours are far in excess of the average manual worker. It is hardly an exaggeration to say that it is a seven-day week with a 12-hour day.

I refer, you may perhaps have guessed, to Hunt servants.

A huntsman, of course, benefits as a rule from the sale of skins, grease, bones – a perk for which he has probably waited 20 years. In addition he has the rewarding and satisfying job of hunting the hounds.

He also carries an immense responsibility. Not only is he expected to show sport and be a good hound-man, but he is also expected to be a good horseman and, much more important, he is expected to be able to get on with everybody: subscribers, farmers, earthstoppers, farm workers, foot-followers – and Masters.

Often today, with regrettably quick changes in Masterships, the huntsman is the one continuous link. Almost every other year he can be expected to have to work for and co-operate with a new employer – which, obviously demands great tact and great patience.

At least he has the compensation of hunting his hounds. Not so the whipper-in or the kennelman. The perks are fewer, the work is less rewarding; often the hours are longer, the responsibilities more frustrating. Much of the work, in industry, would be considered of a high-risk nature, or of a dirty nature, let alone designated as working in unsociable hours.

Hopefully the whipper-in's time will come and the kennelman, too, will work his way up; but it can be a long apprenticeship. At least the whipper-in has the pleasure of riding to hounds, even if much of his time is spent on chores which cannot accurately be described as riding to hounds.

The kennelman just has a rough job, his only satisfaction being to see his hounds looking well and showing sport.

Obviously from time to time a Hunt servant will complain – but one does not often hear them do so. They just get on with their job: their job being to provide sport for an ever-increasing number of people, people of a demanding nature who want to be sure that in these days of increased subscriptions, rising costs of forage and labour they are getting their money's worth.

Most huntsmen, who have risen through the ranks to attain the position, are men of great character, and as such are generally respected on their local Hunt. There is, of course, a danger that the position they hold, sometimes the adulation, can turn their heads; but one does not, not altogether surprisingly, come across many huntsmen with big heads.

If a huntsman does get swollen-headed it is usually the fault of his employer not having helped him as he should have.

When one thinks of the value today of both horses and hounds, when one realizes how much is involved in hunting a country and how much large numbers of people are laying out in the hope of being provided with enjoyable sport, then one realises the responsibility of a Hunt servant, the great onus on his perhaps not very highly-educated or experienced shoulders.

How much is expected of him. How lightly, as far as cash is concerned, is he rewarded.

All this, of course, is a preamble to the responsibility of everyone who follows hounds on Boxing Day.

The origin of Boxing Day is "Christmas Box day." This is the day, when, from time immemorial, people who follow hounds give a Christmas "box", i.e. a present in cash, to Hunt servants as a small token of appreciation to those who have done so much to provide them with sport.

Most people, one hopes, accept this obligation conscientiously, and at the meet on Boxing Day make a point of giving to each Hunt servant the appropriate "tip".

Most people; unfortunately there are many who do not do this.

When a few years ago Boxing Day was lost because of frost or snow, the "tips" received by Hunt servants was down by a third, simply because hunting people forgot, when hunting was resumed, to honour their obligation. Is not this rather despicable?

Even more unfortunate there are, apparently, quite a large number of people who "forget" to give Hunt servants a present, even when there is a Boxing Day meet.

Naturally, Hunt servants, being the sort of people that they are, never complain. Indeed, the likelihood is that they never mention the matter – to anybody.

I know of one Master who, mistakenly in my opinion – as this is a very private matter between Hunt servants and Hunt followers – asked the Hunt staff for a list of those who had given them a present. The number of defaulters was really revealing.

It must be remembered, too, that for some 12 or 15 years, it has been accepted that these Christmas boxes are liable to tax, and no Hunt servant today would be so foolish as not to declare his "takings," which obviously reduce substantially his gross Christmas box.

Everyone, therefore, should most conscientiously make it a point of honour to give the Hunt staff of their local pack their Christmas box, if not on Boxing Day itself, on the next day that he or she is out hunting.

Leaving out of it one's own personal expenses in hunting – the cost of keeping a horse, the forage, the labour, one's hunting kit – it is surely generally agreed that the actual subscription to the Hunt is, in most cases, not only the smallest of one's liabilities but also, quite frankly, an unrealistic one. To put up, therefore, a few extra pounds to recompense those who bear the ultimate responsibility for providing the sport for which one is subscribing is no great imposition.

It should never be forgotten that Hunt servants, because of their nature, will work just as hard, continue to do all in their power to show sport, whether they receive a good Christmas box, a poor Christmas box, or even no Christmas box at all.

Surely, then, it is incumbent upon everybody to see that their generosity, their willingness to oblige, is not abused.

Many today give presents no bigger than 10 or even 20 years ago – or even before the war. Yet Hunt servants are affected by inflation and rising costs no less than the rest of us.

To put it very simply, spelt out virtually in words of one syllable. Hunt servants are the salt of the earth. At all times and in all conditions they do their very best to provide us with sport. Whether they get a Christmas box or not there is no thought of their going on strike.

Surely, then, they deserve a Christmas box commensurate with their loyalty, their cheerfulness, their readiness to work and to work hard, throughout the year, for our sport. They are worth every penny that they receive. And on behalf, I hope, of all readers of *Horse and Hound*, I say to them "A very happy Christmas – and thank you!"

LORINER

* * *

The Duke of Beaufort, in his 52nd year of Mastership, gave a fascinating talk at a conference at Cirencester, held by the Association of Masters of Harriers and Beagles. Foxford tape-recorded the talk and published most of it. The Duke chose the classic hunting work Thoughts on Hunting *by the Dorsetshire squire Peter Beckford to provide the theme for a talk which will long be remembered by all those fortunate to be present.*

Handling Hounds on the Field

I LOOKED at my diary, in case it might amuse you, and discovered that I had hunted hounds on 3,895 days. I am very disappointed I did not reach the 4,000 but I had two very bad falls, and I could not go on another season.

I never hunted a pack of harriers or beagles. It is true that in earliest childhood I had two or three couple of beagles which I used to hunt whenever the holidays came along. I used to have meets in the Park and people would come along and say: "Good morning, Master. Where are you going to draw today, Master?"

And from that rather poor joke to a young boy, my nickname became Master, which most people call me today.

I did whip-in to the Eton Beagles. It was the winter of 1916-17 when the war was at its worst, and I expect quite rightly the headmaster decided the beagles were not to be kept in being.

I had hoped to hunt them the next season, but all of us had to join the Army, and since then I am afraid I took to hunting foxhounds, and only unintentionally, without my permission, have I hunted the hare since then.

These are the qualifications which Peter Beckford in his great book wrote about the huntsman, and this is my text: *He should be young, strong, active, bold and enterprising, fond of the diversion and indefatigable in the pursuit of it.*

Well, those who have hunted hounds know there is nothing they enjoy more in life. They will leave their work, their business, their wife, their children, their home and everything else in order that they can carry on hunting hounds.

A large mid-week field of the Duke of Beaufort's Hunt, led by His Grace and (left) his Joint-Master, Major G. A. Gundry, leaving a meet at Tormarton.

There is nothing like it, and I will argue this is true with anyone if they have once hunted hounds, and enjoyed doing it, whether or not they have been a great success. I don't know that I have been a great success, but I have just loved those more than 3,000 odd days I have told you about, although some of them were not very good ones.

Having thought it all over, one just longs for the next day.

Beckford went on to say the huntsman "*should be sensible and good tempered; he ought also to be sober*".

Well, that seems an obvious remark, but there is quite a

lot in it. Sensible is the most important of those qualities, better than good tempered; everyone can have a drink at times, and everyone gets angry at times.

He "*should be exact, civil and cleanly . . . his voice should be strong, and he should have an eye so quick as to perceive which of his hounds carries the scent; and should have so excellent an ear as always to distinguish the foremost hounds, when he does not see them*".

I quite agree: a strong voice which carries a long way is of great use, and if you can see which hounds have changed the scent that is the way you will probably know whether you have changed the hare. There is no doubt there are hounds which won't change their quarry, and you must rely on them tremendously.

Now, here's an important point: "*He should be quiet, patient, and without conceit . . .*"

Everyone likes a good holloa, and nobody likes it better than myself, but too much noise is very bad indeed in handling hounds. The hounds have got to make the noise, and the quieter you can be the better, then you can leave the work to them without in any way putting them off, and the better they will hunt.

Beckford finishes up by saying: "*Such excellence constitues a good huntsman. He should not be too fond of display until necessity calls it forth. He should let his hounds alone when they can hunt, and he should have genius to assist them when they cannot*".

The huntsman should certainly let them alone as much as he can. I don't know about genius in helping them, but a huntsman is either born to it, or he is not.

But even if you are not born to it, you can make a jolly good huntsman by carrying out all the advice that Beckford or some of the other distinguished writers have given us.

It is a true saying that a huntsman's fame rises and falls with the sport he shows; it's rather a gloomy thought when you are having a bad season.

Many men may not have the obvious qualifications, may not have a good voice, may not be good runners although they are beaglers, may not be very good horsemen although they seek to hunt foxhounds. Yet there are such men for whom hounds will do absolutely anything; they just worship them from the moment they first handle the pack.

There was a very famous man I am going to mention now who was wonderful with dogs, and equally wonderful with horses: the late Lord Lonsdale, the Yellow Earl, a great huntsman in his day with the Woodland Pytchley, a famous Master of the Cottesmore. He always used to walk about with about six dogs, and when he went into his room to have a meal, or to write, all the dogs knew exactly where they had to go and they went there, with just a nod from him.

He was my godfather and I used to stay at Lowther. He had a stallion there. The old stud groom could not handle it without walking into its box with a big stick, but I saw Lord Lonsdale walk into its box, pat it on the neck, and give it a bit of sugar, the stallion remaining as quiet as could be.

He was a very exceptional man who could really do things with animals, and not many of us are lucky enough to be like that.

I know that one does try to spend as much time as possible with hounds. It is not always easy and I am sure that many Masters cannot spare more than a few hours in a week to be with their hounds. I know it is important if you can be with them, but I don't think it is all that important. Of course, you have got to walk them out and get to know which is which; I would not deny that.

But I believe that when you have shown them sport, caught a hare or a fox, hounds know it and they will come to you perfectly well. As for feeding them, I think it is absolutely unnecessary; cupboard love and hunting love are very different things in hounds and in people.

Hounds will go to their feeder when you come back from hunting, and have their meal, but otherwise having once been with their huntsman they will never look to anyone else. How lovely it is to see a Master having perhaps come a long way to a meet, and to see hounds looking for him, recognizing his horse, greeting him, and showing their pleasure at seeing him.

My hero in hunting was my father, who was a great deal older than me and a very big man, who hunted hounds for many years – the same number as I hunted them, oddly enough. He was wonderful with hounds. I really appreciated the way he hunted the hounds; he had a wonderful horn, and a wonderful voice. He had hounds which he could absolutely trust not to change, not like we have nowadays. I think they had much better scenting conditions in those days.

My father did not ride hard in latter years, as he was old and heavy. Hounds would check and he would come up and ask the whipper-in where they had hit the line last. The whipper-in would tell him, and straight away my father would pick them up, and he would not go round to the right and round to the left like I do – round in a circle – no, my father would take them straight on and hit the line of the fox.

There were a lot of foxes in those days, and if it was not the line of the hunted fox, his old hounds would tell him straight away. They would stop and look back at him, and he would stop the pack, then hold them on a bit

farther, and go away on the hunted fox – and they would probably catch him.

It is a great thing if you can really trust your hounds in that way, but I think to achieve this takes years of breeding them and practice in hunting them. If you do attain it, it is worth anything.

In my kennel there are two great lines which produce road-hunting hounds. One was by a dog called Worcestershire Weaver, which was bred by old Mr. Arthur Jones who was a Master many years ago. Yet still those lines continue, and hounds in the pack which were especially good hunting on roads all trace back to Worcestershire Weaver.

Today, sadly as far as my country is concerned, not counting the M4 which has ruined a great deal of it, so many of the other roads are now so covered in traffic that you dare not let your hounds run along the roads in case some car comes round the corner at 60 miles an hour. So we have lost the means nowadays of really finding out which of our hounds are the best road hunters.

Whenever hunting hounds, I used to try to draw up wind, especially in big woods. Foxes tend to run down the wind a lot more than hares, although you may not agree with me on that.

Nearly always, great hunts that I have taken part in have started slightly up wind, until the fox has found that he is going up wind and they are getting close to him, and he has turned down wind.

With a hare I think you are more confined within what I believe is called "the magic ring" of where a hare will run. Therefore, when drawing with harriers or beagles I don't think it is anywhere near as necessary as it is with foxhounds to draw up wind.

But there is no doubt that if you can get a hare or a fox to run upwind the hounds will probably run very much faster than they would if they ran down the wind.

I hope some of you read *Handley Cross*, in which Mr. Jorrocks says that "none but a huntsman knows a huntsman's cares".

Well that's certainly true. No one, except a general commanding an army has more things to think about than a huntsman. There is nothing, in my opinion, more important than letting a huntsman alone. The huntsman should have as much freedom as possible.

As far as the pack is concerned, foxhounds especially must have drive, a word which is difficult to define accurately in hunting. Beagles and harriers are much closer hunting hounds, but the foxhound is famous for its drive, and I do not believe the foxhound without drive will ever catch its fox.

The fox keeps going on and on, and very seldom squats down anywhere, or stops in a hedgerow for you, unless he is really tired. To tire him, hounds must have drive to go with him.

Yet on the other hand it can be tremendously overdone. There is no greater nuisance than a hound that will drive on right through a couple of fields, taking all the other hounds with him, with the huntsman not knowing what is happening.

Last August I saw the College Valley hounds run into a great flock of sheep right in front of them. Hounds came to a check altogether, and they decided the fox had gone through the flock and got beyond these sheep. We were maybe a mile away on another hillside, and we watched hounds go on and hit the line again beautifully.

Directly they got the other side of where the sheep had turned, hounds threw their tongues and away they went like the devil. I don't call that "wrong drive"; I think that was marvellous. Hounds first tried all round where they last had the line, and some instinct in them took them right on through these sheep.

BEAUFORT

* * *

It is foxhunting's environment and climate which gives the sport its wonderful variety and never-failing freshness. If you hunt for a lifetime you will never find two seasons the same.

The extraordinary changes in terrain and altitude to be found throughout the British Isles within a day's journey afford foxhunting the greatest natural setting in the world.

There are just over 200 recognised packs of foxhounds in the United Kingdom, and more than 30 in the Irish Republic. Each season Foxford visits more than 40 different Hunts.

He has no "favourite Hunt"; all are tremendous fun. Some have better riding countries; some are more suited for sheer hound work; in all of them the sport is flourishing and better supported than ever before.

Here are a selection of reports by Foxford and others. The hunting countries have been chosen purely on a geographical basis to illustrate the extraordinary variety available in these small islands. First, the Quorn, by Ulrica Murray Smith.

Quorn Yesterday – Quorn Today

LET me make it clear from the start that I never saw Tom Firr, and that contrary to my Joint-Master's conviction I never rode with "Skittles"; in fact she hunted in 1860! Nor for that matter did I "hob-nob" with the Empress of Austria, Bay Middleton, The Yellow Earl or other heroes of the distant past.

Before the war (which war? Just guess!) the country round Melton was all grass. I remember returning to tea at Quenby saying "I saw a ploughed field today in the Friday country," and Harold Nutting, aghast, asked "No – where?"

Sir Harold Nutting was a stickler for perfect turn-out and correctness in everything to do with foxhunting, and neither he nor any of his staff ever had a pin out of place. He would positively flinch when anyone said "cubbing" instead of cubhunting, or referred to the whipper-in as the "whip". Without being pedantic, it shocks me to see these misuses of English so often in print.

I must admit that staying at Quenby, I became so confused as to the proper way to describe the colour of a gentleman's coat, that to say it was not black seemed to be the only safe solution. Sir Harold, although an inveterate smoker, never had a cigarette from the moment he mounted his horse in the morning, until he dismounted at the end of the day.

My ex-husband, when he was Master of the Quorn after the war, tried to emulate this, but bent the rules slightly – true he never carried a cigarette himself out hunting, but this did not prevent him cadging them from his friends.

Colonel Colman and Lord Daresbury were Joint-Masters of the Belvoir. In those days Lord Daresbury did not dress as an M.F.H. but acted Field-Master in a top hat, swallow-tail coat and white leathers.

If anyone jumped a fence in front of him before hounds had really settled, he would stop the entire field, then sit and wait for the unfortunate and red-faced culprit to jump back again in full view of the large crowd. When it happened to be a fence with a drop or big ditch on the landing side, the return often proved not to be such an edifying spectacle.

Chatty Hilton-Green was Master and hunted the Cottesmore hounds. He was one of the most renowned amateur huntsman of that era, and set the precedent for that Hunt not having a professional huntsman. The one exception was during the war when Boodley Hilton-Green (later Lady Daresbury) kept the whole Hunt going on her own, with Herbert Norman hunting hounds.

The Quorn and Belvoir were hunted by the two famous Georges, Barker and Tongue. George Barker had a long and wonderful innings from 1929 until 1959. He now lives at Twyford, and tells me that he is writing a book, which should be most interesting. George Tongue hunted the Belvoir from 1928 until 1956 when Jim Webster took over.

To list a few from the pre-war days: Lexie Spencer (Wilson), whose loud laugh often echoed round the hunting field, rode anything and went very well; her daughter Joanna is honorary secretary to the Cottesmore now.

Riding side-saddle, Mrs. Fred Cripps and her sister Mrs. Colin Buist, Lady Fortescue (whose daughter Margaret continues the side-saddle tradition with the Leicestershire packs today), and Mrs. Jack Harrison were all superb. Monica Sherriff and Olive Partridge were first class astride.

A sight never to be forgotten were the "Twinnies" (The Miss Wilsons) with the Cottesmore, in grey habits, with very low, flat top hats, riding to the meet or homewards one always a hundred yards in front of the other.

Philip Cantrell-Hubbersty lived for the Chase, and he was a great man across Leicestershire, though a jealous rider. He later acted as Master of the Quorn for the Committee from 1940 until he fell dead from his horse out hunting in 1947.

Reggie Farquhar (Sir Peter's younger brother), was a beautiful horseman, very courageous, with an eye for the quickest way. He and his wife Betty, who looked very smart side-saddle, lived in Gaddesby.

Donnie and Leila Player were a great asset to any hunting field. They lived at Little Belvoir, and then built Friars Well, Wartnaby, where John King, who did so much for the Belvoir during his years of Mastership (from 1958-1972), now lives. Donnie, Jackie de Pret, Hugh Lloyd Thomas, Flash Kellet, Geoff Harbord and Anthony Head were all immaculately turned out, magnificently mounted and went like hawks.

Directly after the war everyone was so delighted to be hunting again, that no one grumbled at the changes or difficulties, but were blissfully happy to be with hounds.

Very few "carpet baggers" had reappeared, and the fields were much smaller and friendlier. People went out hunting because they were madly keen, and not because it was the smart thing to do.

To start with, no one had more than one horse a day, fewer horses were plaited up, and snaffles were more prominent than the pre-war double bridle. There were few "made" horses in England, but plenty coming over from Ireland, although by old standards these were very green.

Petrol was short so that there were hardly any car followers. Horse boxes or cattle trucks which went on "farm fuel" were used for every purpose. James Hanbury went everywhere in his horse-box at a tremendous speed, which made travelling in the back a terrifying experience. Tim Llewellen Palmer once came to dinner with us, at least 20 miles, apologising for being late as he had come on his tractor.

Sir Henry Tate and Cyril Heber-Percy were Masters and both hunted the Cottesmore Hounds, while Micky Gossage, much loved by everyone, was invaluable as the honorary secretary until his untimely death in 1970.

James Hanbury was Master of the Belvoir; he was always in high spirits out hunting. I remember one day waiting at a meet of the Belvoir in an impenetrable fog. After an hour or so James roared up, shouting "What are you waiting for?" "We were waiting for you – and for the fog to clear." "Had a crash in the fog which delayed me, but it is perfectly all right here," he said untruthfully, so off we went, and as far as I recall lost hounds very quickly in a quite unhuntable dense fog.

Ronnie Strutt (now Lord Belper, Chairman of the Belvoir), was a good amateur jockey. He was Joint-Master of the Quorn from 1948–1951 with Mrs.

Cantrell-Hubbersty and Fred Mee (both of thom had given up riding to hounds by then), and continued by himself until 1954 when my ex-husband took on.

Denis Aldridge was secretary, very popular with everyone especially the farmers. Lord Ashcombe, who had hunted in Leicestershire for many seasons before the war, took a house in Melton and acted Field-Master for the Quorn; the Myddeltons came from Chirck Castle to stay weekends with him to hunt.

Two original Meltonians who still hunted with all three packs were John Wilson and Eric Crosfield. The latter married Joan Balding, who owns a lovely bit of land round Cream Gorse, where she hunts from now.

Pat Weldon whose family has long connections with the Quorn still hunted from Wymeswold. Brigadier Dolly Tilney (who was to be my Joint-Master from 1962 until his bad hunting accident in 1965) was back at Sutton Bonnington, and was always a dauntless rider. Liz and Arthur Pilkington were at Little Belvoir; later as Liz Burke she was a Master of the Meath, and now she runs a highly successful stud at Stackallen.

The Earles had moved to Baggrave and hunted a great deal, both impeccably turned out, she side-saddle. Sir George was particularly kind and courteous to any strangers, Lady Earle, on the other hand, would ask in piercing tones who they were. At Baggrave there was the most wonderful show of daffodils in the spring, but Lady Earle said that she simply loathed them as they meant the end of the season.

The Gemmels lived at Ingarsby and Rosemary, who went like a bomb, was another who rode side-saddle which was becoming more unusual. Her brother Teddy Bouskell Wade was always very elegant on a horse – though he told me that before the war Sir Harold

Mrs. Ulrica Murray-Smith (second from left), one of the Joint-Masters of the Quorn, leading the field with (left to right) Mrs. F. Barker, Captain F. Barker, the other Joint-Master, and Lord Manton, near Lowesby.

Nutting had sent him home on one occasion for coming out late from his office in ratcatcher.

Urkie Newton, who runs the Melton Hunt Club (founded by her late husband Lance) so efficiently, hunted about six days a week with all three packs. She and Migs Greenall usually hunted together, Urkie driving the horse-box at such high speed that Migs always complained that the horses arrived like ice in a shaker! I must say that it cannot have had any detrimental effect on them, as both riders crossed the country with tremendous dash.

Rupert Watson, now Lord Manton, was back on the scene (his father had not returned to Melton after the war), and David Keith, who was later Quorn Joint-Master with me from 1965-1972, appeared for the first time from Norfolk.

Another newcomer was the Irish Doctor, Tom Connors, whom I believe took every night call in his practice so that he could have some time off to hunt. He astonished the natives by walking his horse up to enormous places, and when they thought he was just having a look, over he would pop.

He and George Rich sell most of the best hunters around here at the present time. Tim Molony, who was champion jockey several times, was always in front with a chance out hunting.

George Coombe, who farms at Sanham, hunted every day of the week, was always a help, and was there at the end of every hunt – and still is.

Some of the leading lights with the Cottesmore were Bill and Dinie Rollo, Billy and Malise Smith, Mrs. Kessler and family, and, of course Marcus Kimball, who became Joint-Master there (with Malcolm McAlpine) in 1953 until he went into Parliament.

Perhaps it is sticking my neck out to try to compare the present day with the past, but in my opinion the pre-war pushing in gateways was much rougher than it is now, and a newcomer would be shoved right out, probably ending up last through.

On the other hand I find the manners of today far worse than before, and am amazed how few strangers or even friends, bother to say good morning or good night.

People seem to be quite regardless of other riders, and are extremely dangerous going at a fence.

Personally, I feel very strongly that either rider or horse, preferably both, should be paying some attention to what they are doing when approaching a fence, perhaps even try to "see their stride," in any case see that they are not crossing or baulking anyone else. I do not recall members of the Field being knocked down in the old days as they are only too frequently nowadays.

I know Duggie Bunn will not mind me telling of the day I was trying a very small but brilliant horse which he knew. Duggie told me that I was mad at my weight, not to ride little horses, as they were far better than big ones.

Later in the day, when luckily I had changed on to my own big, strong horse, I was jumping a post and rails when Duggie, who must be twice my weight, riding a huge charger, cannoned into me. As I landed, black and blue, but still on my horse, and both upright, I said to him "That is why I never ride little horses!"

Perhaps it would be fair to add a story against myself. When on a rare visit to Ireland, having not a clue how to manipulate a bank, I shut my eyes and clutched my mount's mane. He elected to jump the bank very cleverly sideways, thus knocking Lord Harrington off his horse.

He was absolutely charming about it, and never said a cross word, though at the next bank he did suggest that we should not jump it together – and as he was Field-Master (Limerick) we decided that he should go first.

It seems strange that the standard of horsemanship should not have improved when you consider how many winners in equestrian world events are hunting with us, and ought to (and in fact usually do) set a good example.

There have always been many visitors who come to hunt in Leicestershire from far away. The great difference is that whereas in pre-war days they took houses in the district and moved up for the winter and became residents in the county, now they come for the day by car or even helicopter.

Some keep their horses at livery in the country, but others send them long distances by horse box each hunting day. In fact they do not even bring the proverbial "carpet bag" now.

As regards the Quorn, I know that there are more farmers hunting at present, both on a horse and by car, than at any other time, and I believe that this is so with the Belvoir and Cottesmore too.

There are only four people hunting with us today who appear on the Quorn subscription list of 1938–1939; Pat Weldon, Urkie Newton, Arthur Gemmel and I.

As to hunting hounds, far be it from me to decry the great names of huntsmen of the past, but I think it is far harder to hunt a pack of hounds with brilliance today. There are so many new hazards.

I believe that when railways first appeared, it was said that they would be the finish of foxhunting. Now, as well as railways with much faster trains, we have main roads with heavy traffic and motorways. Then there are sprays and liquid fertilisers which foil the scent, eager car-followers who head the fox, and whose exhausts hardly help hounds if the fox does manage to cross a road.

The huntsman cannot just gallop on regardless, he has got to look out for wheat, seeds, wire and other difficulties. He is alone in front and needs a bold horse when he must often look first before he turns to jump a horrible place.

Sometimes in our Tuesday Saturday country, when I do not know where we are, I ask our huntsman, Michael Farrin, "Can we get across here?" And he always replies with confidence "I expect we shall find a way," which he always does, but it is sometimes rather hair-raising to follow.

Although in the pre-war days there were far longer points, and more epic hunts. I think there were also more bad days, with coverts drawn blank. Probably the country is better foxed today, except where there are shooting syndicates. I should say that there are more "busy days" with enjoyable short hunts, but not the terrific ones we read of in the old days.

To sum up, for those who just went out to gallop and jump, it was, of course, more fun in the old days. But it is certaily more of a challenge in the present day and age, and I find you need a better horse today. To those dedicated to foxhunting it is fascinating to watch huntsman and hounds overcome difficulties not thought of in the past.

In America culinary skill seems to be considered one of my attributes, as I received a letter from a publisher there asking if the Quorn would donate their favourite recipe for a cookery book.

Without consulting anyone, I offered the following from the Quorn, which from personal knowledge is as good today as it ever was. "Take a large tumbler – add ice to taste – half fill with whisky – and consume." They published it!

ULRICA MURRAY SMITH

In February, 1977, Foxford visited the celebrated Shires pack, the Fernie, and enjoyed the best run he had encountered that season.

Here's to a Great Day with the Fernie

"Ooray, Jack! Hoo-ray!" exclaimed Lord Scamperdale. His Lordship was the picture of delight. He had had a tremendous run. The hounds had behaved to perfection; his horse had carried him well and he stood with his crownless flat hat in his hand and one coat lap in the pocket of the other – a grinning, exulting, self-satisfied specimen of a happy Englishman.

I HAD more than an inkling of how Lord Scamperdale in *Mr. Sponge's Sporting Tour* felt when his hounds had achieved a first-class 14-mile hunt. For when I visited the Fernie hounds the other day, they treated me to as good a day's hunting as I have had for a long time.

From the first draw until home was blown at 4.40 p.m. life was a matter of seemingly endless galloping and jumping, in following a superb pack of hounds working brilliantly throughout. From the first draw we had a good 60min hunt. Then after changing horses there followed a wonderful 2hrs 30min. run, with a six-mile point and some 16 miles as they ran. Only about half a dozen of the field finished the day which had started with some 150 riders at the meet.

Thanks to being extremely well mounted I was able to finish the run, plastered in mud and with a great rent in the knee of my breeches. I can only echo Lord Scamperdale again when his friend Jack Spraggon pointed out that he was "mud from head to foot".

"Never mind the mud you old badger," roared his Lordship. "The mud will come off or may stay on; but such a run as we have had does not come off every day".

It was certainly one of the best scenting days I have experienced for a long time, in a season which has generally been noted for poor scenting conditions everywhere. But you need a first-class pack of hounds, a good huntsman, and a well managed country to take best advantage of good scent – and I had every opportunity to observe that the Fernie has these in abundance.

Lt-Col. G. A. (Tony) Murray Smith has been Joint-Master of these hounds since 1960 and was previously Master of the Quorn from 1954.

Col. Murray Smith hunted the Fernie hounds himself from 1962-65 and it would be difficult to find anyone with more experience in providing sport in Leicestershire nowadays. He is keenly interested and involved in breeding both horse and hound, and is the current President of the Hunters' Improvement Society.

Joint-Master of the Fernie since 1972, is Mr. Joe Cowen, a member of one of the most dedicated of hunting families. His father, Major Dennis Cowen, is chairman of the Fernie, is a former Field-Master, and owns some of the best hunting country you could wish to ride; but more of this later.

Bruce Durno, son of the distinguished ex-Heythrop huntsman Percy Durno, joined the Fernie as kennel-huntsman in 1962 and has been hunting the hounds since 1966. He is a quiet, extremely effective huntsman, and I can quite see why he has acquired such a solid reputation among all those who have had the good fortune to follow his hounds regularly. Percy Durno was an observer from a car on this extremely good day from Foxton.

Michael King whips-in, having joined the Fernie in

1973, and is going north to hunt the Lauderdale hounds next season.

It has been exceptionally rainy, lately, and scent everywhere has been unreliable, so everyone was quite gloomy beforehand about the prospects of a good day from the Fernie meet at Foxton, although this is in such a splendid piece of country. This attitude encouraged me tremendously; during visits it is usually when people are utterly confident they are about to have a splendid day that things may go sadly awry. Such is the fickle nature of the Chase.

Privately I was sure things were going to be just right as we jogged to the meet on a damp, raw morning. At Foxton Grange Mrs. Holland's hospitality enabled us to drink the health of her daughter Cecilia on this, her 21st birthday. I am sure she will not easily forget her birthday hunt.

We had quite a long hack to Bunker's Hill, where hounds found straight away and the fox behaved as if he, too, knew it was a good scenting day, moving off sharply along the hills nearly to Saunts Close. Here he turned left and swam the canal, running over Ivy Lodge Farm and left again, past his starting point to go on to Laughton Village.

Here the fox swung right and ran by the Belts to leave Gumley Covert on his left, running up to Lubenham Lodge and so back to Bunker's Hill and to ground. This had been an excellent 60min. hunt with hounds running well all the way. Some of it was on fairly holding arable ground, and I was grateful to be so well mounted by Col. Murray Smith on a nice chesnut hunter which gave a good steady pull no matter what the going, or how steep the incline.

We changed horses and I mounted one of the cleverest

little hunters it has been my good fortune to ride in the hunting field. It was barely 16 hands and is normally ridden by the whipper-in; a smallish mount for a 6 foot 2 inch hunting correspondent, but I was never conscious of this, and the little horse gave me a grand ride throughout, no matter how big the fences nor how demanding the pace.

I have always wanted to see a fox go away from the famous John Ball Covert in the Fernie country. This covert was made early in the last century for the great Squire Osbaldeston by Mr. Oldacre, a man skilled in creating thorn coverts; he also made the Jane Ball Covert on the other side of the Welford road. According to Charles Simson in his wonderful book *The Harboro' Country*, the naming of these coverts has always been a mystery.

But it is thought that the name John refers to a child of Mr. Oldacre's christened at that time, and Ball may refer to a Leicestershire term meaning to cake or gather in lumps, like snow on a horse's feet, which would be appropriate on account of the rounded summit of the hill on which the covert stands.

This hill affords one of the most famous views in the kingdom of foxhunting. I was impressed by the way the Cowen family have maintained this famous covert, with plenty of bottom which may harbour a fox.

It was a wonderful moment when Bruce Durno put his hounds in at one end and they were soon speaking. There was one of those splendid holloas which make the hairs stand up on the back of your neck, and suddenly we were galloping along the top side of the covert to come round the far end and be confronted by a wonderful sight – a classic "gone away".

The Fernie hounds were running beautifully together

over the grass with a wonderful head, and the pace was fast enough to make you sit down and ride, but not too fast to spoil the pleasure of jumping the delectable variety of timber and fly fences criss-crossing the downhill grassy slopes ahead.

Lord Stalbridge, a pre-war Fernie Master, has written of the country's "mile upon mile of beautiful grass, that, even after a week's rain, hardly shows the mark of a horse's foot and yet seems to have all the spring and elasticity of highly tempered steel".

Since his day, much of Leicestershire has gone under the plough, but thanks to the Cowen family much of the permanent grass around John Ball remains, and we had a wonderful 20min. riding away from the covert, the fox making a big left-handed circle by Furnivals and Saddington, nearly to Fleckney and back to the John Ball Covert.

We had had some road work in the middle of this run, but it had been a wonderful ride and it seemed almost too good to be true when hounds pushed their fox straight through the covert and across the grass again.

He ran left-handed this time to cross the Mowsley road by Foxons Farm, over the Laughton Brook and between Gumley and Laughton up to Bunker's Hill. Then the line continued along the hills and right again by Laughton Village, Gumley Covert and Lubenham Lodge, but this time crossing the canal and going on with Gartree Prison on the right.

At this stage hounds were hunting better than ever; it was a joy to watch them making the line good and putting on the pressure, but their fox just got to ground by a few yards in the badger holes below the A.6 on Gallow Hill. It had been a wonderful hunt to ride and to watch hounds all the way and I am so grateful to all concerned for having had the opportunity to take part in it.

The Fernie are indeed an impressive pack to observe in the field, and on the flags. They have retained a strong pure English line and the hounds have more tan colouring in their coats than you will see in many other packs nowadays. They seem to me an excellent blend of the forthright qualities of the older English line with some of the best post-war breeding as well.

There are substantial Beaufort and Heythrop influences, but I note that the 1975/76 entry includes hounds sired by Sir Watkin Williams Wynn's Playmate ('70).

There is an interesting tail-female line in the Fernie kennel through a Green Spring Valley hound, Darkness. The Green Spring Valley hounds are cross-bred English and American hounds, the latter going back to the wonderful scenting and speaking hounds with which Americans used to hunt the fox in the early hours of the morning.

The Green Spring Valley hunts in the beautiful grasslands of Maryland, and the Darkness line goes back to a Mr. Bywater's Lizzie ('25).

Col. Murray Smith tells me the American line has been most successful in the kennel and was introduced when Mr. Fife Symington was Master of the Green Spring Valley. He was given a couple of bitches from the Quorn by Col. Murray Smith, and in return two doghounds and a bitch were supplied from the American pack, the bitch going to the Fernie.

I was much impressed by the way the Hunt has met the requirements of modern farming, and yet rendered the country crossable by building some of the best Hunt jumps I have seen anywhere.

The Fernie was originally part of the Quorn country

and was made over to Mr. Richard Sutton, son of the Quorn Master, Sir Richard Sutton, in 1853. The Hunt owes its name to the great Mr. C. W. B. Fernie who was Master from 1888-1919, with his wife continuing in the Mastership until 1923.

It is a great country with a distinguished history of foxhunting at its best, and it was wonderful to hunt there for the first time and to discover the Hunt still maintaining excellent standards and capable of providing such sport, and such fun.

FOXFORD

The Belvoir

THIS report might appropriately have come "from our meteorological correspondent" . . .

Such was my gloomy observation, laced with a few unprintable adjectives, as I searched for my Land-Rover and trailer in a swirling, blinding snow storm in High Leicestershire the other day.

The mare hunched her back and twitched her ears back and forth, and I would have been glad to have done the same, as a freezing wind hurled the snow against us while we trudged along Landyke Lane.

It is just north of Melton Mowbray, above Holwell Mouth, and one of the highest spots in the Shires. I had a distinct feeling that to the east there was nothing much between me and Siberia.

Suddenly, like theatrical scenery, the snow clouds rolled away, and the sun beamed down from an incredibly blue sky, with a spectacular spread of storm clouds on the horizon.

Forgive me for chuntering on about the weather, but it

was a major factor in my recent day with the Belvoir, a day of strange and remarkable contrasts. I find that a bit of snow does a red coat a lot of good afterwards, but it really is rather early in the season for such climactic histrionics. Coated in half an inch of snow, I alighted from my shivering hunter like a bit player in a Christmas card scene.

Jim Webster and the Belvoir hounds provided us with a lot of fun on a day of such tricky weather: a considerable feat by a huntsman and his pack in any setting, but especially with a keen Saturday mounted field out for galloping and jumping in one of the most celebrated pieces of the Shires. And before I report the sport let me refer to the appalling threat facing this unique part of England.

The appalling threat of the National Coal Board's plans to dig up the Vale of Belvoir for coal, are storm clouds over the future of the Belvoir Hunt.

Three new mines, says the Coal Board, will be needed to gain access to about 500 million tons of coal under 90 square miles of mainly agricultural land.

They want to sink mines near the villages of Hose, Ashfordby, and Saltby. All sorts of promises are being made to "protect the environment," but of course such a massive expansion of the coal industry will have a devastating effect on a beautiful, rural area.

Apart from the colliery sites and tipping, there will be new housing estates for mineworkers and immense increases in local traffic.

There can be no doubt that the Vale of Belvoir, as we know it, will be destroyed forever. Britain's energy needs are obvious, but alternatives *can* be found.

Is it really in the national interest to devastate this wonderful stretch of the Midlands, where so much rural landscape has already been consumed by urbanization?

If you believe, as I do, that the Vale of Belvoir should be saved, then it is surely worth rallying to support the strong body of local people who are fighting against Government permission for the Coal Board to go ahead.

Of course, you would expect that strange anachronism, a hunting correspondent, to advocate saving one of the best pieces of hunting England. Foxhunting is but one aspect of the Vale of Belvoir, but the biggest threat to all the precious elements which make up English rural life will suffer the same fate under such threats as that now facing this stretch of the Midlands.

It will not be the shrill voices of a few abolitionists which will sound the death knell for hunting and other field sports; it will be the sound of excavators as the last shreds of genuinely rural Britain are transformed into suburbia and ex-urbia. In case you think I exaggerate, just think how much country has been "lost" or has deteriorated seriously since the war. And, of course, it is a loss which must be measured in far wider terms than field sports.

T. F. Dale's fascinating history of the Belvoir Hunt traces a great sporting tradition which has adapted and survived in the face of all kinds of changes in rural England. Change is one thing; destruction of the very fabric of the countryside is totally different, and must be opposed.

Dating from 1750, the hounds were held by the reigning Dukes of Rutland, apart from one break, up to 1896. The Hunt Kennels are still in the grounds of Belvoir Castle, and as T. F. Dale wrote:

> " . . . Belvoir has an unrivalled situation. From the towers and terraces of the Castle, woods and plains, tillage and pasture,

in short almost every variety of hunting country, may be viewed.

"For the land of the Dukes of Rutland shows foxhunting in all its phases. The follower of the Belvoir hounds may one day hear the immemorial woodlands ring with the note of the horn and the melody of the hounds, and on the next may see the flying pack race over the Leicestershire pastures, while on the third he may set his teeth and sit down in his saddle to ride from Stubton to Wellingore, while the pack works out the line over the stiff fences and across the deep ploughs of Lincolnshire".

A foxhunter's paradise indeed . . . but the nature of the pasture land has changed somewhat with the post-war agricultural emphasis on arable farming. Of course, the Belvoir country, like most others, bears witness to the 20th century's imprint.

Yet from Belvoir Castle you will still hear hounds, and see them running hard over a country designed by our forefathers with hunting in mind.

Whatever may or may not change, it is indisputable that the Belvoir shares the modern flood of enthusiasm for foxhunting, and continues to provide enormous fun for so many people following hounds on horses, wheels or feet.

Mrs. Ann Reid Scott and Lord Belper are Acting Joint-Masters for a Committee, and the Hunt chairman is former Joint-Master Mr. John King. With Mr. and Mrs. Tom Hudson as joint secretaries, it is a Hunt organization which provides sport four days a week for large mounted fields, and above all it has produced a very happy and successful atmosphere.

This is clear when you visit the kennels, built at Belvoir in 1809, and still dominated by an octagonal building, bearing the fox weathervane aloft. I am told that at one time a kennel lad would sleep in a room high up under the roof, so as to hear hounds if there was any fighting among them in the night.

The Sixth Duke of Rutland (1815-1888) in later life had a room at the kennels, still known as the Duke's Room, where he would sit in a chair with a rail round him to keep the hounds from him when he was crippled with gout, while he looked at the entry.

There is little room here for the dissertation on hound breeding which the Belvoir kennels deserve, but Belvoir blood was a major influence on Hunt kennels throughout the land, except in Wales, until the immense changes in hound breeding wrought by introducing Welsh blood between the wars.

Yet while others have changed, the famous Belvoir tan remains the predominant colour, and the lines remain virtually the same in the breeding here. Continuity is all at Belvoir; huntsman Jim Webster is only the ninth huntsman since the great Will Goodall began service in 1842.

Jim is firmly, and proudly, an adherent of Belvoir blood, and the evidence of this is clear in the Kennel. Now in his 21st year as Belvoir huntsman, Jim is a vastly popular and well known figure throughout the hunting world.

He had a particularly good season last year and I can bear witness that his hounds are hunting with great drive despite the worst that the difficult 1977 November weather could provide. My word, they can fly. Stallion hounds from the Hurworth and the Brocklesby, which stayed true to traditional English lines, are among those in the kennel, and Jim is particularly pleased with the introduction of a line from Sir Watkin Williams-Wynn's Playmate ('70) which produced eight couple entered in 1974.

The other notable kennel where I have also seen, and so enjoyed, Belvoir-bred hounds, is that of the Co. Limerick where the former Belvoir Joint-Master Lord Daresbury (in office from 1930–47) remains firmly committed to this breeding policy.

Jim Webster says little, but sums it up briefly as: "In my opinion this is the sort of hound bred for our sort of country".

After a convivial meet at Holwell, and with a fearful wind already blowing, Jim and his whipper-in, Graham Roberts, took hounds to Old Hills, where suddenly the skies became black, and amid the gloom we huddled against the covertside assailed by a fierce storm of hailstones. Not nice at all, and my first horse (a useful mare called Ambrosia, provided by so helpful Miss Mirabel Bedford) whinnied complainingly.

After the storm the first hunt was from the famous Clawson Thorns Covert, where a fox ran from the Parlour towards the Waltham – Long Clawson road, turned right-handed up the hill over the Eastwell – Six Hills road, crossing the old Ironstone railway towards Holwell Village. The wind whipped up tremendously at this point and no more could be made of the line at the back of Holwell Village.

The spin had given us a chance to enjoy some of the nice fences and grass towards the vale below Clawson Thorns – and great fun it was. After another descent of blackness and hailstones the clouds rolled by again, and Jim took hounds to Holwell Mouth, where a fox went away at the top end and ran hard up the hill, giving the mounted field the devil of a job to get away as swiftly as some of the ladies and gentlemen would have wished.

This fox ran strongly up wind, crossing the Eastwell – Six Hills roads, with hounds really flying. They went towards Old Hills, then swung right-handed and checked. Getting hounds together, Jim Webster hit off the line nicely and the pack ran on to mark their fox to ground just short of Ab Kettelby.

On hounds being taken back to Clawson Thorns, another fox went away, this time heading down into the vale, but strong winds made it difficult to press him and he saved his brush by getting to ground in a drain at Long Clawson Village.

It had been a busy and enjoyable day in appalling conditions, soon exceeded by the snow storm which I mentioned above.

In the Vale of Belvoir tradition not merely survives, but flourishes – may it continue to do so for our generation, and generations of sportsmen to come . . .

FOXFORD

The Whaddon Chase

VISITING the Whaddon Chase country is always a special pleasure for your correspondent. I had better record straight away that I used to enjoy hunting regularly with this famous Buckinghamshire pack. So you need not waste time checking to see whether this is an impartial report; it isn't.

The nature of a hunting country's terrain is important, yet the spirit of enthusiasm which the Hunt itself engenders is equally vital.

In both respects the Whaddon Chase has long been fortunate.

Mr. Dorian Williams took over the Mastership in 1954, having previously been Joint-Master of the neighbouring Grafton, of which his father, the late Col. V. D.

S. Williams, had been Joint-Master before the war.

In Dorian Williams's services the equestrian and hunting worlds have indeed been fortunate to receive the lifelong devotion of one with such exceptional talents as a communicator in the spoken and the written word, and with a vast range of active interests in education, the arts and sport.

The British do not always rapturously welcome versatility, and success and popularity in one sphere is certainly not guaranteed by having already achieved these rewards in another area.

Thus Dorian Williams's immense contribution in his own hunting country, and in putting hunting's case so effectively elsewhere, is all the more remarkable in the light of his many other activities.

Some inkling of how this has been done is conveyed in the burning enthusiasm contained in these words which he wrote in recalling his keenness on the formation of Hunt supporters' clubs:

"I loved hunting, and I wanted as many people as possible to get the enjoyment out of it that I did: the air and exercise, the hazard of the unexpected (which must rule out draghunting as an alternative) the challenge to nerve and skill inherent in the attempt to keep with hounds crossing a stiff country, the camaraderie, the opportunity, enjoyed perhaps by more people than is realized, to indulge a little in the art of venery – seeing hounds working, watching a clever huntsman, gauging the influences of wind, weather, temperature, terrain.

"Endless unrivalled rewards in a dozen different ways for hundreds of people every time hounds go out. All at the expense of one fox: a verminous, if handsome creature, an animal too cunning, too elusive to be controlled by any other method, and *pace* the Cruelty to Wild Animals report, no other method – trapping, shooting, snaring, poisoning – is *more* humane than hunting".

The Whaddon Chase has been fortunate indeed in having as Joint-Masters, since 1969, Mr. Peter Stoddart, whose family have such long and close associations with the Hunt, and Mr. D. J. L. ("Puggy") Wyatt, who has been a popular and effective Hunt Secretary for 13 years.

(*Note*: Since my visit, sadly Mr. "Puggy" Wyatt has died, and Mr. Dorian Williams continues in office with Mr. Stoddart.)

Albert Buckle has been the huntsman here ever since he came from the North Cotswold country when Dorian Williams took over the Mastership. The skill and flair with which Albert has for so long produced outstanding sport has rightly won him a major reputation, but mention his name to folk living in the country and you will soon appreciate that he is also a marvellous ambassador for his sport.

Tuesdays and Saturdays are the Whaddon Chase's two main hunting days, and it has long been such a magnet to foxhunters from outside, as well as inside the country, that inevitably restrictions have had to be made on the size of the mounted fields. Dorian Williams says that one of the factors which has pleased him most in his long term of office has been the enormous increase in the number of farmers and their sons and daughters who ride to hounds with the Whaddon Chase. There are some 1,500 farms in the country.

Originally hunted by the Selby Lowndes family, the country always had a reputation as being a challenge to cross: big hedges, well-ditched, and a vale of large enclosures inclined to ride deep when really wet.

Attended by whipper-in John Barnet, who came from the Portman country this season, Albert Buckle took hounds to the village of Weedon for the Tuesday meet last week.

We were kindly entertained by Mr. George Chapman at Weedon Lodge Farm, and at the meet Mr. Ted Fraser, mine host at The Five Elms, produced a silver loving cup with hot punch for the Hunt staff and the field.

Wild nocturnal weather was probably a major factor in making foxes somewhat difficult to find at first, but when one went away by the brook at Nordruck hounds were able to run fast on a good scent.

The line circled towards Aston Abbotts, and left-handed to Bushmead's Lane, where hounds caught their fox a couple of fields off the lane. A second hunt began with a fox going away from Mr. Parrott's drain, running by the Jubilee Covert, and swinging back over Bushmead Lane by Nordruck.

Hounds then hunted slowly, but very prettily indeed, back across the lane to Creslow. This is the huge area of permanent grass dotted with radio masts behind the village of Whitchurch; when undivided, Creslow was one field of some 365 acres, said to be the largest in England.

It is still fabulous to ride on Creslow's splendid going, and I much enjoyed watching hounds making their line left-handed to the farm area by Whitchurch, where eventually the line could not be sustained. With the late afternoon sun slanting down beyond the village church, and hounds hunting in the foreground, the final stages of the run made a fine picture which stays freshly in the mind's eye.

Foxes will run faster, and straighter before the season is much older . . . and in a wet winter when scent is likely to remain serving they must undoubtedly have a tremendous amount of fun still to come in the Whaddon Chase country before next spring.

FOXFORD

The College Valley

FOXHUNTING in the College Valley's country in the Cheviots fortunately involves few problems – and the rewards far outweigh them.

In a testing country for hounds, it goes without saying that the problems are minimized if hounds start hunting in the best condition and as fit as possible. The degree of supervision which can be exercised once cubhunting commences is limited by the roughness of the country. The schooling of hounds on the roads and in the fields to ensure they have an eye for the movements of their huntsman, and that they meet and resist the temptations on exercise that they will later have to ignore in the field, is therefore all the more important.

There can be no holding up of cubs on the hill, and the problem is to locate the litter of cubs before an old fox decides to step in and draw hounds away. A big bracken bed is ideal cover to start hounds off in. It should be thick enough to provide ample shield for the foxes and to keep hounds "on their noses," but not so thick as to allow hounds from working up close to their quarry more quickly than they would in thick brambles or patches of gorse.

On a bad scenting morning the hill huntsman has to be patient, for he could soon bottom a half fit horse attempting to help his hounds out of their difficulties. The remedies are all too plain to see from a vantage point, but intervention is best preserved for the right moment in the closing stages of the hunt when the fox is beginning to tire.

On a good scenting morning, hounds require little help and the main problem is to stop them hunting before the young entry and the horses have had enough! The hills, of course, afford the huntsman great opportunity to study which hounds are doing the work, especially during cubhunting when they run locally and are seldom out of view, and there can be no finer backcloth for a pack than a hillside with the varied tones of bracken, heather and moss on a bright October morning.

Foxes often run far in October – probably as families and cubs are splitting up and some are driven far afield by parents who feel they have done their stint, and by hostile neighbours. A $7\frac{1}{2}$-mile point is the longest we have secured in this month recently.

In November the bracken goes down and foxes have to fly, though increasing afforestation and growth of gorse in the valley bottoms provides much extra cover in the country than there was 10 years ago. The good hill fox lies out in most weather, on the screes on a sunny day or in deep heather on the tops.

He is easily disturbed and is usually on his legs well before hounds draw up to him. He never waits for hounds and if they "fresh find" it is invariably a fresh fox.

Hill foxes are well aware of the advantages of running through sheep, and the Cheviot Hills are much more heavily stocked than most other hill countries, such as the Fells. There is no more graceful sight than a fox running a wall, and they do this often, and when hard hunted often turn over the steepest of going to gain time, or run the stones by the riversides where scent lies badly.

Lack of cover is, of course, the problem for a tiring fox in a hill country and they often tuck themselves away into farm buildings. One of our shepherds got the fright of his life (and lost a pailful of milk in the process) when a fox, hard hunted in the morning, decided at dusk that it was safe to move from his refuge among the hay bales in the byre – and almost landed on the back of a cow as it was being milked!

Terrier work is an essential part of hunting in the hills, for the more foxes you catch the more you have the following year. Shepherds and volunteers put to the largest holes and of course where soil is shallow so are the holes, so digging is not always a lengthy business.

A more skilful pen than mine has described the type of hound Sir Alfred Goodson has bred to hunt the country. Perseverance is a quality that has not, perhaps, received sufficient mention, for a hill hound must try for his fox and mark him without the support of his huntsman, who cannot always be to hand in terms of hours rather than minutes.

Independence can be a fault as well as a quality, and the right degree comes only through careful breeding and handling. A good hill hound, with his independence, high spirits and activity, is not the easiest animal to handle, especially in his youth. Yet if his mettle is steered on the right course, he is a most rewarding hound with which to hunt the fox.

In the time I have had the good fortune to hunt the College Valley I have handled no better dog than Raglan ('66). He was the best of a very good litter of four dogs and two bitches, and combined all the qualities of a good working hound. As well as possessing great fox sense, he was an exceptional fox-catcher, his muzzle being like a hard-working terrier by the end of the season.

Raglan had a great end in late March '71. Hounds found a good fox on Langleeford. After a turn into the West Percy country, they climbed out to Cheviot itself, and after 90 min and a $5\frac{1}{2}$-mile point, the fox was beat and turned off the hill to be overhauled at Coldburn Rocks.

It would be surprising if Raglan was not closely concerned at the finish, but when Mrs. Letts arrived first up, he was just able to greet her before dying of heart failure alongside his last fox.

However there are many of his progeny hunting here and elsewhere. A good many of them have his fox-catching ability, and there are few who do not inherit his enthusiasm for the best of all sports – foxhunting.

MARTIN LETTS

On October 15, 1977, the people of the Fells in the North West of England celebrated the bi-centenary of the birth of John Peel.

It was marked by a joint meet of hounds in the village of Caldbeck whose inhabitants include Horse and Hound's *celebrated correspondent, Dalesman (Bay de Courcy-Parry). Dalesman, a lifelong hunting man and for many years a Master and huntsman in the North, the West Midlands, and Welsh border areas, recorded this memorable anniversary for us.*

John Peel is So Much More Than a Song

We drink to a sportsman and
brother and the Prince of all
huntsmen, John Peel.

HERE in Cumberland (which new decree bids us call Cumbria), and in the village of Caldbeck, we own something precious, out of which any other part of the country would have accounted tremendous prestige – with something similar to Anne Hathaway's cottage in Stratford-upon-Avon and a statue in the centre of the village.

But, with true Northern modesty, all that we have to remind us that the best known hunting figure of all time lived here is a very ordinary white tombstone in our Churchyard, whereby to remember John Peel.

Every year thousands of people from afar travel here to wear down the grass around the grave, standing beside it in respectful reverance, while the local people might merely mention that the "famous auld hunter" once lived here, and then say no more about it.

However, it seems that the intrinsic merit of the old warrior is realized every so often and his spirit, or his memory, is resurrected, and a "John Peel Day" is celebrated in his honour, mind you, not without an eye to the main chance to raise an honest bob or two for the benefit of the village.

This year it was the turn of the committee of the village hall, under the presidency of our sheep baron Mr. Henry Ridley of Wood Hall, to arouse the neighbourhood and organize a celebration of the 200th anniversary of his baptism, for of his actual birth date there is no record.

Caldbeck, with its traditional Green and its duck-pond, lends itself admirably to any form of rural entertainment and so for "starters" four packs of hounds were invited to meet here upon October 15. At 9 a.m. Major Davidson arrived with huntsman Johnnie Richardson and whipper-in Barry Todhunter and the famous Blencathra pack (with the most of them decended from Peel's old pack) to meet outside the Oddfellow's Inn.

No sooner were they gone away to the fells with their enthusiastic following, than Mr. Tom Wales came with the Cumberland Farmers' pack and Jack Taylor took them into Dentonside.

Then along came the Cumberland, with John Peel's

grandson, or may be great grandson, carrying the horn, and away they went, followed by a fleet of cars to Fauld's Brow – and very soon Robbie Hudson was catching a fox.

And now, with the day warming up into a glorious one, for we have, mostly the best of weather in October, John Leigh and David Grayling brought the Bleasdale Beagles all of the 100 miles from their kennels.

The Blencathra found at once on the bottom of the fell, below High Pike, and, catching a brace, ran a third across their accustomed way of travel across the valley and up to where the Cumberland hounds were hunting and they, of course, caught him, making up their brace, which was followed by a good hunt with a third with scent very catchy.

The Farmers' hounds found themselves in thickly-wooded, difficult country and although many were happy – excepting perhaps Tommy Dickinson, who bought a length of ground, and my Lord Inglewood (who busted his nose) – foxes eluded these hounds' best efforts.

The beaglers (including as fair a selection of long-legged young women as ever climbed the fells above Charlton Wath) went to the high ground and chased a hare, who was hard to find, leaving her below Snow Hill much later on a poor-scenting day.

. Meanwhile, back in the village was high canival, and those recovering from the banquet in their honour at Parkend on the previous evening were going about their appointed duties with calm efficiency, our editor himself in charge of the panel judging the horn blowing competition, for which *Horse and Hound* had presented a mounted hunting horn. This was deservedly won by Barlow huntsman Ted Hill, who has twice won first prize in similar events at the *Horse and Hound* Ball. Mr. L. Hudson won the amateur class and Mrs. Lavender Fletcher and Clive Hodgson judged with editor Michael Clayton. The huntsman's son from the Colne Valley Beagles won the singing competition, himself (seemingly about 12 years of age) rendering three verses of John Peel in a very strong class, while his brother was a runner-up in the horn blowing. Second in the singing was Wayne O'Brien.

Sidney Cole had a stand upon which he displayed many remembrances of John Peel, including a coat of Hodden grey, similar to the one Peel wore out hunting, and spent his day answering innumerable questions to which he knew all the answers, for there is no better authority on Peel than Sidney.

Michael Lyne, the famous artist, and Derek Bingham, the editor of *The Field*, judged the terrier classes with Cyril Tyson. There were very strong classes for fell terriers, which I, personally, would so much prefer to call lakeland terriers (whom once upon a time we knew as Patterdale terriers). There was a fine and even selection with the dog class won by Gyp, the property of Mr. C. Hodgson of Apatria, while Mr. Middleton's Candy won the bitch class.

In the Jack Russells' sector, Mr. D. Brightmoor of Brough was first with his dog and Mr. C. Hodgson's bitch won her section.

Candy won the championship and the painting of a fell terrier so well done by Elizabeth Rowley-Williams.

Michael Whitaker did noble work with the B.F.S.S. van, and being an honest man, well known and liked, he made many new friends – and new members too.

Great heroics were performed by tremendous men in the tug of war, but the two hound trails were a disappointment to those who had come to look and not to bet, since hounds were entirely out of sight excepting for the last 200 yards of their eight-mile excursion around Caldbeck Fell.

The ladies of the village provided 1500 "tatie-pot" dinners, which were collected by a shuttle service from the homes of those who had so kindly cooked them. All went well and president Ridley and hon. secretary George Todhunter have the thanks of the many who enjoyed themselves so much.

Next morning Edmund Porter was hunting his hounds in the afforested crags across Ennerdale Lake, so rising early we sped down to see some more sport. It was a perfect autumn morning, with a sun which shone throughout a most glorious day doing nothing to improve scenting conditions.

Perseverance, however, prevailed and hounds rolled a fox over in the top corner of a huge plantation after hunting him for more than 2hrs. Upon the previous day they had failed to find a fox, and this was something which is of very rare occurrence.

"Rich" Bland, untired after the Melbreak opening meet (a brace of foxes was caught) the previous day, was having a morning off to watch his neighbouring pack.

To myself, it always seems that a stranger can watch hounds at work far more easily in the Melbreak country than elsewhere in the Lake District. Although much of the country is very steep, rough going, the roads running down the deep valleys are a great convenience to the motorist-foxhunter.

An old tale says that there are 21 fine days in every October, and it seems that this must be true this year. And now, with all the shows over and John Peel Day gone, we can say once again:

Of all the recreations with which the heart be blest,
A Chase among the mountains is the purest and the best.

DALESMAN

* * *

Bedale and West of Yore

THE glorious uncertainties of foxhunting were never better demonstrated to me than last weekend when I went to Yorkshire. Fortune can be exceptionally fickle on Pomponious Ego days (Ah, if only you'd been here *last* week," the locals usually say ruefully after only one blank draw).

Yet both my days, with the Bedale and the neighbouring West of Yore Hunts, provided most enjoyable sport – each with an entirely different flavour, and with the added spice of unexpectedness in unpropitious circumstances.

The main problem was the wind. As our corpulent old friend would have remarked, it was "werry windy" indeed. I heard it roaring through the coverts on both nights before hunting, and everyone from Pony

Clubbers to the most wizened veterans of the Chase could have been excused for concluding that "nowt good could come of it."

The credit for ensuring that such forecasts were entirely wrong rests fairly and squarely with the Bedale and West of Yore hounds' Joint-Masters Capt. Malcolm Sherwin, Mr. Michael Abrahams, and Miss Susan Fife, and their Hunt staff. Persistently good hound-work triumphed on both days, and this is not a quality achieved overnight.

Captain Sherwin is in his fourth season as Joint-Master and huntsman of the West of Yore, the pack restarted in 1962 by Mr. James Ramsden. Mr. Abrahams joined that Mastership in 1971; then the following year he and Capt. Sherwin also took over the Bedale country, with Miss Fife joining them in both Masterships last year.

Fifty couple of hounds are kept at the same kennels at Leeming Bar, Northallerton, for both countries, and George Cooke serves them as kennel-huntsman. Yet the Hunts retain their distinct identities, with their own committees and supporters' clubs. Captain Sherwin hunts the Bedale pack, and Mr. Abrahams shares with him the hunting of the West of Yore hounds.

Hunting four days a week, the establishment thus provides much sport for a large slice of Yorkshire, and from my own observations deservedly has a large slice of Yorkshire goodwill from the farming community.

This was clear at the meet at Danby Wiske in the Bedale Friday country, and became a great deal clearer later that night! The farmers out hunting that day included Hunt Committee members Mr. Ken Fletcher, father of show jumper Graham Fletcher, and Mr. Gordon Turnbull.

George Cooke had been fighting a painful eye injury

received from a blackthorn and was on his feet. Mrs. Nancy Stavely, who used to carry the horn with the West of Yore, was assisting in polished style with the whipping-in duties.

Although ploughed land is abundantly in evidence among the grass enclosures, the Friday country has the advantages of smallish coverts, and a mildly undulating terrain. It is easily crossable, thanks to immense work in the post war years by successive Bedale establishments. The present Hunt Secretary, Major Robin O'C Moorsom, told me that maintenance of the country includes the care of some 200 bridges enabling the field to cross the steep-sided waterways known locally as "stells".

It was from the side of a stell that our first fox got up, and being abruptly headed, was lost in a short hunt. The Fell Gill covert soon yielded a far more enterprising customer. Despite that dratted wind, which had got up again, and a glaring sun, hounds made the best of none too helpful scent in sustaining a line past Pepper Arden towards East Cowton. Captain Sherwin viewed his fox lying ahead in some plough, and a smart forward cast saw the pace pick up.

Their fox went on round East Cowton, checking in some cattle-foiled ground – a blessing to the mounted field temporarily out of touch after a misdirection in the village. Then hounds hunted much faster to Stripe House and the Forty Acres covert, where I was impressed to see them running through so well together, sustaining the line right-handed below High Whinholm. A check, and a circle in the grounds of Pepper Arden House, saw the line going right-handed away from the house, towards the Arden stell.

The fox was viewed some 30 yards ahead of the pack as they ran on strongly again. When we came up to hounds at the Arden stell it appeared they had accounted for their fox in the water.

This had been a run of some 13½ miles, including a four-mile point, in 1hr 45min. It was an excellent performance on such a day. Among those still out were some who could testify to this with long experience of the country, including former Masters Mr. Arthur Spilman and Major John Howie, the present Hunt Chairman.

Joint-Master Michael Abrahams, a most effective Field-Master, had flown overnight from the United States, arriving in the country at 9 a.m. and had good reason to declare his journey well worth while!

Having been brilliantly mounted by Captain Sherwin on his dark bay, Dai Jones – a half-brother to Harvey Smith's Evan Jones – I had no excuse for failing to negotiate the interesting assortment of timber and other obstacles during the run. It had been an enjoyable ride.

The Hunt's Thirsk Friday Farmers had plenty of sport to discuss that night at their splendid dinner dance when I met a wonderful company of genuine sporting folk. How fortunate is the Bedale to receive such a solid basis of rural support.

Next morning the wind threatened to knock me off my feet before I could put a foot into a stirrup. So the addition of other distillations to the sporting spirit were indeed necessary at the meet if one was to move off with any optimism from the West of Yore's fixture at Grantley. Despite the wind, however, it was a treat to be out in such beautiful country: permanent grass in small enclosures, with a profusion of small hedges patched with timber, and some stern walls, with the green giving way above us to the brown sweep of winter moorland.

Holding on to my silk hat, and devoutly wishing I had

worn a bowler, I was just thinking it impossible to find a fox let alone hunt one in such a gale, when hounds poured out of West Hill Edge, through Laverton big wood on the line of a sturdy fox which insisted on running up-wind on to Skelding Moor. And what a tear-jerking, coat tail wrenching wind swooped on us!

Hounds did marvellously on the moor, but eventually lost their fox in such conditions. Michael Abrahams resolutely took his hounds back to the thick conifer woods at Laverton, and they drew so well that in 20min I saw a splendid fox breaking covert, with Mr. Abrahams putting the pack on most effectively to hunt the quarry running down wind to the lower country.

And what an entertaining hunt ensued!

It was frequently a case of "hark to Romper", as this large doghound, drafted from the Tynedale country, put the pack right when they feathered in the old pastures past Laverton, and then hunted on short of Kirkby Malzeard left-handed, and right to Biggin, where the fox had to be given best after a hunt of some 70min.

We had crossed a splendid line of country, with plenty of opportunities for varied jumping, and I was indeed glad to have been so well mounted by Mr. Abrahams. Miss Fife was Field-Master, and it was good to see George Cooke resuming his whipper's-in duties this day.

The West of Yore followers are indeed fortunate to hunt in such delectable surroundings. I wish them many more travelling foxes of this sort during the remainder of the season.

And I take off my hat to all those who provide the sport in the Bedale and West of Yore countries – devoutly thankful that the said hat was not blown off first!

FOXFORD

A Crisp Day with the Zetland

THE second stage of my journey northwards was to the Zetland country, one of the most attractive in Yorkshire, or anywhere else for that matter. Changes in agriculture had laid their brown ploughed swathes across some of the grass, just as they have elsewhere in Britain. But there are well-placed coverts, plenty of fences to jump, and a fine sporting spirit in the country which it would be hard to beat.

Since the death of the Senior Joint-Master, Mr. Bill Snowdon, his son, Mr. John Snowdon, continues in the Mastership, joined in office this season by his wife Sally, who is one of the nicest and most elegant personalities in the northern sporting scene. Mr. Willie Barker remains in office to complete a trio of Joint-Masters who form a strong and enthusiastic team at the head of a particularly happy Hunt.

Mr. Barker is a member of one of the best known Yorkshire farming and sporting families, and is the owner of that very good hunter 'chaser Jaunty Jane.

I was particularly pleased to have an opportunity to see Cliff Standing hunting hounds, as I have frequently heard such praise of his skills, and when I visited the Hunt two years ago he was temporarily out of action due to a leg injury.

Cliff is a spry lightweight, and throughout the day I admired his quickness, yet sympathy, in handling his hounds, and his good voice and horn were always a pleasure to hear. Young Colin Hicks, who whips-in, is going to the Heythrop country next season when Tony Collins will be hunting those hounds.

There is considerable Hepthrop influence in the

Zetland kennel, and I was much impressed by the way hounds hunted with pace and persistence on a day when patches of ice and snow lay sporadically in most fields, and with scent deteriorating rather than improving as the afternoon drew on.

There was quite dense fog at the meet at Houghton-le-Side and I was resigned to a long wait and a difficult, slowish day's hunting. The glorious unpredictability of the Chase dictated otherwise: we were to enjoy a really good day's hunting, both in hound-work and in endeavouring to ride after them.

We were hunting on the Durham side of the Zetland country, which, of course, also lies in North Yorkshire. This was an area of mixed grass and arable farming with fences of brush and timber, some of them distinctly upright, especially when jumped out of plough.

Hunt Secretary Mr. Bob Wilson's son, Jim, is the keen amateur second whipper-in, and also assisting with hounds was the distinguished former amateur huntsman Capt. the Hon. Colin MacAndrew, who was Joint-Master of the Zetland for 17 years. It was good to see him going so well at "the sharp end" during a very busy day.

The fog began to lift slightly and hounds were taken to the first draw with no delay. I saw three roe deer leap gracefully from the second covert drawn, and there seemed to be plenty of hares about too, so hounds had to be really steady.

There was news of a persistent chicken-stealing fox at Joe Pierson's covert and we did not have to wait long for the signal to go ahead from Field-Master Mr. Chris Spalding, who is going north of the Border to the Lauderdale as Joint-Master next season.

A fox went away from covert running fast across the Goat Field and over the Piercebridge/Gainford road. He

continued to run on swiftly, and, praise be, there was a serving scent, hounds streaking away on the line.

Their quarry crossed Gallow Hill, passed White Cross Farm, crossing the Cock Lane and skirting Fanny Banks Covert.

Hounds soon bustled their fox out of Dyance Covert and he ran on in the open again, swinging left-handed to Headlam. The pace was somewhat slower now, with hounds getting their heads down and working well.

I was much impressed by Cliff Standing's speedy and effective cast at Headlam village green, where there was inevitably a lot of foiled ground. Hounds hit off the line again nicely as a result, and ran faster again across Middleton House Farm to Ingleton Mill. They crossed the Darlington-Staindrop road, and Colin Hicks viewed the tired fox going to Killerby, through the Kilns, getting to ground just ahead of hounds in an earth below a kale field where he was despatched.

This good hunt of nearly 75min included a four-mile point, and was more than ten miles as hounds ran.

As the winter afternoon drew on and the temperature dropped, we had two more interesting hunts. I heard a crash and tinkle as I landed over one fence and thought I had landed on glass – but it was ice. Yet the going on the turf and plough was amazingly good in most parts, and we were able to keep reasonably near hounds during some sharp bursts which were followed by slower hunting as scent continued to get worse.

From Dobinson's Covert a fox ran fast to just short of Kitchen's Covert, where he was lost on sheep foiled ground. Then hounds found in Houghton Ling Covert and got away well on the line of their fox which ran nearly to Elm Grange, then swinging right-handed at the A.68 and back across Walworth Moor, where he was given best in failing scent and with dusk coming in.

It had been a very creditable performance by hounds and their huntsman in anything but the best of conditions. How fortunate indeed are those who hunt behind such hounds, in such a nice country – and in such good company.

Riding strange horses in strange countries is one of the many pleasures, and occasionally terrors, of a hunting correspondent's life.

People are very kind and provide excellent hunters which know the country and often I can ride my own horses. Yet I have never been more privileged than at the Zetland when I was invited to ride one of the great horses of our time, Crisp.

Sir Chester Manifold's Australian 'chaser, in 1973 at Aintree, "achieved a feat unequalled in all the Grand National's long heroic history". These were the words used by John Oaksey in describing the performance of Crisp and Red Rum in beating Golden Miller's record time by 19sec.

Tragically, after leading the field by some 30 lengths with a fabulous display of accurate jumping over the

Aintree fences, Crisp was overhauled by Red Rum and beaten into second place in the last 50 yards.

John Oaksey wrote of Crisp: "Many horses, of course, have jumped boldly and well at Aintree without making a single mistake. But what Crisp achieved – over fences like nothing he had ever seen before – was a unique blend of speed and economy . . . Crisp is far from a normal horse. All obstacles come alike to him – just one more problem to be solved as quickly and neatly as possible".

Such words were carefully stored in my mind when I put my foot into the stirrup and swung into Crisp's saddle at Houghton-le-Side.

Richard Pitman's old partner entered the hunting field for the first time last season when Fred Winter and Sir Chester Manifold agreed that this was the best future for Crisp, who is now rising 14.

Capt. and Mrs. John Trotter, keen hunting folk in the Zetland country and extremely knowledgeable horse keepers, accepted the offer and the challenge of providing a home for this great racehorse and introducing him to the hunting field.

Of course, 'chasers can make excellent hunters, but many loathe the popping and pushing which can be a hunter's lot. Galloping on at a fly fence is one thing; jumping timber off the hocks on to poached ground, perhaps with wire wrapped round the fence, is another matter entirely.

Capt. Trotter, who so successfully organizes the Zetland's annual cross-country ride, tells me that Crisp certainly did not like timber at first. "Then we let him loose in an indoor school," said Capt. Trotter. "The horse neighed at himself in a schooling mirror for some time. Then he scattered some cavaletti.

"We put up a more substantial bar behind cavaletti and

then Crisp obviously decided: 'If this is what you want, I'll show you what jumping is all about'."

"He flew the jump with feet to spare, and since then he has jumped everything out hunting with no trouble at all".

Brakes seemed likely to be a problem in the hunting field, judging by Crisp's record as a front-runner. The Trotters have found that a pelham with a single rein works best, and I rode him in this.

Behind those famous quarters, with such a pronounced "jumping bump," a red ribbon adorned the top of his tail. The illustrious 'chaser did not take too kindly to being crowded in gateways at first, and had kicked out with his off-hind.

I was glad the Press had always been kind to Crisp, for like a true gentleman, he behaved perfectly when providing a "Press seat" in the hunting field for me. There was certainly no trouble on the gateways.

Once in the saddle, it was surprising to find much less "front" than I had expected, and he tended to carry his head somewhat low at the gallop; he gave a nice strong feel, but did not pull inordinately, and I cannot help wondering if he tends to lean somewhat on the pelham.

Those distinctive Crisp ears often stick out sideways, and there seems a lot of fence showing above his head as he gallops towards a jump. Yet, given a squeeze, the old horse will stride on confidently at any sort of fence.

Like all horses with real jumping ability, he gives a wonderful "feel" as he takes off, really using his back, soaring over the fence like a Trident aircraft and landing way out beyond ditches or any other trouble.

At an in-out of two brush fences over a lane, Crisp put a short one in, jumped cleanly out of plough, and took a stride to surge on over the second hedge into a field beyond. Many an experienced hunter would not have done half so well, and after that combination I felt that we were firm friends indeed. Between fences I could go into "over-drive" if necessary to gain ground easily.

We had a very busy morning in the good hunt described above, and there was plenty of jumping. What a tribute to Fred Winter, and now the Trotters, that this great Aintree horse should have been fit enough and temperamentally suitable for his new life in the hunting field which he obviously enjoys so much.

One thing Crisp will not tolerate is being clipped, and he had to be anaesthetised to be clipped just once this season. His coat is already growing through a bit, and he was sweating up somewhat after the good run.

Very sensibly, the Trotters use him for half-days only in the hunting field, and I handed him over at 1 p.m., full of running still after a busy morning and ready to go home and eat his grub to the last morsel.

I am more than grateful for having had the opportunity to ride such a great horse. It is good to think of him emphasizing the very real links between the Turf and the Chase in this splendid sporting part of Yorkshire. May he prick those distinctive ears at hounds for many a day to come. . . .

My second horse on the Zetland day was a superb ride, the chesnut Porchford, brought over from Ireland by Ernie Fenwick, himself a former 'chase jockey, and now one of the most sporting farmers in the country. A stalwart of the Zetland Farmers' cross-country team which has ridden with such success all over Britain, Ernie really knows what jumping over natural fences means.

Porchford was a fabulous ride from first to last, putting the seal on a day's hunting I shall never forget.

FOXFORD

Dalesman in the Dales . . .

So, with the celebrations terminated and poor old John Peel allowed to rest in such peace as was permitted him, we went hunting with Johnnie Richardson and saw his Blencathra hounds catch five foxes fairly in the one day and a brace in the following days of the week that he was in Bassenthwaite.

This was all in glorious October weather, and the unfortunate young lady who clears up the muddles which I sometimes make said, on yet another fine morning, "Come on Grandad, it's high time you stopped talking and did something useful. For the last six months you have been nattering about writing a tremendous fine book yet never the one line do you write."

May the Lord save us, she is mostly Irish with only slight knowledge of English, who does not understand the word "no" and she brought out the collar and the chain.

"You will go over into Yorkshire and take a look at the packs whose names end in 'Dale' and write something heroic about each one of them, and I will be typing it all out neat and tidy, correcting the spelling and putting in the commas and full stops."

When one is young and strong-minded it is a waste of time to argue with women, and when one is old and senile they just do not listen at all.

"Come on Grandad," said she pushing me into the transport and putting a net over me. We went along the Eden Valley, lamenting that no longer did any hounds hunt beside this, the most beautiful of all rivers, and through Appleby, once a county town and still a very fair one, and over Stainmoor, where our Yeomanry used to camp. The road continued through Warcop and into the Lunesdale foxhunting country and through Kirkby Stephen and along such a glorious hill road with great rolling hills all round us.

On we went through some grand hunting country of big fields and good thorn fences, and away in the distance were all manner of hills and woods clothed all in autumn glory. Then there was Thirsk with its famous racecourse, its grey town and grand market square.

So up Sutton Bank, which once held such terrors for motorists, and across some high ground that looked as though it never could carry a scent, and so to Sproxton and to such a grand, thick-walled cottage of the utmost comfort and warmth, which was to house us for a fortnight.

Then we must find out where hounds were to meet and there was no better nor wiser man from whom to inquire than Mr. Alfred Brown, who has been hon. secretary of the Farndale for over 20 years and chairman of their Supporters' Club since it was first started.

What an afternoon we enjoyed, to be sure, with Alfred and his wife, and we left filled with information and tea. And what do you think, when we turned out of the yard there, on the top of his garden hedge, was a great dog-fox and a couple of hounds in close pursuit, plain to see in our headlights. Gospel true, nor was I ever a man to tell a falsehood.

On the Monday, unable to find hunting anywhere, we went up to Chop Gate to see Britain's oldest pack, the Bilsdale, at Beak Hills, and once again we were welcomed in a most hospitable manner by Nancy Cook, whose husband George has hunted them for the past 15 seasons.

This is a very good pack of fell hounds, looking quite

splendid and reflecting the greatest credit to Nancy, who told us that these most friendly hounds are entirely her own when at home, but belong to George when they are out hunting.

We left this grand place to travel to the Farndale country, which pack lays claim to being the oldest-established pack in Britain, being formed by the Duke of Buckingham in 1670 at Helmsley, though this claim is strongly disputed by the Staintondale, who boast of a warrant to hunt foxes from King John in the 13th century.

On the next morning we climbed up through fog and along Blakey Ridge, which is one of the many ridges dividing one dale from another, and came to Bank Top in good time, as befits foxhunters.

Hounds looked very well and much on their toes after a tremendous hunt on the previous Saturday, when they pulled down a hard-run fox after 1 hr 45 min.

It is unfortunate that lack of suitable kennels compelled hounds to be moved from Farndale almost 20 years ago to Harry Weldon's farm at Great Broughton, where Harry has looked after them and brought them into their own country to hunt them twice a week.

Foxes, it is said, may often be hard to find. However, regardless of the myth, Harry took his hounds or perhaps they took him, straight to a fox who gave us a grand opportunity of appreciating the merit of this most musical pack and of the worth of the grand, weight-carrying Irish horse who took Harry across bog and rock as nimbly as a Connemara might have done.

"Confound these motor cars!" and ourselves as much to blame as any, but they turned this good fox from his chosen point, making him go down by the Goat Hole to climb out above the wood and over the higher ground almost to the top of Farndale, then down to the Oak House Farm.

Here there was considerable confusion, with sheep and cattle gathered in the yards, and our fox was mistaken for a large, ginger tom cat, or else the cat was mistaken for the fox.

Advice was freely given by one and all, while the younger men, almost brothers to hard-running "lads" who used to delight us so much in far away Co. Kerry, went up the steep fell like greyhounds, where Harry, in some miraculous way, put the greatly surprised fox on his legs again, to the astonishment of us far below, still hunting the tom cat.

Now all was hope and glory and the fox came down through Farndale Village and, ignoring the temptations of the Feversham Arms, we watched them climbing up on to Bracken Bank, where the fern covered the smaller horses entirely and, although hounds could be heard loud and clear, it was impossible to see them.

Our fox would have crossed the valley had he not been chased back again whence he had come by a dog, but Harry, undaunted, held hounds forward until they marked their quarry to ground in a mass of rocks.

Then came Wednesday in this eventful week with "the dusky night riding down the sky and ushering in the dawn," and a very dull, unpromising one it was, to be sure.

"A great scenting day," proclaimed those who know these things, as we stood expectantly beside the village green in Sinnington's most glorious old-time village, to see this pack of such ancient lineage arrive at their opening meet.

Mr. and Mrs. William Poole joined the Countess of Feversham in the Mastership last season, coming from the Taunton Vale Foxhounds, which is a very different country from the Sinnington.

Her Ladyship, whose husband, the late Earl, died most prematurely while making history for this pack which he hunted so well, has been Master and Joint-Master for the better part of 30 years and is greatly beloved in all this grand part of England, which well could be called "the Feversham Country," for the family connection with foxhunting over it goes back to the dawn of history.

Willie Poole is a great hound man and most musical upon the horn, which is always a delight, but, alas, he is one of the latter-day-saints in this era of "silent men."

B. Dobson, coming from the Cheshire last year, turned out a very fit and happy pack of hounds, and although a "purist" might, possibly, have looked slightly askance at the broken-coated Welsh immigrants, these are not the old-fashioned woolly-coated "Taffies" with the long ears and sad expressions, but quick and active hounds – and so they ought to be, coming from the Vale of Clettwr, one of the best packs of hounds in all of wild Wales.

Risboro' was the first draw and since it was not possible to cubhunt there the long bank held sufficient foxes for everyone to see at least a brace, all of whom were reluctant to go far away. So hounds were taken away from this vast ruined house, about which no one seemed to know very much, and caught a fox from Sherbrooks Thorns and then made up the brace with another from Skeltons Whin.

Next morning, in sunshine and high spirits, we took that grand hill road past Rievaulx Abbey and, going over the hill by Chop Gate, were soon looking across a wide vale to where, in the distance, the smoke and greyness of industrial Teesside could be seen. Overtaking "horsemen and steeds on their way," we were soon in Stokesley at the opening meet of the Cleveland, where Charles Wrightson is Master. Charles hunted the Stokesley Beagles for 12 seasons before taking over the foxhounds from Mr. Pickering two years ago.

Foxes were hard to find after a very stormy night and it was most disappointing that Constantine was unexpectedly blank, as were a great many most likely-looking places which had held foxes during cubhunting. It was after one o'clock before a fox was found near Broughton and, being headed on the main road, turned to make for the cliff woods below Roseberry Topping, a most fascinating pinnacle standing out above Guisborough Moor.

Hounds, having run fast and well, came to a check above the old railway line above Great Ayton. They were taken back to safety beyond the meet, in some very good country, but did not find again.

On Saturday, a dull morning, we went again to see the Bilsdale at Thirlby, just below Sutton Bank. These are an even nicer pack of hill hounds out hunting than they are at home, and George Cook is quite the right man in the right place at the right time.

The Bilsdale were to draw all that great circle of hill and woodland around Donald's grand mansion, Southwood Hall, and what a wonderful re-echoing place it is to hear hounds, to be sure, with foxes everywhere.

This is a countryside made famous by the Herriot books and the author himself lives nearby the meet, while Donald is, of course, the somewhat cantankerous senior partner, Siegfried, and Thirsk must be the town in these stories.

Hounds found at once and, apart from the Dumfriesshire, I have never heard so glad a chorus as they raced this fox around these wood banks where George blew them away in capital form. But the fox, not risking the open country, came back in view on the driveway below the house and dived into an impenetrable thicket to emerge no more he probably went to ground in the rocks.

Another fox was put to ground behind the Hall and we rushed for home, hoping to see our friend Willie and his Sinnington hounds, who had met at Helmsley, before light stopped play. We dropped right in with them at the closing of a disappointing day of very little scent and, although hounds had caught a fox in the morning at Duncombe, they had not been able to run since.

The ever-hopefuls, looking both cold and hungry, still remained and Willie battled on with enthusiasm undimmed to find a fox who ran resolutely across fields to the River Rye, where a great flock of sheep, taking away what scent there was, made Willie reluctantly blow that last sad call.

So ended quite an inspiring week enlivened, no less, by so many young people coming out hunting, continuing in the old Yorkshire tradition.

DALESMAN

The Suffolk

THOSE Hunts which proudly bear county names are usually among the oldest, and the Suffolk is no exception.

It is more than 200 years old, the Duke of Grafton hunting the country in the middle of the 18th century. I believe in 1745. His Grace's hounds hunted a fox for seven hours, crossing 28 parishes before a kill near Stowmarket.

At the risk of causing the late Duke to revolve fiercely

in his coffin, I would not be surprised if hounds *did* change during that seven hours. However, it is certainly evidence of the open, accessible nature of the country.

And after my recent visit to the Suffolk, one of the features which remains strongest in my mind is the fine sweep of the terrain, allowing one to see a fox run for miles ahead of hounds.

In this incredibly dry spring, the Suffolk acres – virtually all arable – were almost powdering in places under the feet of horses and hounds. I saw a fine dust hang in the air as hounds ran across some of the plough.

Suffolk, of course, has a subtle pastoral appeal which Constable captured: its willows and sprouting oaks standing amidst those gently rolling vistas. And I enjoyed my day with the Hunt as an exploration on horseback, just as much as a splendid chance to see a good pack of hounds working hard.

On all sides I heard nothing but praise for the efforts of Mr. Paul Rackham, now having completed his second season as sole Master. I saw tangible evidence, such as the new Hunt staff cottages and additions to the kennels, but there were also many to bear witness to his hard work in opening up country for new fixtures, and cementing relations with land-owners, farmers and Suffolk's strong shooting interests.

It is always an excellent sign when gamekeepers are among regular Hunt followers, as they are in this country.

Mr. Rackham's expertise and success in producing show hunters is well known in these pages, and at the meet I attended he was mounted on Heron's Phase, now 13 years old, a superb lightweight which twice won the Horse of the Year Show hunter championship. His daughters Jane and Sarah are keen followers and were among the mounted field at the meet at the Old Rectory, Welnetham.

I was sorry to learn that our host, Mr. Martin Corke, was abed with flu, but Mrs. Corke ably dispensed excellent hospitality. General Sir Richard Goodwin, secretary of the British Field Sports Society, and Lady Goodwin are keen Suffolk Hunt members, and Sir Richard was out on this, the last day of the season. Major Gerald Astley-Cooper, the B.F.S.S.'s indefatigable area representative, was also in the mounted field, his 50th day this season on one horse.

Tom Batterbee is in his second spell as huntsman here, returning from the East Essex to carry the horn for Mr. Rackham. And Tom blows that horn exceptionally well; one of those huntsmen who summon hounds out of covert with a proper "gone away" which it is a real pleasure to hear, and to follow.

A Yorkshireman, Tom's early hunting experience was in totally different types of country, but he is now much experienced in getting the best out of hounds on plough. The Suffolk pack had to be largely reconstituted two years ago, and with a draft Tom brought from the East Essex there was also obtained an excellent draft from the Duke of Beaufort, and from the Meynell.

They have some nice young hounds coming on, and I thought the bitch pack worked extremely well on a bad scenting day, with glaring sunshine and a gusty wind.

Fortunately, there was an excellent show of foxes, and we had busy and most enjoyable sport. It is a pretty stiff test to visit a pack on its final fixture of the season, and the Suffolk showed up very well indeed.

In these days of equal opportunities I suppose I ought to forbear special mention that the Suffolk hounds have a girl whipper-in, but I must record that Sarah Turner is a smartly turned out and effective whipping-in person.

After some local hunting in Link Wood we had a short, sharp hunt after a fox which went away to Melfields, running at the back of Bradfield towards Rougham, then swinging right-handed to Tinker's Grove where he was given best.

Some famous hunting correspondents habitually claimed that they viewed away the best fox of the day, but since Foxford is rather inclined to coffee-house when visiting, the claim can seldom be made in this Diary.

However, I really did have first view of the good dark red fox which went out from Breech Wood. Hounds hunted him in the open, then back through the wood towards Bradfield, crossing Capt. Player's stud, right-handed to Chensil Grove. This strong fox then went back to the stud, and on to a stick heap in the covert beyond.

From the thick Rawhall Covert a good fox went away very quickly, and I had a wonderful view of him running with that grace and deceptive ground-covering lope which is so characteristic of Charlie. Hounds were hampered by the poor scent in the open, but made the line very well, going on past Bradfield St. Clare Church to Bradfield Park where he was eventually lost.

We had three useful hunts, and I was indeed content as I rode back behind hounds on the excellent grey hunter kindly provided by the Master, with Tom eloquently blowing for home for the last time this season – always a particularly sad sound in the hunting calendar, but encouraging us all to anticipate the pleasures of cub-hunting in the autumn, and the joys of next season.

Suffolk hunting folk have clearly much to look forward to under their present regime, and I wish them well, having so greatly enjoyed my visit.

FOXFORD

The Eridge

IN this curiously dry early season weather the South and the North appear to have fared rather better for good scenting conditions than the Midlands.

It is a generalisation to say so, but it is certainly my own impression in travelling up and down the country.

Thus I found a decent scenting day when I had the good fortune recently to go down to Sussex for a day with the Eridge. And what a lovely pack of hounds they have to take advantage of such a day.

They look like a pack, and they work like a pack, and so they should, having been so carefully bred by Major Bob Field-Marsham ever since he became Joint-Master just after the war.

His Mastership was completed in 1961, but Major Field-Marsham has continued to be responsible for hound breeding policy with notable successes "on the flags" as well as in the field. Major Field-Marsham has judiciously used the great Badminton, Heythrop and Portman lines which figure so prominently in modern hound breeding, believing that it is not the role of a two-day-week pack to experiment with untried outcrosses, leaving such exercises to the larger kennels.

The Eridge's Actor ('74) who is by Cottesmore Actor, was champion doghound at this year's South of England Hound Show, and was among the pack which huntsman John Cooke brought to the meet at Whiligh, home of the Hon. Miss Daphne Courthope, former Master and a great Hunt supporter who entertained us most handsomely.

It was good to meet again friends I knew some years back when I had greatly enjoyed visits to this country of foxhunting enthusiasts, where some of the best known huntsmen in Britain have served their apprenticeship.

I saw former Masters Col. Thorne-Thorne and Capt. Henry Brierly at the meet, and Sir Henry d'Avigdor-Goldsmid was among the mounted field.

The Marquess of Abergavenny's family established the Hunt country in its present form in 1880 and ever since the family has figured frequently in the Mastership. The Marchioness of Abergavenny has performed great services as Joint-Master in the post-war period, and the Hunt kennels are still on the family estate. Her daughter, Lady Rose Nevill, continues to hunt enthusiastically with the Eridge.

Since 1969 Mr. Rodney Benstead has been an immensely enthusiastic Joint-Master, and Mrs. Moira Schicht joined him in 1971. They continue as Joint-Masters for the committee, and much is owed for their hard work and dedication in keeping foxhunting flourishing and in good heart in a country in the busiest corner of England.

In fact, the Eridge has suffered less from the South-East build-up than I had expected, and has fared better than some other Hunts, but the pressures of urbanisation can never be discounted in this area.

Yet from the meet at Whiligh we were on grass nearly all day, and the going was lovely. I was kindly provided by Mrs. Schicht with a good grey hunter, whose confidentiality I particularly appreciated as I must confess tiny hammers were at work behind my forehead, as I had rashly attended a Hunt Ball elsewhere the night before.

After negotiating the solidly built park rails at Whiligh we watched John Cooke put hounds into the covert appropriately named Happy Valley, since it proved to hold a good fox who went away with determination.

Martin Thorne, whom I saw whipping-in to the Portman last season, now whips-in for the Eridge, with lifelong local hunting man Mr. Bill Swift as second whipper-in.

As I have observed before, John Cooke lets nothing stop him in keeping near his hounds, and I was reminded of this as he led the way over a five-bar gate on to a rather slippery downhill roadway.

The Eridge have put an immense amount of work into providing Hunt timber wherever possible, and it is usually possible to get about with enjoyment and ease, especially at Whiligh.

Our fox ran to Foxhole Farm and Long Wood, going on to Little Pell Wood and Great Pell, then going back towards Wadhurst Village. He turned left-handed over Stone Cross Farm and eventually went back to the Park at Whiligh again where by way of the hunter trial course we followed hounds to Beechfield Covert. Hounds pushed their fox on, and another circular line followed, ending with the fox being marked to ground on Chesson's Farm, where he was accounted for.

We had some local hunting around the Park to follow, and then I particularly enjoyed an evening hunt in undulating country from Little Pell, listening to the Eridge hounds hunt with a beautiful cry as they ran in failing light up the Bewl Valley where work is underway to drown it in a new reservoir.

More country will be lost, but Hunt members take such problems philosophically and look forward to a new bridle track round the water's edge. It was a lovely evening and the pack hunted a difficult line so well, eventually being stopped in the dark towards Wisketts Wood just short of the A21.

Proof of the tonic effect of such an enjoyable day in good company was that I was able to attend the Eridge Hunt Ball that evening at the Spa Hotel, Tunbridge Wells, feeling refreshed and ready for the thoroughly successful party it proved to be.

FOXFORD

The Berkeley

ONE of the countries I have long wished to explore is the Berkeley in Gloucestershire. Parts of it are as big to ride as any country in Britain. I fulfilled this ambition the other day, and although it was a most difficult scenting time for hounds I had a memorable visit.

The building of the M5 carved a severe problem across this hunting country, but the Hunt has done extremely well in recent years to fence the motorway in part, thus making some areas available for sport again.

But the best known and favourite meet of many Berkeley followers is Ham Green, which lies in below Berkeley Castle – in the famous vale country alongside the River Severn – and is unaffected by the M5.

I was most fortunate in being a guest at the Castle of Major John Berkeley, who has been Joint-Master since 1960 and continues his family's remarkable record of ownership and control of this pack.

The Earls of Berkeley hunted all the way from London to Bristol in the 16th and 17th centuries, and the Hunt servants and Masters of the present Hunt – which dates from 1807 – still wear the tawny yellow coats of the Berkeley livery, instead of scarlet.

Standing on the battlements of the 12th century Castle, I gazed in fascination over the view towards the

Severn, a vista which has broadly changed remarkably little over the centuries – apart from the Berkeley nuclear power station sited by the river, yet doing surprisingly little aesthetic damage.

It is still an expanse of grass: the more trim areas of Berkeley parkland below the Castle, where the stone-built kennels stand, and beyond are the pastures and reclaimed marshland which still offer a delectable swathe of grass.

Grazing this land successfully over the centuries was only made possible by extensive drainage, and it is the ditches, dikes and distinctive reens, or rhines, of this area which pose a special challenge to horse and rider in following hounds.

Such wet, low-lying land encourages the growth of hedges, and few can be taken for granted. It reminded me to some extent of parts of Dorset or Ireland, but the Berkeley Vale certainly has a formidable character of its own and hunting folk in these parts are justifiably proud of it.

From the battlements I looked just behind to the church roof where Cromwell placed cannon to blast open the Castle keep. Fortunately, the Castle escaped massive interior sacking in the Civil War and its furniture and other historic contents make it one of the most fascinating buildings in Britain. Thousands of the public visit it during the summer months.

Artist John King and I shuddered in the cell where Edward II was murdered, admired the Castle's tapestries and paintings, and then sallied out into a sunny morning to study a living link with history – the Berkeley hounds.

The pack owes a considerable amount in the post-war years to the neighbouring Duke of Beaufort's and Heythrop kennels. Heythrop Craftsman ('69) and Duke of Beaufort's Tory ('70) are among sires used in the Berkeley pack, and Tipperary Bacchus ('71), which would nick in with the "Green jacket" lines, is another stallion hound used here.

Tim Langley has spent the greater part of his career with the Berkeley, which must be testimony not only to his own loyalty and liking for the country, but to the immensely high regard in which he is held by those fortunate enough to have observed him hunting hounds.

He was kennel-huntsman from 1951, and whipped-in to Capt. Brian Bell who hunted these hounds, and then Tim became huntsman in 1967. It is very much a grass country still, but those big hedges are virtually all coverts and hounds and huntsman need to work most effectively in finding outliers, and in pressing their fox to prevent him finding ample sanctuary.

It is all too easy to describe a huntsman as popular, but the adjective really does apply in the Berkeley country.

Mr. W. J. Barclay Watson has hunted in the country all his life and has been Joint-Master since 1971. This year Mrs. J. "Buster" Daniell, another with a life-long knowledge and enjoyment of the country, has joined the Mastership, to form a strong triumvirate.

Tim Langley, with Richard Perry whipping-in, first drew a covert very close to the Kennels and which often holds, proving that foxes are indeed cool customers and are not perturbed by hound music on moonlit nights.

Charlie was not at home on this occasion, but another fox got up near the meet and was unfortunately chopped.

From the Deer Park a fox got up and ran across the Park into Hillswoods, going to ground at Roundhouse. A warm sun blazed down relentlessly from an almost cloudless blue sky; very pretty, but not hunting weather,

and I was not at all surprised to see hounds finding it difficult to own a line for long in the open. A blue haze in the mid-distance confirmed that it was a particularly bad scenting day.

All the more credit to the pack, then, when a fox from Shepperdine provided an interesting hound-hunt, the line going through Longpools and Fishing House. We trotted along the flood defence wall of the Severn as hounds continued to World's End Farm and over Hill Lane to Hills Woods, where this fox was lost.

Although the pace was not hard, I saw quite a bit of grief in a short distance in the vale, possibly because horses need to warm up a bit to tackle some of those fences with the boldness which is the best insurance against disaster.

A horse which dwells or hesitates at one of those Berkeley deep ditches-towards is not likely to have the momentum to arrive safely on his feet on the far side of ditch and hedge. Such thoughts, and quite a lot of my past life, flashed through my mind as I faced up to one or two of these obstacles.

Fortunately, I was well hunted on an excellent gray hunter kindly loaned by Mrs. Diana Brylis, who is a former Joint-Master of the Croome. Her husband Jack, who I was also pleased to see out with the Berkeley, was sole Master of the Croome from 1951-1961.

At the end of the day we repaired to what was described to me as "the real reen" country, and, although hounds did not find, I had further opportunities to observe these open water obstacles.

I must confess that after two horses and riders in front of me had flopped into a reen, it was discretion as well as chivalry which prompted me to dismount immediately and take a small part in the rescue of one of these unfortunates. The steep sides of the reen, filled with perhaps four or five feet of foul-smelling water, make the whole thing an unforgettable experience.

And a still, small voice at the back of my mind kept whispering: "By the time you get this horse out, it will hardly be worth attempting to jump the reen yourself. . . ."

Sometimes those still, small voices are very wise, and I

took this one's advice and hacked away from the reen. I had not gone far before I observed an element of the Chase which had been lacking for some time – a fox – but my holloa did not carry well enough across the reens, as hounds were by now drawing far away.

More than half the fun of visiting Hunts is exploring their country; if hounds had been able to run harder, I am pretty sure my exploration would have included the bottom of a few ditches and reens.

Yet I can confirm that it is quite something to ride, and the Berkeley hounds continue to maintain high standards in keeping alive one of hunting's longest and most illustrious links with the sporting past.

I doubt whether I could keep Tim Langley's yellow coat in view for long when hounds really run in their marsh country – but I dearly hope for an opportunity to try.

FOXFORD

The Portman

SELDOM is optimism repaid as quickly as occurred after my wish last week for improved scent and longer points.

My Christmas Eve hunt was one of the most enjoyable I can ever remember in the festive season, thanks to both the elements of the Chase so devoutly wished for being present in full measure.

Since the local correspondent, Ballyn Garry, has been somewhat dilatory this season, he kindly allowed me to record the hunt in question, achieved by the Portman hounds in their deep, grass vale which lies below Bulbarrow Hill. This area of North Dorset, smallish dairy farms below and broad downlands above, with occasional secret places in tree clad coombes, has a touch of wildness and even mystery about it which makes it a delight to explore at any time, but never better than when following hounds.

Hunting history abounds: more than 2,000 years ago the pre-Roman iron age settlers hunted from their hill forts of which traces remain at Rawlsbury where Portman foxes so often run; and in the late 18th century Peter Beckford, who wrote *Thoughts on Hunting*, followed his hounds in these North Dorset hills and valleys. From his observations was born one of the classics on the noble science of venery.

We enjoyed the warm hospitality of Mr. Martin Mayne at Chitcombe House, Woolland, on Christmas Eve, and almost inevitably our first fox soon took hounds up the steep slopes of Bulbarrow Hill, behind Woolland. As you ride after them, hounds look like seagulls wheeling against a green sky, but most of your attention is needed to nurse your panting horse up the 900ft slope.

This was a short-lived hunt, however, and soon we were following hounds in the vale again, as they drew the formidable, wide hedges set on banks which harbour foxes as frequently as the coverts. The natural obstacles to be jumped in this vale can never be trifled with, since even the most innocent looking flyer may easily hide a yarning ditch and a big drop. The growth is too thick to permit them to be banked, and the horse which takes liberties with width or height soon pays for it with a fall.

Joint-Master Mr. John Woodhouse, who has also been the Portman's Hon. Secretary for 21 years, holloaed away the fox which provided the day's major hunt. He saw it in Whitecombe Lane after hounds spoke on Mr. Frank Kent's farm at Stoke Wake. Huntsman Geoffrey Harrison had the pack nicely together on what proved to be an excellent line, with a fast improving scent.

They ran towards Droop, swinging left-handed to Park Gate, back across Mr. Kent's farm and over Stoke Common. Then it was puff and pull again for the horses as we ascended Bulbarrow's neighbour, White Hill, but there were smiles all round as the fox sank the vale again, running by Rawlsbury Wood and over the Ansty-Mappowder road into the neighbouring South Dorset country.

Our fox pressed on down the vale, crossing Hatherly Dairy Farm, and skirting Melcombe Park to run through Humber Wood. Here, two and a half couple remained, marking at a drain under a gate, but the main body moved on quickly and there is every reason to believe they did not change.

The line continued across the Mappowder-Plush road, then going through Ball Copse on to Ball Wood, swinging left-handed round the back of the Old Fox Inn Folly, and crossing the valley bottom before ascending Lyscombe Hill. Here, the few remaining mounted followers were cheered on by two gentlemen on foot who proved to be the Joint-Master and huntsman of the South Dorset Hunt, Mr. Alastair Jackson, and fellow Joint-Master, Mr. Edgar Tory. They watched our sport with the extra benevolence of those who had just enjoyed a seven-mile point with their own hounds.

Fortunately for the horses, in view of the "mountaineering" now required, the pace decreased considerably, but the Portman hounds continued to make the line across Lyscombe Bottom, up over Hog Hill and the stretch of arable land beyond the Cheselbourne-Piddletrenthide road, where the fox had to be given best in darkness at Kingcombe. It had been a five-mile point, with hounds running more than twice the distance, in less than 90min.

Just as in the great days when J. J. Farquharson hunted most of Dorset in the last century, one of the chief joys of this sort of line was the wonderful variety of terrain, almost entirely on grass, but changing from deep riding vale, and stiff fences, to narrow tracks through woodland, to soaring hills with wide expanses of grass.

Of the dozen or so who finished I especially noted young Charlie Gordon-Watson, riding his brilliant grey pony, Shade – both rider and mount aged 14 – formerly ridden by his elder sister, the Olympic gold medallist, Mary Gordon-Watson, who earlier this season brought Cornishman out with the Portman. Their father, Brig. Gordon-Watson, was also one of those who finished this enjoyable hunt.

Jogging through several of the vale's little villages, guided by cheerful lights beneath their low-thatched roofs, it was indeed worth rejoicing that we would soon be changing to a New Year bearing ample proof that some of the countryside's traditional pleasures remain as enduring as ever – offering so many more pleasures in the year ahead.

FOXFORD

The South Devon

It seemed a good idea to head for the moorland countries again. Many a hunting vale is still waiting for the corn to be fully gathered in owing to the harvest rain so cruelly timed for a farming industry already beset by so many other problems.

I was delighted to be invited by one of the longest serving Masters and amateur huntsmen in Britain, Mr. Claude Whitley, to join him on Dartmoor as he took his doghounds in pursuit of the fox for the first time this season.

It was in 1938 that Claude took over as sole Master of the South Devon Hunt, until joined by Mr. Dennis Ferens for seven seasons from 1953. This season Mr. Ferens again rejoins the Mastership and is hunting the bitch pack. It is 60 years since the senior Joint-Master's father, Mr. William and uncle Mr. Herbert Whitley, took over the South Devon's Mastership, the former continuing for varying periods until 1938.

Altogether it is a wonderful record of service to hunting in this wild, rugged part of the West by one family, and I am glad to hear they are going to mark Claude's own enormous contribution with a "right good hunting dinner" early in December.

Up there among the granite and heather of Dartmoor the mists can descend with the suddenness of a theatre curtain. So I was exceedingly relieved at 7 a.m. last Saturday to find myself strolling through the charming village of Haytor on a shining, clear morn. Captain Woof's excellent riding establishment in the village not only provided me with a safe mount, but a hearty hunting breakfast as well.

So I trotted across the moor with that happy combination of a light heart and a heavily fortified constitution. Deep purple heather clothed the hills, with the browns of the tors, and patches of green fields making up a superb backcloth stretching up to the pale blue morning skies. Dartmoor had decided to show me her friendliest face.

I was heading for Bone Hill, which lies above Widecombe-in-the-Moor, and I was certainly going all along, down along, out along lee because it was the very route taken by Bill Brewer, Jan Skewer and friends (not forgetting Old Uncle Tom Cobbleigh and all).

And on coming over the brow of the hill one of the first things I saw were the white tents of Widecombe Fair which had taken place that very week.

The Master was riding a grey horse, but clearly such coincidences were not on his mind; he was properly engaged in the current preoccupation of casting his hounds into a kale field belong to his younger brother, Mr. Wallace Whitley, who was among the mounted followers.

With the tower of Widecombe church and cottages sitting neatly among the spread of Dartmoor's autumn finery beyond, it was indeed pleasant to sit listening to the sweet cry of hounds as the pack pushed a fox from the kale into an adjoining small wood.

They certainly rattled the woods to good effect. Within a few minutes there was a resounding whoop from the far side, signalling that the South Devon doghounds had just caught their first fox of the season.

There really was not a great deal of scent, but the pack was working diligently. There were no puppies out on this first morning which had to be a fairly restricted excursion owing to Mr. Whitley's need to hurry off to Newton Abbot Racecourse, where he is Clerk of the Course.

Among the hounds to be entered is the splendid doghound Pagan, who is by Fitzwilliam Paragon ('66), and was awarded the Honiton Cup for the best doghound from local packs taking part in this year's West of England Hound Show. There are some happy links between the South Devon and Earl Fitzwilliam's hounds, since this pack has paid some welcome visits to this country in the West, and there have been useful exchanges of hound breeding lines.

The South Devon's stallion hound Acrobat, who was

out on Saturday morning, has sired some Fitzwilliam litters and has been on loan to that country as a working hound.

The Master, with kennel-huntsman David Strivens whipping-in, jogged next to Bell Tor bog, and it was not long before hounds had another fox afoot. It gave us a chance to enjoy a canter round the edge of the bog as hounds hunted on beyond. Within a few minutes there was a crash of hound music as the pack accounted for the second fox of the day.

The mounted field, who included the sporting artist Mr. Richard Dupont, and other keen followers, had ample proof that cubhunting really had begun. Among those out on foot was Rear Admiral J. H. F. Eberle, Joint-Master of The Britannia Beagles, who told me they had not yet been able to start hunting their country because of late harvesting.

Although the Master had his racing duties elsewhere, the end of the successful cubhunting morning was by no means the cessation of hunting for the day for all members of the Whitley family. The Master's son, Mr. Timothy Whitley, has just taken over as Master of the North Dartmoor Beagles. They had their opening day of the season on the moor at Cator, and I heard they had plenty of sport with a nice 75min. run.

FOXFORD

The Tipperary

IRISH eyes are not smiling much when they discuss the weather nowadays.

During my visit to the Republic last week I heard this winter's rainfall frequently described as "the worst in living memory." Standing in a Tipperary bar with the rain drumming on the windows one could but fervently agree with the gentleman who drank his stout and proclaimed of the Irish weather: "Sure, t'would break the heart of Noah in the Ark".

Sportsmen have lately had to contend with packs of hounds drastically altering meets, or cancelling days, in order to protect local farming interests. The season looks like being curtailed in some countries.

Yet cheerfulness will always keep breaking through in Ireland, and as usual during a visit there, I found plenty of that commodity even in the rural communities where water-logged land, and the dire effects of dearer foodstuffs for cattle fetching depressed prices, have brought no joy to the farmers lately.

The hospitality and friendship of the sporting fraternity was as warming as ever. And despite all the difficulties I found splendid sport at my first stop – in Tipperary. For 19 years Capt. Evan Williams was Master of the "Tipps," renowned for breeding a distinguished pack of hounds, effective in the field – and highly successful on the flags, being so often admired and rewarded at Clonmel and when they have crossed the water to visit Peterborough.

Following such a Mastership is daunting indeed, but everyone in the Tipperary country seems in no doubt they have had good fortune in the appointment of their new Master and huntsman, Mr. Michael Higgens, who took over this season.

Much of his early hunting experience was with the Puckeridge, where he whipped-in for Capt. Charles Barolay, to whom he pays much tribute. ("Anything worthwhile I may know about hounds, I learned from him.")

Coming from an English plough country to Ireland's

grass and banks was an exciting challenge, which this red-headed young foxhunter seized with the utmost enthusiasm. He started by whipping-in and hunting the Island hounds, and then had three seasons as Master and huntsman of the revived East Galway Hunt; he has brought $10\frac{1}{2}$ couple of those hounds to Tipperary.

With experienced and congenial staff in the persons of Micky Flanagan, kennel-huntsman and first whipper-in, who has been 14 years in the country, and Pat O'Brien as second whipper-in, the Tipperary's huntsman has a formidable team with which to provide sport in a wonderful four-day-a-week country.

Insinuating rain – it soon found its way to the skin – attended the meet at Moyglass, near Killenaule, but in no way dampened the enthusiasm of a small, keen field. I was most grateful to be united with Callan, a chesnut hunter kindly provided by Miss Yvonne McClintock.

Callan, named after a TV special agent, will not be five until August but I admired his precocious wisdom, his agility, and his powers of detection in puzzling a safe way across a positive textbook of most of the shapes and sizes in which banks and ditches could possibly be fashioned.

It was to be an "all go" day, certainly one of the most enjoyable I have had this season. And how those Tipperary foxhunters do go! Following hounds across their all grass country means tackling a fresh bank every few minutes. The country became wet even before Christmas and had good scenting conditions, enabling hounds to provide some excellent early season sport.

Mr. Higgens modestly ascribes this to "the wonderful ready made pack of hounds which I am privileged to hunt, plus a marvellous country originally laid out with hunting in mind." These are indeed plus factors, but his own handling of hounds and ability to stay with them have earned much admiration already. He even has the asset of riding light.

The first draw of the day quickly produced a fox in the Knockingglass Covert and in a trice the huntsman's horn was blowing hounds away on a good line in the open.

A lurching drop down what seemed like a cliff, into knee deep mud, gave me a taste of the future, and after a check hounds ran on strongly across a swollen brook to Arbour Hill, and on to Paddy Brown's pit where this fox had to be given best.

A high wind and drenching rain were not preventing hounds making good use of a serving scent, and this opening burst was merely the overture. In a few minutes there was a slower hunt on the line of a fox which had got well ahead early, but it provided an interesting selection of hairy banks for the followers.

The notable Irish National Hunt jockey Tim Hyde, on a numble grey, was showing just how neatly and quickly such obstacles can be conquered. The Field Master Mr. Tom Ronan and others also afforded a visitor excellent pilotage, but I still managed to be swept off once by a low tree branch growing on top of a bank. A seat in the mud below the bank merely emphasized the inroads already made by the rain!

The second hunt having petered out, hounds were put into the excellent Powers Wood Covert, standing like an island amid a sea of grass; a delight to any foxhunter's eye.

Frankly I thought it would take a long time to find a fox and see it go away, but I was completely wrong. Within minutes a ringing holloa signalled the good news, and the Tipperary mixed pack was speaking gloriously and running hard on the line of a bold, travelling dog-fox, going upwind with the utmost determination.

The pack seemed to me to hunt together beautifully all day, with plenty of drive and a splendid voice at just the right times. They owe much to Heythrop and Badminton lines; the stallion hound Portman Lorimer has been introduced as an outcross recently.

From Powers Wood hounds ran on to Ann's Gift, and to the Prospect Stud where they swung right-handed across Coolmoyne road, and on to Tullamaine Moat. This is a grassy knoll bearing an old ruin, not far from the Hunt kennels at Fethard.

"He's gone to ground," I heard someone say, but before one could ease one's horse after a gruelling ride, the crash of hound music told us that Charlie had found the earths closed and was heading back on his line. The fox had gained valuable time in heading back, and after some slower hunting on the grass, from bank to bank, the Master wisely decided it was time to blow for home.

Hounds had run at least 10 miles, with a farther point of nearly four, in 80min; a capital hunt to conclude the day.

Even if the "Tipps" have had to "take water with it" this season, the spirit of hunting is indeed potent in their country – and clearly, they have an exciting future likely to prove worthy of their illustrious past.

FOXFORD

The Limerick

ONE of the great pleasures of my recent hunting trip to Ireland was an opportunity to meet Lord Daresbury, senior Joint-Master of the Limerick Hunt; an M.F.H. of some 40 years' experience, and one of the most engaging personalities in the sport today.

His reminiscences are spiced with a great deal of wit,

and have the special depth born of a great knowledge and love of hunting art and literature. Lord Daresbury's sporting library and paintings are of immense interest and value. It was a special pleasure to view his original Ferneleys and other paintings, recently restored to remarkable effect.

Yet although Lord Daresbury can speak captivatingly of the pre-war glories of all-grass Leicestershire, and the post-war challenge of the Limerick's grass and bank and walls country, he is very much a foxhunter of today, with firm ideas on how the sport should be conducted now – that firmness always leavened with more than a glint of humour. His self-designed hunting stable block is one of the most modern and efficient I have seen.

Having been a Joint-Master of the Belvoir since 1934, Lord Daresbury went to Ireland in 1947 and hunted the Limerick pack as sole Master until 1970 when Mr. A. R. Tarry joined the Mastership, with the Earl of Harrington later forming the present trio at the helm. Hugh Robards was engaged as professional huntsman in 1970, at first hunting hounds two days a week and nowadays carrying the horn on all four Limerick days.

Robards had six seasons with the Heythrop before going to Ireland, and so it hardly needs emphasizing that he is exceptionally well versed in the science of hunting hounds and ensuring their fitness. He crosses the country "like smoke" his admirers assured me. His whipper-in, young Pat Meehan, was brought up at Hunt kennels, but was something of a stranger to the pigskin when he took to the hunting field for the first time this season – yet he rides this big country with amazing aplomb already.

Lord Daresbury has never espoused the Welsh outcross which has so influenced English hound breeding in this century. Thus in contrast to the light coloured packs you will see in so many kennels nowadays, the Limerick hounds are Belvoir tan in colouring, and a distinctive and brave sight they make.

Inevitably Belvoir stallion hounds figure prominently in the blood lines, their Marquis and Warwick being among those used to produce the 31½ couple of 1973 hounds, although the greatest influence on the entry was the Limerick's own stallion hounds, Capital '67 and Valesman '68. Another Limerick stallion hound, whose first litter was in the '73 entry, is Slasher '71, drafted from the Waterford pack where he was sired by Lifeguard '67.

He appears to have a particularly good nose and a distinctive voice since I heard and saw him working particularly well during one of the wettest day's hunting of my life, the first of two days I had with the Limerick.

I have already reported in these columns of Ireland's exceptionally wet winter, and the consequent problems of the Hunts. For this reason Lord Daresbury took hounds up to the coniferous forest-clad hills at Mulareik. In drenching non-stop rain hounds did remarkably well not only to find, but to push their first fox well out of the forest to Glanduff Castle, and eventually kill him above ground. Their huntsman took hounds back into the forest and they found again, and hunted well in the appalling conditions.

Emptying a boot full of water later, I was glad to follow a hot bath and dinner with the still more warming opportunity of stamping a foot at the Limerick Hunt Dinner and Ball, one of the jolliest Hunt occasions I have attended. Irish hospitality and friendship is as delightful as ever it was.

Next morning, praise be, the sun was shining on the Limerick's meet at Drumore House, a Rhineland style edifice looking from a hilltop down to a lake, a fair vista

Mrs. Mary Tarry shows her experience of conditions to be found only in Ireland as she tackled a hairy bank while out with the Limerick Hunt.

of Irish greens and blues, and an immediate prospect of smallish enclosures separated by craggy walls. How fervently grateful I was to the Senior Joint-Master for once again providing me with a superb mount, capable of matching agility with sagacity.

After some local hunting in covert, hounds pushed a

fox away, the holloa being given by Miss Muriel Atkinson, one of the nicest and most experienced hunting people you could wish to meet, who has whipped-in to Lord Daresbury's hounds for many years. They ran to Ballynacarrigh, turned left-handed by Kennedy's crags, then left to Courttown, and back to theDrumore coverts, where other foxes intervened. I thoroughly enjoyed the hunt and the ride; negotiating the walls provided plenty of interest and some challenges, and following the Master I had a magnificent and unusual view of the hunted fox, slipping quietly through a corner of a covert and craftily changing his point.

A memorable visit indeed, proving once again the truth of James Pigg's observation: "There's nowt like huntin'."

FOXFORD

* * *

The prime responsibility of a Master of Foxhounds is to show sport, but what an extraordinary range of activities is involved in achieving this end.

The quality of the pack, the manner in which they are hunted, are vital. But of what avail is this, if the country itself is unsuitable to hunt? The modern Master has to work immensely hard throughout the year in maintaining good relations with landowners and farmers, and in a host of other ways, to ensure that sport is of the best during the hunting season.

Captain Ronnie Wallace in 1977 retired as Joint-Master and huntsman of the Heythrop after 25 years in office. He set standards in the hunting field, and in organising a hunting country, which were admired everywhere.

A tribute to a remarkable record of sporting achievement was paid in Horse and Hound *by Michael Berry.*

Tribute to a Great Mastership

It is only too easy, we all know, to sing the praises of days gone by. The foxhunting historian can, without fear of contradiction, hark back to Squire Osbaldeston or Lord Henry Bentinck as having in their turn made outstanding contributions to the art of hunting the fox and to the science of hound breeding.

To assess the contributions of the great figures in the hunting field over the past 50 years and to compare them with the heroes of the 19th century is obviously far more difficult.

But the past 50 years have certainly produced Masters worthy to rank with the most illustrious of their predecessors. When "Chatty" Hilton-Green died, not long ago, the Duke of Beaufort wrote a delightful appreciation in these columns, claiming that between the two wars, when England still had plenty of wild, well-fenced grass countries and when, for instance, Chatty was hunting the Cottesmore hounds, we enjoyed (perhaps without appreciating it at the time) "a golden age of foxhunting".

There is no necessity yet to consider what we owe to the Duke of Beaufort himself and to Sir Peter Farquhar – not forgetting Mr. Isaac Bell.

But this is certainly the moment, when Captain Ronnie Wallace is just resigning his Joint-Mastership of the Heythrop hounds after 25 years in office, to pay tribute to the constant help that he has given to all of us, to offer our thanks and to express a hope that in years to come his genius may still make itself felt from the more distant heather-clad slopes of Exmoor.

Ronnie Wallace was born in the year 1919, son of a

foxhunting father who for many years was secretary of the Eridge hounds. He duly went to Eton, where he whipped-in to the beagles in 1935-36 and hunted them for the two seasons 1936-37 and 1937-38. In those three seasons sport with the Eton College pack reached a very high level.

Statistics, for what they are worth, record that in 1937-38 he killed 75 brace of hares and three foxes in 104 days – a record for any pack of beagles until in 1966-67 Mr. Alastair Jackson (now Master of the South Dorset Foxhounds), hunting the Royal Agricultural College Beagles at Cirencester, killed 76 brace in 82 days.

Ronnie went on to hunt the Christ Church Beagles at Oxford in the season 1938-39 and, of course, made it more obvious than ever that he was a young man with an amazing flair for hunting hounds, catching hares and organizing a hunting country.

Very soon after that he changed from a green to a scarlet coat, becoming Master of the Ludlow Foxhounds in 1944 and hunting them for four seasons – need one add, with great success. In 1948 he moved rather nearer the "fashionable" countries and took the Cotswold hounds.

At that stage he showed such consistently good sport as to establish himself firmly as a highly efficient Master and a first-class huntsman. One more move, four years later in 1952, enabled him to return to a green coat, as Master of the Heythrop, to take over a much bigger establishment and, hunting hounds himself four or five days a week, to show wonderful sport to a very large and well-mounted field.

Moreover, with much greater scope for breeding hounds his kennels began to be one of the fountain heads of the very best foxhound strains and, through his generosity in helping other Masters, it has had a very great influence indeed on foxhound breeding in the past 20 years.

It would not be accurate to suggest that the Heythrop hounds are alone in their glory. We all know that the Duke of Beaufort has been brilliantly successful in hound breeding and equally generous in helping other packs. He, too, has shown sport of the highest order, hunting hounds himself for many, many seasons and, of course, he has held the highest offices in his own country and in Court circles, in addition to playing a leading part for innumerable good causes.

Ronnie, like Master, has travelled far and wide, judging here, speaking there, finding time for everyone. But his main work, of course, has been organize sport in the Heythrop country to the highest possible pitch, solving difficulties with charm where charm alone can succeed, but in general relying on an organization which he has made so regular and so efficient that there is not much left to chance except the weather and the whims of the foxes. Indeed many of the foxes must have found their minds made up for them.

Even hunting hounds four or more often five days a week for so many seasons is itself a feat of courage and endurance. That the Heythrop hounds and their big field should be able to go virtually wherever they wish and to make long points all over their own large country – and sometimes make incursions into neighbouring countries – with barely a murmur of dissatisfaction from landowners and farmers is a wonderful achievement. Happily, numerous other packs could be quoted as equally well received, but not many who have such large fields of hard-riding supporters.

Until quite lately Ronnie devoted many summer days to hunting the otter – again, need we add with remarkable success. Either he or his father were Joint-Masters of the Hawkstone Otterhounds for 30 years from 1936-1966. Since then he has topped up his services to fox-hunters as a whole, not only by invaluable work for the British Field Sports Society, but also as chairman for the past seven years of the M.F.H. Association.

Anyone who has attended the annual general meeting of the M.F.H. Association and listened to Ronnie's survey of the year, dealing with perhaps 15 or 20 difficult subjects – relations with Government bodies, humane killers, Humane Societies, motorways and so on – must be amazed at the work involved and at the patient logic of the suggestions put forward by the chairman and his committee.

Lord Henry Bentinck was a great hound breeder, but he was apparently a solitary bachelor, and indeed the politics of hunting just did not exist in his day.

Why do the Heythrop hounds make such long points and catch so many foxes? Of course, they are beautifully bred, so as to ensure, as far as possible, that they can gallop and stay and have good noses and fine voices. But Heythrop drafts, just as well bred, go to other packs and they do not automatically have as good sport as the Heythrop. Breeding is not everything. If it were, then a man whose two grandfathers each won a V.C. would necessarily be a brave soldier.

We know that he will, in fact, be a brave soldier only if he serves under brave, efficient and inspiring officers. It is the handling that makes the difference. The morale of the Heythrop hounds is very, very high. They expect every day to be a good scenting day and they expect to catch foxes.

If the present pack disappeared and Ronnie was presented with a fresh pack, no doubt the morale of that new pack would very soon be just as high. And how does one attain that high morale?

Technical efficiency, first-class kennel management, confidence, mutual trust – and no doubt, in order to maintain a first-class pack in a first-class country, the Master must be autocratic, perhaps even ruthless.

After all, the best commanding officers are not always smiling. Think of Monty – or Frank Freeman. Yet in Ronnie's case, under the formal exterior, there is a streak of real generosity and human kindness.

But we have said enough. Fresh superlatives are hard to find. The Heythrop foxhunters are saying goodbye to a very exceptional Master who, through his devotion to their sport and also through his services to foxhunting as a whole, has certainly secured a place among the great Masters of all time. And if I were an Exmoor fox I should certainly now be considering emigration.

MICHAEL BERRY

* * *

Towards the end of each season, the Melton Hunt Club holds its annual ride across one of the most delectable pieces of Leicestershire – alternating each year between the Quorn, Belvoir and Cottesmore countries. More than 70 riders ride the line, and afterwards there is a meet of the appropriate pack of hounds, and everyone enjoys a day's hunting.

Here Ivor Herbert describes a Melton Ride in the Cottesmore country.

How They Finished – or Fell

LIKE an orange gush from a giant's hose 72 contestants, compressed on Col. Billy Smith's starting line high on the hill-flank, suddenly burst forward. They swept on to the first hedge in a flood.

It was a bullfinch, "splashed" down to the height of a stout schooling fence, wide enough to take 30 horses abreast and very thick indeed. A huge swathe of blackthorn cuttings filled take-off and landing sides to the brim.

A troop of half-a-dozen detached itself instantly from the main body and galloped at an angle downhill as if sucked by gravity. They thrust at two post-and-railed jumps lower down in the scratching bullfinch. The rattle of legs on grey rails, a sharp cry, and several bitten-off shouts wafted half-a-mile southwards across the Cold Overton to Somerby lane.

Red coats, racing colours, black coats and sweaters of variegated taste, all thundered onward. But the overall colour was orange, from the huge number-cloths carried on the chests and backs of competitors in last week's annual Melton Hunt ride.

Grouping, scouting, wheeling before the start they had looked like French cuirassiers before Waterloo. As they spurted across the green sloping hill behind Somerby Lodge Farm, you could see the hats: some bold devils with rakish top hats, many black caps, and a host of sensible crash-helmets under a confetti of different coloured covers.

No one was riding racing length, but most leaned forward much farther than those game "thrusters" of last century's sporting prints. All shapes and sizes were galloping across as fine a line of Leicestershire hunting country as ever Lionel Edwards painted. And natural. So far only one hedge had needed to have an oxer of wire cut back.

By the time the leaders had raced over the sixth fence –

three fell in a tangle behind Oaklands Farm buildings – the orange mob tailed backwards across three wide Leicestershire fields. They were on a cavalry charge front: a furlong of turf and difficult but jumpable fences covered the riders highest up the hill and those – we spotted Chris "Pardubice" Collins and Elizabeth "Killer" Boone – going down the shortest but wettest way lower down to the first lane crossing.

The pace of the landing posse was tremendous.

"Good two-mile 'chase speed," grunted former leading amateur Bob McCreery. "Faster than a point-to-point," Chris Collins calmly noted. Both would know. Both were in the first half-a-dozen. Behind them two refused.

This was no neat course, but 4½ miles of tough Leicestershire hunting country inviting one to cross it again on a bold horse – at one's own speed . . .

The ground, drying after weeks of rain, was tacky and holding. The line, riders opined, was the toughest in the series. It was a tremendous one to watch, for the route – the first red marker-board gleamed distantly high on the green ridge south – struggled up four hills, two of such severity that out hunting one would certainly trot. Walking round on the contest's eve, we blew like grampuses. Three times the line crossed contours 150 feet apart.

Confusion, as we'd expected, on the first lane crossing: boggy take-off, slippery landing, rails and hedge opposite. Several refusals. One loose one. A policeman on guard. Clatter of hoofs, smash of timber, screech of iron shoes on tarmac, a few cries of frustrated rage.

The leaders jinked west again – a water-logged paddock – to fan out round Somerby football pitch, past a clump of astonished council houses and then over the

steep in-and-out of rails guarding both sides of the narrow Owston lane.

Several falls silhouetted in jerky black and white on the farthest green sky-line: a gaping ditch with insecure footing at the top of a pumping incline. The horses swung left, due south, over some of the sharpest ridge-and-furrow, then left again, eastwards at the top of a diving incline past some foxholes down to Somerby Brook.

Someone – a speck of red whirling against the sky like a shot bird – turned a terrifying cart-wheel and crashed down, still.

The field vanished into the cleft of the brook. Watchers, all local country people, some splendid farmers, a quiver of elderly ladies, somersaulting children, broke out in a spate of speculation: who might be leading?

There were all sorts riding. Little Barry Hills, the great flat-race trainer, with 102 horses awaiting his return to

Lambourn, sat neat as a wren at not much more than 9 stone natural weight (but all had to carry at least 11st. 7lb.). Douglas Bunn – the Master of Hickstead – loving it all the way, thundered along at 16st., backing himself to win the heavyweights.

A handful of farmers: Michael Chatterton, Michael Coulson, William Cross, Bob Hislop, Michael Ings. Some sporting invaders: the Woodhouses up from distant Dorset, a team from the Mid-Surrey Drag, Jeremy Bagge and Christopher Barclay from Norfolk, Mrs. Brocklehurst down from Cheshire, Jerry Dennis, a dashing stockbroker from Gloucestershire, Tim Hart from Essex, a Smith from Yorkshire . . . Cambridge undergraduates and graduates, serving officers from the King's Troop and Capt. Gavin Musgrave, their adjutant, men from the Blues and Royals, and Capt. Tony Goodhew, adjutant of The Life Guards.

Then there were popular locals like the Humfreys (he of the Desert Rat moustache and typical air of a Major) who, on astonishingly inexpensive horses and doing it all themselves, won a sheaf of victories in the ride last year.

Some famous names, too, from distant and different backgrounds: the Hon. Bridget Astor from Hever Castle, Neil Wates, the builder, Lord Vesty, Capt. Willie Long of Blades the tailors, Miss Mary Gordon-Watson, Mrs. Sally Everitt, and international property man Charles Mackenzie Hill.

They are a good mixed bunch in the Melton Hunt Club, founded by the late Lance Newton, that popular and energetic man whose widow "Urkie" (Lord Rank's daughter) runs the whole caboodle with marvellous dexterity, firm heels and light hands.

"Ask Urkie" is the universal cry.

The Club's "rides" – not *races*, please," say the foxhunters "whatever they look like!" – began in 1956. They've missed only two years. Riders contribute at least a fiver towards the sporting farmers' costs.

Urkie Newton, whose telephone had been squeaking since 6 a.m., said, "The Hunt Club spends three thousand a year on fencing within ten miles of Melton".

The line last week lay over 10 different farmers' land. All were enthusiasts about the extraordinary event. None was keener than Dick and Michael Reynolds, father and son, over whose land the distant finish lay, flanked by rich horse-boxes and humble trailers, shimmering Aston-Martins and dog-dirty Minis.

Now the leaders hove in sight again, breasting the stake-and-bound above the brook where the new binders, thick as footballers' thighs, gleamed like hawsers.

"Pardubice" Collins and the nubile Suzanne Lumb (who had scrutinized the land with the microscopic earnestness of gold-prospectors) crossed the brook on a slippery wood bridge. They and Barry Hills squeezed over, jostling together.

The leaders swung round a telegraph pole, recrossed the Somerby-Owston lane, struck on eastwards over the old hunter-trial course and came down on an in-and-out of nasty fixed timber flanking Rubbish Dump Lane.

A grey horse stood out in the first three galloping strongly. There was a girl in a pale blue cap and a man in a red coat. They were like the first questing hounds of a pack. Their pursuers tailed backwards in a loop of a mile.

The leaders leapt into and out of the Somerby-Knossington road, with Tommy Philby keeping the pressing cars back. Behind there were several refusals, a horrid fall, two loose horses pounding away, then the leaders came up to us perched on our hill. They were cantering steadily.

Pretty Elizabeth Boone, a novice riding Off Centre, squelched past under her pale blue cap just ahead of the experienced Mrs. Sally Everitt on Vanwall. Both were moving easily. In third place galloped that good eventer Miss Katherine Wills on Rabicane.

Tense and crouched in fourth place "Pardubice" Collins moved past us well-mounted on his point-to-point and event winner Barbers Piece. He gave his fans a curt nod and strode on by. He was to comment later that he waited too long.

Close behind galloped Mrs. Rosie Samworth, who had won five of the rides on the trot. Then in sixth place appeared Mary Gordon-Watson, with Bob McCreery, seventh, looking as if he loved it with a great grin, and Mrs. Jennifer Phillips, eighth (who before and since her marriage has won many point-to-points.)

Not more than a field behind the leaders (and the fences, though battered, were not yet flat) came Lord Vesty and Barry Hills.

Barry had declared at Urkie Newton's dinner party that his horse wouldn't be good enough. He was right; it was barely cantering and blowing horribly. Barry shouted back "I'll pull up soon. . . . "

Douglas Bunn came past a little later, going amazingly easily for a heavy man. "How's my money ahead?" he called. He had negotiated a mass of complicated wagers with James Teacher.

After the first group, the next pursuers were trotting past our vantage point, two hills from the finish. Then behind those came weary riders almost walking. Gasping heads and necks extended, nostrils wide and pink, the last of the horses wobbled up the slope. A few arrived still taking it easily.

"I'm really loving this," called a grinning man in red coat. Another greeted by mirth from a giggle of friends, snapped back, "Well, at least I've got *this* far. Half of 'em haven't".

Nor had they. More too would fall, pull up, refuse on the run to the finish up one last desperate hill and across the slippery Cold Overton-Knossington road.

In the last field Jim Cunningham, well in the rear a mile from home fell in the last small ditch. "I was going well," he announced in the bar.

Ten minutes after the leaders finished Dr. Parry from Market Rasen was hammering up the lane from Knossington, wheeling right across the smashed rails only to refuse again at the second last hedge.

Forty-six finished, a score of them reporting (as has become the habit after these Melton rides) that they – "had finished about twelfth".

At the finish the crowd of horses steamed. Cameras poked. Bottles of Martell – the only prizes – were presented. The winner, Sally Everitt from Colston Basset, said her arms had been pulled out all the way, that she'd had Vanwall since he was an unbroken three-year-old, that he'd been fifth in the Foxhunters at Aintree and had been reserve champion showing at Leicester.

"So now he's done *everything*," she sparkled, "and twice he was reported dead!"

Excited voices retold horrifying crashes. Jeanette McCreery had fallen early, squashed out by two fallers beyond a fence. She had remounted and finished, looking a trifle shaken.

"Horses fell everywhere," she said, "some awful falls. I couldn't look, or I wouldn't have dared keep on".

"Teach" Teacher and his slim wife Chloe had both completed. He had won money off Bunn and stood long drinks in the clamorous tent.

Outside the Cottesmore hounds, under their highly-praised Master Simon Clarke – "*easily* the best up here this season" several people murmured – met and moved off.

Six vets and three doctors – "Urkie got her priorities right," said someone – were caring for the fallen. A few stitches had to be put in, but no horse or rider was seriously hurt.

And the rest of these remarkable thrusters, treating this grinding, frightening marathon as a mere hors d'oeuvre, trotted off to enjoy a proper meal of foxhunting.

IVOR HERBERT

Spring

This is a time for endings and beginnings. The hunting season concludes, but Masters and Hunt staff are appointed at this time. It is a time for renewal in the hunting world, as it is throughout the rural scene.

Many hunts finish their fixtures in early April; on the moorland countries it is still possible to continue throughout that month, and even to kill a May fox before the season finally ends.

It is a time for taking stock, and planning begins already for the next season.

Here Foxford records his last day of the season.

With the Heythrop on Dartmoor

NEVER have I ended a season with more regret than this one. Constant heavy rain has been a problem in many countries in the New Year, but what an open season – and better still, what a remarkable scenting season!

Some of those with memories going back well before the last war tell me they have never known better sport.

It was not a happy story everywhere. Some deep vales in the South West found the heavy rainfall too much of a good thing right from the start.

Yet, since we had virtually had a drought in many areas for several years previously, generally the moisture in the ground did improve scenting conditions marvellously.

My last day was in the South Devon's country on Dartmoor, on Friday last week, when Capt. R. E. Wallace, Joint-Master and huntsman of the Heythrop, brought his bitch pack for a visit.

Ronnie Wallace's annual Spring hunting tour of Exmoor and Dartmoor with the Heythrop hounds is famous in the hunting world. Other packs, of course, visit different countries occasionally, and although it must involve quite a lot of organization such trips produce immense fun.

Watching another huntsman and hounds hunting your country is enormously interesting for the local supporter, and for the visitor there are so many novelties to be discovered.

Widecombe was the scene of the meet, and on a sparkling sunny morning, it was indeed a sight to gladden any foxhunter's eye, with the green coats of the Heythrop Joint-Master and his whipper-in, Anthony Adams, surrounded by the red coats of their hosts and other visiting Masters and huntsmen.

Mr. Claude Whitley and Mr. Dennis Ferens, Joint-Masters of the South Devon, both carry the horn, in their country, on different days. They welcomed Capt. Wallace, and also Heythrop Joint-Master Mr. Ted Marsh and Mrs. Marsh, and Mr. J. W. Painter, a Joint-Master of the Woodland Pytchley.

Mr. Painter had come to Devon with Tom Teanby the Woodland Pytchley huntsman who was formerly with the South Devon.

Mr. Jim Broom, Master and huntsman of the Dart Vale and Haldon Harriers, was also in the mounted field, and there were three professional huntsmen, Rachel Green from the Monmouthshire, John Creed, kennel-huntsman from the Blackmore and Sparkford Vale, and South Devon kennel-huntsman David Strivens..

Mr. Michael Renny, Joint-Master and huntsman of the East Devon was out on foot.

So altogether the front row of the stalls held a strong contingent keeping a particularly close eye on the centre of the stage. This sort of limelight is absolutely no strain

Captain Ronnie Wallace, Joint-Master and Huntsman of the Heythrop since 1952, leading hounds away for the last time on March 26th, 1977, with (right) his Kennel Huntsman Tony Collins.

to the elegant bitches we had all come to see, the Heythrop bitches, and they proceeded to show us how to make the very best of a particularly difficult day.

There proved to be very little scent in the open, and foxes tended to be "not at home." Sunshine did not abate all day, and this never aids scent. The going was remarkably good in places, but those Dartmoor granite slabs and ruts can make you catch your breath when you try a smart gallop.

The Heythrop pack got on excellent terms with their second find, a fox which went away from Honeybag Tor. It was essential to get on good terms and really press a fox to sustain a run in the open in such conditions, and this they did.

After going into Goodlays Wood the fox went on to Hedgebarton Newtake, going over Belltor Bog towards Widecombe Hill. Hounds ran fast over Pudsdum Down, going on over Ruddycleave Mire to Buckland Beacon where a holloa enabled hounds to be held on from Cold East Cross to Halshanger Mire, hounds running on to mark to ground at the Thornbushes. This was a splendid moorland hunt, with a four-mile point.

Hounds found another brace, and marked them to ground in a long and enjoyable day, with Capt. Wallace blowing for home well after 5 p.m. I had been particularly well mounted by Mrs. C. N. Evans, on an excellent Game Rights mare who flew swiftly and safely over any sort of going, good or gruesome, and jumped obstacles with assurance.

Dartmoor offered us ever changing fabulous views all day, but to attempt to convey it one would need the sort of talent of our Field Master, the sporting artist Mr. Richard Dupont. He has been hunting four days a week this season, and I do wish I could match that . . . (the brush is mightier than the pen).

After such a day we all owed our best thanks to our hosts in the South Devon country, and to Capt. Wallace and his hounds. They certainly proved that even the best of scenic attractions is all the better for having a pack of hounds working well in the foreground. . . .

FOXFORD

* * *

Richard Pitman, the leading National Hunt jockey, made a transition from the saddle to the microphone when he retired from race riding. He became a successful B.B.C. T.V.

commentator – but he also had time to find a new recreation: foxhunting. At the end of a season he looks back on his new experiences in the hunting field.

How an Ex-Jockey Discovered Hunting

WHEN a professional steeplechase jockey retires from the saddle he is unable to relive the glories of yesteryear via the medium of point-to-points, having once ridden for hire.

But one year after my retirement – having written a book, been seated behind a microphone throughout the winter, and clacking away at a typewriter for three days a week – I must admit that I would be no danger to even the most "novicey" amateur, and would weight-wise, nearly qualify for the heavyweight division of the members' race at the Heythrop.

So, excluded from point-to-points by my professional status and the state of my body, I decided my future recreation lay in the hunting field. For the past few seasons the Old Berkshire Foxhounds, who are extremely well hunted by Colin Nash, one of the Joint-Masters, has allowed me to qualify my wife's pointers and hunter 'chasers with the Hunt.

This, however, did not give me a proper insight into the hunting scene, mainly because so many Thoroughbreds kick out from excitement, others bite, and worst of all, some of them treat the majority of obstacles with disdain, or even utter horror!

On one of my earlier qualifying days, I was merrily cavorting among the leaders when my mount, Road Race, decided that the fifth tiger trap was far more frightening than the previous one, and promptly refused, both front legs being caught in the jump.

My predicament was not helped by the fact that Mike Allsopp, another Joint-Master, had been right behind me and in "full cry" at that moment. After backing his horse off Road Race's quarters, Mike left me in no doubt as to my rightful place. "You, you * * * * excuse for a jockey, should be at the back of the field with the older women and small children where there's time to think and holes in the fences!"

At his next attempt the Joint-Master's horse sailed over the tiger trap to disappear into the woods. A scruffy 12 hands pony gave me a lead over the cause of my embarrassment. Fifteen years as a jockey had taught me that horses make fools of men, but it is also true that men make fools of themselves.

The day with the V.W.H. when Pat Eddery borrowed Peter Walwyn's own hunter for his "maiden hunt" was one to remember!

My host was Michael Henriques, permit holder and then a Joint-Master who mounted me on a Grade A show jumper. Armed with the knowledge of his achievements, I felt confident that a good day was in store.

Pat, sporting fancy black walking boots, was riding only two holes longer than he did on Grundy in the Epsom Derby. Dry conditions causing little or no scent led to a situation whereby the field had remained on terra firma for the first half hour.

So, with a twinkle in his eye, Michael Henriques motioned to the field to follow him over a hedge, not quite in the direction that hounds were working. Having waited so long for the first jump, the field came alive at the chance to perform and surged forward 20 abreast and five deep!

The inviting 4ft hedge concealed an enormous drop on the landing side, waiting to claim its usual proportion of victims. As he felt the turf defy his bodyweight and his topper crumple under the strain, Peter Walwyn heard his Number One jockey shout: "If that's the proper way to land Guv'nor, I'll do it my way".

Pat was becoming airborne for the first time in his life, and when a halt was called seven fields later he was among the elated band recounting their thrills and pay left-handed compliments to the fallers who were slowly rejoining them.

The day became more lively and, apart from giving Ann Backhouse a close look at my show jumper by hitting her broadside on, nothing went wrong until the hounds crossed the river over a dilapidated footbridge.

Peter Walwyn led the way into the river only to sink immediately up to his horse's girth in thick mud, and, as if one, the followers turned down stream at the gallop where a safe bridge stood some one and a half miles away. Five of us stayed to see Peter safe, then he too headed for the bridge. The bank was sheer except where the first attempt had failed.

We leapt into the river and, despite much frantic threshing about, scrambled triumphantly on to the far bank soaked but intact. Smug with the knowledge that we had left the field far behind, we attacked the next hedge as if it were non-existent. It was at this point that I realized what hunting is all about (I hear M.F.H's everywhere asking: "Hasn't he ever watched hounds work?")

For me, it was the answer to my quest to find a replacement for the excitement and satisfaction which steeplechasing had provided in the past.

Several kindly people invited me to visit their Hunts

during last winter. My first visit was to the Berkeley, between Gloucester and Bristol, a country comprising nearly all grassland in small parcels bordered by hedges, each accompanied by a broad ditch.

With the Berkeley, jumping is the name of the game, and survival of the fittest is the order of the day. The penalty for landing short over a hedge is to be dragged backwards into the vertically-sided ditch, which not only loses you the hunt but also covers the recipient with a film of black mud, inflicting its pungent smell on the intruder for several days!

My host, Mike Irish, mounted his two sons, his wife Jenny and myself, and to his eternal credit all five of us completed the day smelling only of aftershave and talcum powder.

The Earl of Radnor was kind enough to give me a day on his wife's superb hunter with the Wilton Hunt, who boast a large grassland country near Salisbury. The obstacles were post and rail or Hunt jumps inserted in wire fences.

This day a young jockey repeatedly showed the field how stupid it is to qualify a horse on a racing saddle with his knees under his chin, giving little or no assistance from above. The horse refused eight or more times at each fence, providing the field with a source of conversation when the main purpose of the day lulled.

My next visit was to the Zetland Hunt in North Yorkshire as the guest of John and Joy Trotter, who house Crisp, the 1973 Grand National second, amongst their string of hunters.

Always one to show his well-being by rolling in his stable, Crisp injured a hock prior to my visit, rendering himself unfit to resume our partnership.

Having always scurried through Yorkshire solely by

means of the A.1 I did not quite know what to expect of the people or the land, but now, having met so many genuine folk and hunted their country, I cannot wait for a return visit.

There are no Hunt jumps inserted in the huge stone walls, and the railway sleepers that sometimes form the post and rails defy even the largest horses. If a partnership is careless enough to clout either, they learn by the mistake – if they are still intact after the impact.

To the casual observer, Ernie Fenwick, John Ormston and Harry Johnston looked to have the instincts of Kamikaze pilots, but as the day wore on I realized they were real hunting folk and knew just what they were doing.

I admired them for their prowess, and the ladies of the Hunt rode at the black stone walls with as much grit and fervour as the men.

My final visit was to the Cotswold Hunt on a drizzly Thursday, and in the small field were Col. Chris Sidgewick, his wife Jill, Rosie Hambro, Pam Cowley, Annabell Owen, Barbara Scudamore and George Exell. Hunting their Thursday country can best be described as a jolly day out. Jill Sidgewick was even able to laugh when the horse she had lent to me came over backwards in a gateway, breaking the saddle's sprung tree and rendering it useless!

Within several minutes Rosie Hambro emulated my feat when attempting to jump a set of rails down a 1 in 4 hill which had surface water rushing down it. She established a new British record of 107 yards for unaided travel on one's back in the mud – which was 100 yards farther than her horse.

So I have found a pastime both rich and poor can enjoy, which provides wonderful exploration of the countryside, produces breath-catching excitement, and leaves one tired but fulfilled at the close of the day.

RICHARD PITMAN

* * *

For all foxhunters the end of season is a time for making decisions about horses. Do I sell him? Do I keep him? What are his needs?

A leading veterinary surgeon, under the nom de plume 'Horse Doctor' advises on the options for the end-of-season hunter.

Those Vital Decisions About Your Hunter

THE end of the hunting season is a time of re-assessment and decision making as far as one's hunter is concerned. Indeed it may be a watershed in his working life: time for a number of pertinent questions to be asked.

Is he too old to do another season?

Will he stay sound through another season? Worse still, can I get him sound before next season? Is he worth the trouble and expense of Hobdaying – firing – X-raying, etc.? Can I stand another season having my arms pulled out? If I send him to a member of the show jumping fraternity could he be cured of stopping – breaking timber, etc., etc.? Will I be able to afford to hunt next year? Shall I sell him now, or when he looks better at the end of the summer? If it's a mare, shall I try to get her in foal?

These questions reflect the close relationship between a man and his hunter and are not just objective enquiries about the horse's ability to function properly. They also include considerations of cost, suitability and even affection.

It is extraordinary how sentimentally attached you get to a horse that has regularly carried you to the front; memories of when everyone else refused but he jumped that hairy place in the corner, or the day you gave both the Master and the huntsman a lead over that upstanding gate. These memories affect your judgment. An old favourite will be kept on for just one more season when common sense dictates that he or his owner – or both – should be retired.

This is a good time to consider some of the practical considerations involved. To provide all the answers would require not only a vet but an economist – psychologist – tax adviser rolled into one. Even then the wrong answer would probably emerge.

When the season finishes there is the opportunity to treat various unsoundnesses that you have patched up or put up with during hunting. Some particular conditions will be obvious and may have been causing problems for weeks.

Discuss with your vet what should be done. You have a tendon or suspensory ligament, a fetlock joint or a hock swelling up or causing lameness that you have been controlling with poultices, etc. Now you must decide whether to blister or fire it. Possibly your vet can recommend some modern surgical treatment.

Some horses with ringbones, spavins or chronic foot lameness will have been kept going on butazolidin. Now is the time for a detailed diagnostic examination, probably including X-rays.

Some of these conditions can be treated surgically, some can be shown to be so bad they will not be likely to respond to reasonable doses of butazolidin next season. It is worthwhile to spend time and money in a detailed consultation with your vet about a hunter who cannot be kept sound without drugs, and to ask for a second opinion if he appears at all uncertain about his diagnosis, or the development or treatment of the lameness.

The great mistake at this time of year for a horse with leg problems is to turn him out without doing anything. You lose valuable time during which effective treatment could be working. Even if you have had no specific leg problems it is still well worth examining his legs closely before turning him out. After a hard season with lots of road work or the odd bang on the legs, it is surprising how general wear and tear causes enlarged fetlock joints, big knees and various thickenings to appear without causing lameness.

At the end of term the opportunity should be taken to help disperse these by blistering, which only takes a few days whilst a horse is being let down, and if the horse is properly controlled with side reins or a cradle, no problem should arise.

If you have not blistered horses before you should obtain the blister and some advice on application and control from your vet.

The major end-of-season overhaul involves the legs. However, certain other problems can well be attacked now: a horse with a bad tooth can have it removed, unsightly warts can be operated on, saddle-sores and cuts, which have only undergone running repairs so far, can now be attended to properly. Whilst hunting the true state of a horse's wind will have become apparent. Some horses that seem to make a noise when unfit will no longer make it when they are hunting fit and doing plenty of fast work. Other horses that appeared to be sound will very obviously make a noise after galloping through the fifth or sixth field of plough. Moreover, one gets a pretty good idea out hunting whether the whistle or roar a horse makes affects his ability to gallop and jump through a fast and long hunt.

If you find that your hunter makes a noise and it stops him performing as well as he should, now is the time to consider having him Hobdayed. There will be plenty of time for him to get over the operation and get big and well before next season.

When and how should hunters be turned out? This is dictated by a number of factors, and seasons finish at different times in different parts of the country. Hunting seems to be finishing earlier than it used to with few packs killing the proverbial "May fox" nowadays.

After the unprecedented wetness and deep going this winter, at least one famous Midland pack finished the season in the last week of February.

Hunters can only be turned out when the grazing is dry and the weather not too wintry, though it is quite possible to turn them out before the grass is growing, so long as they are provided with hay. Occasionally, for reasons of labour shortage, hunters are turned out in cold weather with New Zealand rugs on. If you intend turning your horse out fairly early, don't be in a hurry to give him another clip after the middle of January.

When you have finished hunting and are not aiming at a final fling over the hunter-trial course, you must start "letting down" or "roughing off" your hunter.

This involves a variety of things. First of all, a radical drop in the quantity of oats or nuts in his diet to be replaced by a series of mashes. This dietary change is accompanied by a rapid reduction in the amount of exercise he gets.

In order to prepare him for his new environment, he should have a rug removed every two or three days until he is in the stable with no rugs at all. Simultaneous with these changes in his management, he should stop being groomed as grooming removes the protective greases and matting from his coat.

When he is wearing no rugs, getting no exercise and no corn, is no longer being groomed and has been blistered, he is "let down" and ready to turn out. Incidentally, he should not be blistered until he is completely "off" corn or nuts, and should have his legs greased with vaseline five or six days after blistering and before he is turned out.

If there is an early finish to the season and if the horse has fairly recently been clipped and the field he is going into is very exposed, it may be necessary to turn him out gradually by leaving him out by day and bringing him in at night for a week or so.

Apart from an extreme case like this, it is surprising how well horses adapt to being turned right out "at a stroke" if they have been carefully let down first.

Horses at grass should have their shoes removed and their feet trimmed regularly. It just may be worthwhile having front shoes put on with brittle feet or rough, hard ground later in the summer, but generally speaking all foot conditions, and particularly corns, pedal ostitis and ringbone, improve a lot with a few weeks on the soft without shoes.

During the period at grass, any troubles that occur will arise from injuries from barbed wire fences, kicking horses or foot troubles. Horses at grass often pick up nails, stones or bits of grit which work their way into their feet and cause inflammation. Sometimes they also sustain cracks in the walls of their hooves.

Some ponies, and the occasional rather cobby horse, suffer from laminitis during the period of rapid spring growth of grass, so regular inspection by the owner, and occasional trimming of the feet through the summer are necessary to control these problems.

Some people hunt all winter and show jump or event all summer. I am sure a horse is better for six or eight weeks complete holiday in the spring. Oats, nuts and hay do not contain all the dietary requirements of a horse and by the end of a hard season, a horse has often lost condition which is demonstrated by his lower haemoglobin levels and blood count. A rest, and the iron and vitamin content of spring grass, can put this right.

Any keen hunting man, thankful at the end of a good season to his horse, will feel that part of the contract involves a run at grass.

HORSE DOCTOR

* * *

The end of a season may well be the end of a Mastership, or even a hunting career.

Here, Dermot Kelly, at the end of his last season with the Meynell, looks back on his memorable term as Master and amateur huntsman with this great pack in one of the best countries in Britain.

What Fun It Has All Been

I WELL remember during 1961 reading *Horse and Hound* and seeing that the Meynell required a Master for the next season. At the time I was in Yorkshire as A.D.C. to

General Lord Thurlow who was the most delightful man and a most distinguished soldier.

My predecessor in the job had been Captain Fred Barker, who is now Joint-Master of the Quorn.

Mr. Douglas Bunn told me recently he once met the General, who told him he had spent more time being A.D.C. to Messrs. Barker and Kelly, than they had to him!

I remember saying to the General: "I think I have had enough of the Army. I see the Meynell want a Master, I think that I'll put in for it".

I then got a tirade on the fact that he'd always known I was mad, but this was the finishing touch, and ended up by saying that the Army was the only organization that could possibly employ me and I would be best advised to remain in it!

I then spoke to Captain Colin MacAndrew, who had allowed me to whip-in to him hunting the Zetland hounds. He said: "Well you might as well put in for it. It will be good practice, but you'll never get it!"

I then composed a letter to the Chairman, and showed it to the General, who said it was illiterate and rewrote it for me! To my amazement I was accepted.

It had always been my ambition to hunt some hounds, so May 1, 1962 was an exciting day in my life. However, I wondered whether the General was right, and came to the conclusion that he probably was. To be taking on the Meynell, knowing very little of the art of hunting hounds, let alone breeding them, and running a famous country I must be mad. But there we were, the Meynell was stuck with me, anyway, for a season.

During the first summer I did my best to meet as many people as possible – landowners, farmers, keepers, earth-stoppers, puppy walkers and so on. Hound exercise came and went without anything too ghastly happening. Cubhunting went fairly well. Hounds managed to catch a few foxes, and I learned something every day. The opening meet was a disaster, scentless with everything going wrong, and the foxes headed everywhere.

In spite of everything we had a few good days up to Christmas. Then the big freeze-up put a stop to hunting for virtually the rest of the season, which was probably very lucky for me. We had some days on foot in the snow, and I was taken on again for the following season. I also took the opportunity of marrying a local girl, which seemed to improve my image!

One was still largely in the dark for the second season, but it was a good scenting one, so the sport was adequate, and one kept on learning all the time.

Thereafter things went well, the hounds produced good sport with the minimum of assistance, and a satisfactory number of foxes was caught. The country was getting organized as one wanted it. Leslie Johns came to do the terrier work and organize the earthstopping, which had been a weak link.

It is sometimes said that with good kennel management, more foxes are killed in the kennel than out of it. I think this is true; equally the management of the country is vital. The Master must know everything that happens in his country almost before it happens. Good contact must be maintained with the farmers. Shooting interests must be considered and consulted; any damage to fences mended up as quickly as possible. I was once on a tired horse in the dusk, and hounds were running where we had been earlier. Heading for a gap which I knew had been made, I had a proper fall when my horse hit a stiff post and rails, which my damage man had erected where the gap should have been!

Certainly a lame horse is of greater concern than a lame hound, I was lucky that my wife undertook the organization of the stables, and we were fortunate to have an up-to-date and helpful vet, and a good blacksmith.

An awful lot has got to go right with a day's hunting before you have a really good day. The more you can organize beforehand, the better chance you have of producing good sport, and doing your job of controlling the fox population.

It has been said that the more foxes you kill, the more you will have to hunt. I think this is true, as if you do your job efficiently, other people will be less inclined to do it for you.

It has also been said that there is no such thing as luck. I think this is true taken over a period of years, although some seasons are bound to be better than others, however good is your organization.

Breeding a pack of hounds is a fascinating task. Over the years it is interesting to see characteristics coming through from generation to generation. The training and handiness of your hounds starts when they come in from walk and continues from kennel to hound exercise, and on through cubhunting. It is vital to have your hounds handy and responsive.

I well remember the 1968-69 season. We had a particularly good cubhunting and caught a record tally, then the blow of foot and mouth disease struck the evening before the opening meet, and it was not possible to hunt at all that season. One will never forget the depression of the countryside as herd after herd had to be slaughtered. One realized how completely foxhunting is linked to the farming industry.

By Christmas I was unlivable with, so we arranged to go to East Africa to see the wildlife with Major and Mrs.

Lindsay Wallace. Mrs. Wallace was hunting the South Shropshire herself at the time. Believe it or not, the first wild animal we saw was a fox. We stayed in Africa for four weeks and enjoyed every minute, but it still was not comparable to foxhunting.

How lucky one has been to hunt the hounds for 18 seasons, something no one can ever take away. The problems of modern foxhunting are there to be faced and sometimes worried about, but how much the rewards outweigh them.

How much better one remembers the good days than the bad ones; a few great hunts.

Hunting correspondents nowadays write of three-mile points. I had always understood there was no such thing as a point of less than four miles, and a great hunt must be at least a six-mile point, and the *hunted* fox must be caught.

I shall never forget my best hunt from Longford Carr which included a seven-mile point, and 11 miles as they ran in 70min, the fox caught on the outskirts of Derby, with the field and even the cars, scattered in every direction over miles of countryside. Just sometimes it felt as though one was leading an old-fashioned Cavalry charge.

How well one remembers the excitement of the final judging at Peterborough if one's hounds were in the shake up; the few triumphs, the more frequent near-misses.

What pleasure it gives one to see some Hunt servants who helped one so much hunting their own hounds; John Cooke at the Eridge, Johnny O'Shea at the Cheshire, Cliff Standing at the Zetland, and Jimmy Laing at the Burton.

What has one achieved? Probably not very much, but

over 1,500 foxes, caught, one likes to think a top class pack of hounds bred, and one hopes the country and farmers at least as good as when one took on the amalgamation between the Meynell and South Staffs achieved, and one hopes the whole operation set to go well for one's successor.

One final thought: The fox is a very clever, cunning and pretty unpredictable wild animal, and contrary to what the antis will tell you, he starts with most of the high cards in his hand. To minimize this advantage is the objective of an M.F.H.: a top class pack of hounds well managed in kennel, and well disciplined in the field; top class horses well managed in stable; efficient earth-stopping; good liaison with landowners, farmers and keepers; a good Field Master to control the field, and yet see they enjoy themselves; and finally the back up of the Hunt chairman and his committee, to see that the finance is there to do the job properly.

If all the above is there, the fox can still disappear into thin air within a quarter of a mile! But at least you have attempted to see that it does not happen.

Looking back, what fun it has all been. How much there is still to be learned. On scent alone, the more you *think* you know, the more you realize how little you know; what awful mistakes one has made . . . and finally dare one think, and hope, for a second innings after a breather, somewhere, sometime in the future?

DERMOT KELLY

Appendices

Glossary of Terms

ALL ON The expression used by the whipper-in to tell the huntsman that every hound in the pack is present.

ACCOUNT FOR To kill or run the fox to ground.

AT FAULT It means that the hounds have stopped during a hunt because they have lost the scent.

BABBLER A hound that gives tongue (or bays) when it has not picked up the scent of a fox, thus misleading the huntsman and the rest of the pack.

BAG FOX A fox loosed from a bag for hounds to hunt; a deplorable practice forbidden by the Master of Foxhounds Association and *not* undertaken in modern foxhunting.

BILLETT A fox's droppings.

BINDER The top strand of a cut-and-laid fence; you may hear of a horse falling after 'catching its leg in a binder'.

BLIND A 'blind' ditch is one covered with grass or weeds; the country generally is blind and 'hairy' in early autumn.

BLOWING AWAY The huntsman's series of quick notes on his horn when hounds leave a covert on the line of a fox. A most stirring sound.

BLOWING OUT An approximately less exuberant note on the horn which the huntsman blows to bring hounds out of a covert which is blank, or empty of foxes.

BOB-TAILED A bob-tailed fox is one with little or no brush.

BOLT To bolt a fox is to drive it from an earth or a drain, usually by putting a terrier down.

BOTTOM A deep gulley or steep ravine which cannot be jumped, and must be skirted on horseback; to say that a covert has plenty of 'bottom' means that it has much thick undergrowth.

BREAK A fox breaks covert when it runs from it.

BREAK-UP When hounds kill the fox and eat its carcass, an extremely quick process.

BRUSH The fox's tail. Sometimes a guest is presented with the brush at the end of a good run; or it goes to a member of the field who has done well to stay with hounds during the hunt.

BYE-DAY An additional day's

hunting to those normally hunted by a pack.

BULLFINCH Often a formidable jump. It is a high hedge with a spreading, thin top; you have to jump boldly *through* the upper part.

CAP As well as being the headgear of the huntsman, the Master, farmers and children, it is the term used for the sum paid by a visitor for one day's hunting; or the smaller amount, paid by regular subscribers each time they come out hunting, usually in aid of the fund to take down wire nowadays.

CARRY THE HORN To be a huntsman.

CARRIES A SCENT The ground surface 'carries a scent' if it is good scenting country such as clean pasture land.

CARRY Plough, or some other sticky surface, 'carries' when it sticks to the feet of a fox or a hound, usually after a frost.

CAST The hounds' efforts to recover a lost scent; a huntsman casts hounds when he tries to help their efforts.

CHALLENGE The hound which first gives tongue on striking the scent of a fox, can be said to 'challenge' or 'open'.

CHECK To lose the scent either temporarily or permanently. After they have checked they have to cast (see above).

CHOP To kill a fox before it has had time to run from covert.

CLEAN GROUND Land which is free of distracting scents such as sheep or cattle stains, or the foil of horses.

COLD LINE An old scent.

COLD SCENTING COUNTRY A country which does not carry scent readily.

COUPLE Hounds are always counted in pairs; thus a pack may be 15½ couple, or 31 hounds; the traditional way to put hounds on a leash is to couple two hounds together with links of chain joining two collars.

COURSE When hounds pursue a fox which is in view.

COVERT (pronounced 'cover' without the 'T') Any stretch of growth where a fox resides: usually a coppice, a stretch of gorse, or a wood; in addition foxes are found in a 'woodland' which in foxhunting terms is always a big area of trees.

CRY The noise made by hounds when they are hunting.

CUB A young fox.

CUBHUNTING The preliminary period of hunting, mainly September and October, before the season proper starts on November 1st.

DOUBLE A 'double' is the short term for a fence with a ditch on both sides: a double bank is a big, wide bank with a ditch on both sides. The huntsman 'doubles' his horn when he blows a succession of short notes on it.

DRAFT Hounds which are sent out of the pack are 'drafted', either to be sold or given to another pack.

DRAG The scent line left by a fox when it returns to its bed after a night's hunting on its own account.

DRAG LINE An artificial line used by trailing some suitable substance across country for a pack of hounds to follow. Hence the title 'Drag Hunt' for packs which habitually follow artificial lines to provide guaranteed runs for the mounted followers.

DRAW The process of sending hounds through a covert to look for a fox; 'the draw' is the area of country where the huntsman intends to search for foxes during a particular day's hunting. To 'draw' a hound from a pack is the practice of hunt staff in calling an individual hound's name and making it come forward from the other hounds.

EARTH A fox's underground home.

ENTER To enter is to initiate young hounds in the skill of hunting a fox by taking them cubhunting for the first time.

FEATHER A hound feathers when it is uncertain of the line it is following; usually it waves its stern and keeps its head down, but it does not give tongue under these circumstances.

FIELD The mounted followers of the hunt – not including the Master, and Hunt servants.

FIELD MASTER Either the Master himself, or someone he appoints, to be in charge of the mounted field. He tells followers when to stop and when to gallop on, and he keeps them off cultivated land etc.

FLYING FENCES Those fences which can be cleared from a gallop, preferably a collected gallop.

FOIL Any odour which tends to obliterate that of the hunted fox; if a fox doubles back on its tracks he is said to be 'running his foil'.

FRESH FIND To rouse the hunted fox anew after losing him.

GOOD HEAD Hounds 'carry a good head' when they run well together and are not strung out.

GUARANTEE The sum of money which a Master receives from the hunt committee towards his costs in hunting a country.

HACKLES The hairs along the ridge of a hound's neck and spine.

HAIRY A hairy hedge is an overgrown straggly one which can be a tricky jump.

HARK FORWARD (pronounced on the lines of 'Harrk For-or-orrard') The huntsman's shout to the hounds indicating that one or several hounds further on have spoken on finding the line of the fox, or it could indicate that the fox has been seen further on.

HEAD To head a fox is to turn it from the direction it is running; cars on roads are very likely to do this.

HEADS UP Getting their heads up, refers to the hounds lifting their heads from the scent.

HEEL To run the heel way, or to hunt the heel-line is to follow the scent in the opposite direction to which the fox is travelling – something the huntsman must always be careful to prevent.

HIT THE LINE To hit the line is what a hound does when it finds the scent.

HOLD UP To surround a covert with horsemen and prevent foxes leaving it; usually done during the cubhunting season.

HOUND JOG The half-trot pace of a horse which is accompanying hounds along a roadway.

HOLLOA (or 'View Holloa', pronounced 'Holler') The shout or screech given by someone who has just seen the fox; the intention is to inform the huntsman and hounds of the fact.

HUIC HOLLOA (Pronounced 'Hike Holler' – 'Huic' means 'Hark') A shout or screech to draw hounds' (and perhaps the huntsmen's) attention to a holloa further away. Thus a whipper-in might hear a good holloa two fields from a covert where hounds are drawing. The whipper-in might canter up a ride inside the covert shouting to the huntsman and hounds: 'Huic Holloa! Huic Holloa! Huic Holloa!'

KENNEL-HUNTSMAN A huntsman who looks after the management of the kennels where hounds are kept. This applies only to a pack where hounds are hunted by an amateur. A professional huntsman is his own kennel-huntsman.

LAY ON To start hounds on a scent.

LARK To lark in the hunting field is to jump fences when hounds are not running; or to do it on your way home unnecessarily. Usually frowned upon unless you have no other way of going from one field to the next.

LIFT This is what a huntsman does when he calls his hounds to him, and takes them to a point where he thinks the fox has gone, and where they can hit the scent again without having to try to find the scent over the ground in between. He may take them some considerable distance if he is sure that he knows the route the fox has taken. To lift hounds and then disappoint them is bad practice.

LINE The scent trail of the hounded fox.

MAKE 'Making' the pack is counting it.

MARK Hounds are marking when they give tongue at the mouth of an earth or a drain after the fox has entered it.

MASK A fox's head.

MIXED PACK A pack comprising both bitches and dog-hounds.

MOB To mob a fox is when hounds surround a fox in covert and kill it without giving it any chance to escape; this could happen when a covert is held up during cubhunting.

MUSIC A commonly used term for the cry of hounds, e.g. a 'crash of hound music'.

MUTE Hounds often run mute, without giving tongue, when they are running hard on a good scent. When a hound habitually runs mute and never speaks to the line it is a serious fault.

NOSE To breed hounds 'for nose' is to breed them for their scenting qualities.

OPEN To give tongue on hitting the line.

OPENING MEET The first meet of the season proper, usually on or soon after November 1st.

OVER-RIDE To over-ride hounds is to ride in among them; a hunting misdemeanour.

OWN THE LINE To speak to the line, e.g. 'a bitch named Rambler owned the line first.'

OXER An ox fence: a thorn fence with a rail on the side of it; a double-oxer has a rail on each side.

PAD A fox's foot. This is sometimes presented to followers for the same reasons as a brush (see above).

POINT The distance in a straight line between the start of a run and its end, e.g. 'Blankshire Hunt score 6-mile point . . .'; Hounds, and the followers, will usually run much further than six miles in achieving a six mile point.

QUICK THING A very fast run is sometimes called a quick thing; a popular phrase in the galloping grass countries where some huntsmen have been renowned for providing 'a quick thing'.

RASPER A splendidly avocative name for a formidable fence.

RATE To rate a hound is to tell it off; a function strictly reserved for Hunt staff.

RINGING Running in circles; it is applied to a fox which will not run straight.

RIOT A foxhound riots when it hunts any animal other than a fox; it is strictly trained not to do so as a young hound; but the temptation to hunt, say, a hare or a deer is often very strong for a foxhound.

SCENT The smell given off by the hunted animal.

SKIRT A hound which cuts corners instead of following the exact line of the fox it is hunting is said to skirt, or to be a skirter.

SPEAK To give tongue, or bay.

STAIN A sheep stained field is one which is foiled by sheep for scenting purposes.

STALE LINE An old line of scent left long after a fox has gone.

STERN A hound's tail.

STOPPING To stop earths is to block them at night so that the fox which is out foraging cannot get below ground when he returns. One system of earth stopping was to stop the earths within the area of the day's draw, and to put to others adjacent. Thus the foxes it is hoped to hunt will be above ground and cannot run to ground nearby; nor can hounds change during a run to a fresh fox nearby.

STUD-BRED Stub-bred foxes are those which are bred above ground rather than in an earth.

TAIL HOUNDS Hounds which are behind the main body of the pack when they are running.

TALLY-HO Same as 'View Holloa'. 'Tally-Ho back' is a shout which means that the fox has been viewed coming out of a covert, but he has headed back into the covert.

THROW THEIR TONGUES When hounds are in full cry.

TONGUE When hounds 'give tongue' they are baying.

TRENCHER-FED The old system whereby each hound was kept by an individual farmer at home and then brought to the meet to form a pack with other hounds on a hunting day, i.e. 'a trencher-fed pack'.

UNENTERED A hound is unentered when he has not finished his first cubhunting season.

VIEW To sight the hunted fox.

VIXEN A female fox.

WALK To walk a foxhound puppy is to rear it at your own home.

WHELPS Unweaned puppies.

WHIPPERS-IN The first Whipper-in and Second Whipper-in are the huntsman's assistants in the field.

List of Hunts

WITH LOCATION OF KENNELS

England and Wales

ABER VALLEY
Felin Uchaf, Aber, Gwynedd

AFONWY
Pentre-Ceithon, nr. Rhayader, Powys (Tel: Rhayader 202)

ALBRIGHTON
Whiston Cross, Albrighton, Wolverhampton, W. Mid. (Tel: Albrighton 2270)

ALBRIGHTON WOODLAND
Hurcott, Kidderminster, Heref./Worcs. (Tel: Kidderminster 3069)

ASHFORD VALLEY
The Forest, Hothfield, nr. Ashford, Kent (Tel: Ashford 21248)

ATHERSTONE
Witherley, Atherstone, Warks. (Tel: Atherstone 3385)

AVON VALE
Spye Park, Chippenham, Wilts. (Tel: Lacock 277)

BADSWORTH
Hillthorpe, East Hardwick, Pontefract, Yorks. (Tel: Wentbridge 325)

BANWEN MINERS'
C/o Hon. Sec. Mr. D. R Hopkins, 47 Southdown Avenue, Mayals, Swansea, W. Glam. (Tel: Swansea 4221)

BARLOW
Horsley Gate, Holmesfield, Sheffield, Yorks. (Tel: Sheffield 890245)

BEAUFORT'S, DUKE OF
Badminton, Glos.

BEDALE
Low Street, Northallerton, Yorks. (Tel: Kirkby Fleetham 242)

BERKELEY
Berkeley, Glos. (Tel: Berkeley 239)

BERKSHIRE, OLD
Faringdon, Oxon. (Tel: Faringdon 20153)

BEWCASTLE
North Gill Bank, Ainstable, Cumbria (Tel: Croglin 601)

BICESTER AND WARDEN HILL
Stratton Audley, Bicester, Oxon. (Tel: Stratton Audley 610)

BILSDALE
Beakhills, Chopgate, Middlesborough, Clev. (Tel: Wainstones 368)

BLACKMORE AND SPARKFORD VALE
Charlton Hawthorne, nr. Sherborne, Dorset (Tel: Corton Denham 214)

BLANKNEY
Blankney, Lincs. (Tel: Metheringham 20250)

Blencathra
Gate Ghyll, Threlkeld, Cumbria (Tel: Threlkeld 219)

Border
Overacres Farm, Otterburn, Newcastle-upon-Tyne, Tyne & Wear (Tel: Otterburn 646)

Braes of Derwent
Whittonstall, Consett, Co. Durham (Tel: Ebchester 789)

Bramham Moor
Hope Hall, Bramham, Wetherby, Yorks. (Tel: Boston Spa 842167)

Brecon
Canal Bank, Watton, Brecon, Powys. (Tel: Brecon 2091)

Brocklesby
Brocklesby Park, Humberside (Tel: Roxton 214)

Burton
Riseholme, Lincoln, Lincs. (Tel: Lincoln 22798)

Cambridgeshire
Caxton, Cambs. (Tel: Caxton 213)

Carmarthenshire
Old Kennels, Llysonnen Road, Carmarthen, Dyfed (Tel: Carmarthen 7269)

Cattistock
Cattistock, nr. Dorchester, Dorset (Tel: Maiden Newton 210)

Cheshire
Sandiway, Ches. (Tel: Sandiway 883004)

Cheshire Forest
Water Farm, Sandy Brow, Tarporley, Ches. (Tel: Little Budworth 368)

Chiddingfold, Leconfield and Cowdray
Petworth Park, Sussex (Tel: Petworth 42193 or 42540)

Cleveland
Tocketts, Guisborough, Clev. (Tel: Guisborough 2025)

Clifton-on-Teme
Tedstone Delamere, Bromyard, Worc. (Tel: Bromyard 3493)

College Valley
Langham Toll, Kilham, Mindrum, N'land (Tel: Mindrum 223)

Coniston
Green Bank, Ambleside, Cumbria

Cornwall, East
Little Gimble, St. Cleer, Liskeard, Corn. (Tel: Liskeard 42018)

Cornwall, North
St. Brewed, Bodmin, Corn. (Tel: St. Tudy 223)

Cotswold
Andoversford, Cheltenham, Glos. (Tel: Andoversford 206)

Cotswold, North
Broadway, Worcs. (Tel: Broadway 2379)

Cotswold Vale Farmers'
Boddington Manor, Cheltenham, Glos. (Tel: Coombe Hill 326)

Cottesmore
Ashwell Rd., Oakham, Rutland, Leic. (Tel: Oakham 2829)

Crawley and Horsham
West Grinstead, Sussex (Tel: Cowfold 275)

CROOME AND WEST WARWICKSHIRE
Croome Hunt Kennels, Kinnersley, Severn Stoke, Worc. (Tel: Severn Stoke 215)

CUMBERLAND
Westward Park, Wigton, Cumbria (Tel: Wigton 2391)

CUMBERLAND FARMERS'
Welton, Dalston, Carlisle, Cumbria (Tel: Raughton Head 248)

CURRE, THE
Itton, nr. Chepstow, Gwent (Tel: Chepstow 2965)

CURY
Grigland Green, Cury, nr. Helston, Corn. (Tel: Mullion 634)

DARTMOOR
Woodlands, Ivybridge, S. Devon (Tel: Ivybridge 2478)

DAVID DAVIES
Llandinam, Mont. (Tel: Caersws 348)

DERWENT
Snainton, nr. Scarborough, Yorks. (Tel: Snainton 253)

DEVON, EAST
High St., Andrews, nr. Cullompton, Devon (Tel: Kentisbeare 267)

DEVON, MID
Factory Cross, Chagford, Devon (Tel: Chagford 2280)

DEVON, SOUTH
Pulsford, Denbury, Newton Abbot, Devon (Tel: Ipplepen 229)

DORSET, SOUTH
Bere Regis, Wareham, Dorset (Tel: Bere Regis 213)

DULVERTON, EAST
East Anstey, Tiverton, Som. (Tel: Anstey Mills 229)

DULVERTON, WEST
Stoke Beera, Stoke Rivers, nr. Barnstaple, Devon (Tel: Brayford 470)

DURHAM, SOUTH
Hardwick Park, Sedgefield, Stockton-on-Tees, Clev. (Tel: Sedgefield 20229)

EGGESFORD
Wembworthy, Chulmleigh, N. Devon (Tel: Chulmleigh 230)

ENFEILD CHACE
Birch Farm, White Stubbs Lane, Broxbourne, Herts. (Tel: Hoddesdon 66299)

ERIDGE
Hamsell, Tunbridge Wells, Kent (Tel: Frant 352)

ERYRI
Hafod-y-Llan, Natgwynant, Caern. (Tel: Beddgelert 228)

ESKDALE AND ENNERDALE
Sword House, Eskdale, Holmrock, Cumbria (Tel: Eskdale 295)

ESSEX
London Road, Harlow, Essex (Tel: Harlow 29448)

ESSEX, EAST
Earls Colne, Essex (Tel: Earls Colne 2208)

ESSEX FARMERS'
Althorne Lodge, Althorne, Essex (Tel: Maldon 772153)

Essex and Suffolk
Layham, Ipswich, Suffolk (Tel: Hadleigh 3129)
Essex Union
Billericay, Essex (Tel: Billericay 22808)
Exmoor
Balewater, Simonsbath, nr. Minehead, Som. (Tel: Exford 254)
Farndale
Great Broughton, Middlesbrough, Clev.
Fernie
Great Bowden, Market Harborough, Leics. (Tel: Market Harborough 2081)
Fitzwilliam (Milton)
Milton, Peterborough, Hunts. (Tel: Castor 263)
Flint and Denbigh
Cefn, St. Asaph, Clwyd (Tel: St. Asaph 2421)
Four Burrow
St. Day, Corn. (Tel: St. Day 820 487)
Garth and South Berks
Goddards Green, Mortimer, nr. Reading, Berks. (Tel: Burghfield Common 2323).
Gelligaer Farmers'
Blaenantwen, Bedlinog, Glam.
Glaisdale
Castle House, Danby, Yorks. (Tel: Castleton 361)
Glamorgan
Llandough, nr. Cowbridge, Glam. (Tel: Cowbridge 2583)
Goathland
Alumgarth Farm, Eskdale, Sleights, Whitby, Yorks. (Tel: Grosmont 251)
Gogerddan
Ffynnon, Caradog, Aberystwyth, Dyfed (Tel: Bow Street 354)
Golden Valley
Sheepcote, Clifford, Heref./Worcs. (Tel: Clifford 221)
Goschen's, Mr.
Isnage Farm, Bentley, Hants (Tel: Bentley 2181)
Grafton
Paulersbury, Towcester, Northants (Tel: Paulersbury 214)
Grove and Rufford
Barnby Moor, nr. Retford, Notts. (Tel: Retford 5131)
Hambledon
Droxford, Hants (Tel: Droxford 402)
Hampshire
Ropley, Alresford, Hants (Tel: Ropley 2306)
Haydon
Settlingstones, Newbrough, Fourstones, Hexham, N'land. (Tel: Newbrough 267)
Herefordshire North
Bodenham, Heref./Worcs. (Tel: Bodenham 238)
Herefordshire, South
Wormelow, Heref./Worcs. (Tel: Wormelow 319)
Heythrop
Chipping Norton, Oxon. (Tel: Chipping Norton 2552)
Holderness
Etton, Beverley, Yorks. (Tel: Dalton Holme 250)

HURSLEY
Braishfield, Romsey, Hants (Tel: Braishfield 68330)

HURWORTH
West Rounton, Northallerton, Yorks. (Tel: East Harsley 213)

IRFON AND TOWY
Llwynderw, Abergwesyn, Llanwrtyd Wells, Powys

ISLE OF WIGHT
Gatcombe, nr. Newport (Tel: Chillerton 238)

KENT, EAST
Elham, nr. Canterbury, Kent (Tel: Elham 236)

KENT, WEST
Home Farm, London Road, Southborough, Tunbridge Wells, Kent (Tel: Tonbridge 350683)

LAMERTON
Stowfold, Lewdown, Okehampton, Devon (Tel: Lewdown 346)

LEDBURY
Bromberrow, Ledbury, Herf./Worcs. (Tel: Bromsberrow 207)

LEDSBURY, NORTH
White House, Suckley, Worc. (Tel: Suckley 215)

LLANDEILO FARMERS'
Milo, nr. Llandeilo, Dyfed (Tel: Crosshands 842639)

LLANGEINOR
Derwin Goppa, Coity, nr. Bridgend, Mid Glam. (Tel: Bridgend 3310)

LLANGEITHO
Gellyllyndu, Llanio, Tregaron, Dyfed (Tel: Llangeitho 273)

LLANGIBBY
Llangibby, Gwent (Tel: Tredunnock 245)

LONSDALE, NORTH
Pennybridge Hall, Ulverston, Cumbria (Tel: Greendodd 212)

LUDLOW
Cayntham, Ludlow, Salop (Tel: Ludlow 2898)

LUNESDALE
Hole House, Cautley, Sedbergh, Yorks. (Tel: Sedbergh 591)

MELBREAK
Miller Place, Lorton, Cockermouth, Cumbria (Tel: Lorton 233)

MENDIP FARMERS'
Priddy, nr. Wells, Som. (Tel: Priddy 271)

MEYNELL AND SOUTH STAFFORDSHIRE
Sudbury, Derbys. (Tel: Sudbury 203)

MIDDLETON
Birdstall, Malton, N. Yorks. (Tel: North Grimston 209)

MILVAIN (PERCY)
Beanly, Alnwick, N'land (Tel: Powburn 275)

MONMOUTHSHIRE
Llanvihangel, Gobion, Abergavenny, Gwent (Tel: Gobion 225)

MORPETH
Rivergreen, Meldon, Morpeth, N'land (Tel: Whalton 212)

NEW FOREST
Furzey Lawn, Lyndhurst, Hants (Tel: Lyndhurst 2585)

NORFOLK, WEST
Corbetts Lodge, Necton, Swaffham, Norfolk (Tel: Swaffham 22047)

NORTHUMBERLAND, NORTH
Stainsfield, Cornhill-on-Tweed, N'land (Tel: Crookham 215)

NOTTS, SOUTH
Epperstone, Notts. (Tel: Lowdham 3388)

OAKLEY
Knotting Road, Melchbourne, Bedford. (Tel: Bedford 781825)

PEMBROKESHIRE
Slade, Haverfordwest, Dyfed (Tel: Haverfordwest 3672)

PEMBROKESHIRE, SOUTH
Cresselly, Kilgetty, Dyfed (Tel: Carew 214)

PENMAEN
Penmaen Kennels, Cilparc, Bryncrug, Towyn, Clwyd

PENNINE
Harden Hill Farm, Holmfirth, Huddersfield, W. Yorks. (Tel: Holmfirth 3787)

PENTYRCH
Tydu Farm, St. Fagans, nr. Cardiff, Dyfed (Tel: Pentyrch 280)

PERCY
Canongate, Alnwick, N'land. (Tel: Alnwick 2047)

PERCY, WEST
Beanley, Eglingham, Alnwick, N'land. (Tel: Powburn 275)

PLAS MACHYNLLETH
Bryn Tudor, Aberhosan, Machynlleth, Powys (Tel: Machynlleth 2507)

PORTMAN
Bryanston, nr. Blandford, Dorset (Tel: Blandford 2050)

PUCKERIDGE AND THURLOW
Brent Pelham, Buntingford, Herts. (Tel: Brent Pelham 241)

PYTCHLEY
Brixworth, Northampton, Northants (Tel: 880204)

PYTCHLEY, WOODLAND
Brigstock, nr. Kettering, Northants (Tel: Brigstock 202)

QUORN
Barrow-upon-Soar, Loughborough, Leics. (Tel: Sileby 2258)

RADNORSHIRE AND WEST HEREFORDSHIRE
Titley, Kington, Heref./Worcs. (Tel: Kington 433)

ROYAL ARTILLERY
Bullford Camp, nr. Amesbury, Wilts. (Tel: Bulford Camp 3371 ext. 4405)

RUFFORD FOREST
Shireoaks Hill, Cuckney, Mansfield, Notts. (Tel: Warsop 2554)

SALTERSGATE FARMERS'
Warren Farm, Lockton, Pickering, Yorks. (Tel: Pickering 60244)

SEAVINGTON
Seavington St. Mary, Ilminster, Som. (Tel: South Petherton 479)

SENNYBRIDGE AND DISTRICT FARMERS'
Cefn Rhosen, Sennybridge, Brecon, Powys (Tel: Sennybridge 212)

SHROPSHIRE, NORTH
Annscroft, nr. Shrewsbury, Salop (Tel: Wem 32555)

SHROPSHIRE, SOUTH
Annscroft, nr. Shrewsbury, Salop (Tel: Hanwood 255)

SHROPSHIRE, WEST
Glanyrafon Hall, Llanyblodwel, Oswestry, Salop (Tel: 0691 81 545)

SILVERTON
Drews Clieve, Stoke Hill, Exeter, Devon (Tel: Stoke Canon 216)

SINNINGTON
Lund Lane, Kirbymoorside, Yorks. (Tel: 31208)

SNOWDON VALLEY
Pen-y-Bryn, Pentir, Bangor, Gwynedd

SOMERSET, WEST
Bowerhayes, Carhampton, nr. Minehead, Som.

SOMERSET VALE, WEST
Farringdon Hill, Stogursey, Bridgwater, Som. (Tel: Nether Stowey 404)

SOUTHDOWN
Ringmer, Sussex (Tel: Ringmer 812392)

SOUTH WOLD
Belchford Horncastle, Lincs. (Tel: Tetford 213)

SPOONERS AND WEST DARTMOOR
Marston Gate, Stampford Spiney, Tavistock, Devon (Tel: Yelverton 2178)

STAFFORDSHIRE, NORTH
Hill Chorlton, Baldwins Gate, nr. Newcastle, Staffs. (Tel: Stoke-on-Trent 680232)

STAINTONDALE
Stainton Farm, Staintondale, Scarborough, Yorks. (Tel: Scarborough 870289)

STEVENSTONE
The Old Kennels, Torrington Station, Devon (Tel: Torrington 2297)

SUFFOLK
Copy Farm, Whelnetham, Bury St. Edmunds, Suffolk (Tel: Sicklesmere 292)

SURREY AND BURSTOW, OLD
Felbridge, E. Grinstead, Sussex (Tel: E. Grinstead 25168)

SURREY UNION
Boswells Farms, Oakwood Hill, Ockley, Surrey (Tel: Oakwood Hill 370)

SUSSEX AND ROMNEY MARSH, EAST
Catsfield, Battle, Sussex (Tel: Battle 2022)

TAF FECHAN
Cwm Farm, Ponsticill, Methyr Tydfil, Mid Glam. (Tel: Methyr Tydfil 2753)

TALYBONT
Duffryn Mawr, Gilwern, Powys (Tel: Gilwern 293)

TANATSIDE
Trawscoed Hen, Guilsfield, Welshpool, Powys (Tel: Welshpool 3520)

TAUNTON VALE
Henlade, Taunton, Som. (Tel: Henlade 442223)

TEDWORTH
Westcourt, Burbage, Marlborough, Wilts. (Tel: Burbage 234)

TEME VALLEY
Knighton, Powys (Tel: Knighton 279)

TETCOTT
Rowden, Kilkhampton, Corn. (Tel: Kilkhampton 398)

TETCOTT, SOUTH
Tetcott, Holsworthy, Devon (Tel: North Tamerton 240)

TICKHAM
Wren's Hill, nr. Faversham, Kent (Tel: Teynham 264)

TIVERTON
Hensleigh, Tiverton, Devon (Tel: Tiverton 2670)

TIVYSIDE
Cefn Lodge, Cilgerran, Dyfed (Tel: Llechryd 216)

TORRINGTON FARMERS'
Stevenstone, St. Giles, Devon (Tel: Torrington 2326)

TOWY AND COTHI
Nantfforest, Cilycwm, Llandovery, Dyfed

TREDEGAR FARMERS'
Tredegar Park, Bassaleg, Gwent (Tel: Rhiwderin 456)

TYNEDALE
Stagshaw Bank, N'land. (Tel: Corbridge-on-Tyne 358)

TYNE, NORTH
Ealingham, Wark, Hexham, N'land. (Tel: Bellingham 20207)

ULLSWATER
Grassthwaite, How, Glenridding, Cumbria (Tel: Glenridding 230)

UNITED PACK
Bishops Castle, Shropshire, Salop (Tel: Bishops Castle 480)

VALE OF AYLESBURY
Dodds, Charity Kimblewock, Aylesbury, Bucks. (Tel: Stoke Mandeville 253423)

VALE OF CLETTWR
Blaenpant, Pencader, Dyfed (Tel: Pencader 200)

V.W.H
Merseyhampton, Cirencester, Glos. (Tel: Poulton 232)

VINE AND CRAVEN
Hannington, Basingstoke, Hants (Tel: Kingsclere 298282)

WARWICKSHIRE
Kineton, Warwicks. (Tel: Kineton 640220)

WARWICKSHIRE, NORTH
Rouncil Lane, Kenilworth, Warwicks. (Tel: Kenilworth 54584)

WESTERN
Madron, Penzance, Corn. (Tel: Penzance 2667)

WEST OF YORE
Low Street, Kirby Fleetham, Northallerton, Yorks. (Tel: Kirby Fleetham 242)

WEST STREET
Thornton Farm, Tilmanstone, Kent (Tel: Dover 204230)

WHADDON CHASE
Ascott, Wing, Bucks. (Tel: Wing 243)

WHEATLAND
Eardington, Bridgnorth, Salop (Tel: Bridgnorth 2263)
WILLIAMS-WYNN'S, SIR WATKIN
Wynnstay, Ruabon, Wrexham, Clwyd (Tel: Ruabon 2296)
WILTON
Wilton, nr. Salisbury, Wilts. (Tel: Wilton 3156)
WILTS, SOUTH AND WEST
Motcombe, Shaftesbury, Wilts. (Tel: Shaftesbury 2149)
WORCESTERSHIRE
Fernhill Heath, nr. Worcester, Heref./Worc. (Tel: Worcester 51024)
YNYSFOR
Ynysfor, Penrhyndeudraeth, Gwyn., N. Wales (Tel: Penrhyndeudraeth 282)
YORK AND AINSTY, NORTH
Myers Barn, Cundall, Yorks. (Tel: Topcliffe 689)
YORK AND AINSTY, SOUTH
Moreby Hall, York, N. Yorks. (Tel: Escrick 394)
YSTRAD
Penyrheol Farm, Stanleytown, Mid Glam. (Tel: Ferndale 730865)
ZETLAND
Aldborough St. John, Richmond, N. Yorks. (Tel: Piercebridge 330)

SCOTLAND

BERWICKSHIRE
Brieryhill, Duns, Borders (Tel: Duns 3241)
BUCCLEUCH'S, DUKE OF
St. Boswell's Borders (Tel: St. Boswell's 3578)
DUMFRIESSHIRE
Glenholme, Lockerbie, Dumfries and Galloway (Tel: Kettleholm 207)
EGLINTON
Earlston, Kilmarnock, S'clyde (Tel: Kilmarnock 25428)
FIFE
Harlswynd Ceres, Fife (Tel: Ceres 232)
JED FOREST
Abbotrule, Bonchester Bridge, Borders (Tel: Bonchester Bridge 277)
LANARKSHIRE AND RENFREWSHIRE
Houston, S'clyde (Tel: Bridge of Weir 612022)
LAUDERDALE
Trabroun, Berwickshire, Borders (Tel: Lauder 205)
LIDDESDALE
Twiselhope, Hermitage, Hawick, Borders (Tel: Steel Road 272)
LINLITHGOW AND STIRLINGSHIRE
Threemiletown, Linlithgow, Lothian (Tel: Phillipstoun 200)

Lochaber and Sunart Farmers'
Lockuisge, Kingairloch, Ardgour, nr. Fort William, H'land (Tel: Kingairloch 228)

Wigtownshire
Culhorn, Stranrear, Dumfries and Galloway (Tel: Lochans 335)

Ireland

Avondhu
Cregg Fermoy, Co. Cork (Tel: 025 31053)

Ballymacad
Grennan, Dromone, Oldcastle (Tel: Oldcastle 4)

Bermingham and North Galway
Bermingham House, Tuam, Co. Galway (Tel: 093 24133)

Bree
Ballynadara, Ensiscorthy, Co. Wexford (Tel: 054 2340)

Carbery
Old Military Barracks, Bandon (Tel: Bandon 41525)

Co. Clare
Rour, Adare, Co. Limerick

Down, East
Seaforde, Co. Down (Tel: Seaforde 267)

Duhallow
Blackrock, Mallow (Tel: 022 21552)

Dungannon
Donaghmore Road, Dungannon, Co. Tyrone (Tel: Dungannon 2347)

Galway County ("The Blazers")
Craughwell, Co. Galway (Tel: Craughwell 3)

Galway East
Raford, Athenry, Co. Galway (Tel: Kiltulla 2)

Island
Glandoran, Gorey, Co. Wexford (Tel: Gorey 055 2116)

Kildare
Jigginstown, Naas (Tel: Naas 7344)

Kilkenny
Mount Juliet, Thomastown, Co. Kilkenny (Tel: 056 24212)

Kilkenny North
Ballyring, Freshford, Co. Kilkenny (Tel: Freshford 109)

Laois (Queen's County)
Beechfield, Abbeyleix (Tel: 0502 31265)

Limerick, Co.
Clonshire, Adare, Co. Limerick (Tel: Adare 94220)

Louth
Lissrenny, Tallanstown, Co. Louth (Tel: 042 74193)

Macroom
Ballyverane, Macroom (Tel: Macroom 9)

Meath
Nugentstown, Kells, Co. Meath (Tel: Kells 30)

MUSKERRY
Cloghroe House, Blarney, Co. Cork (Tel: 021 85121)

ORMOND
Mordeeney, Cloghjordan (Tel: Cloughjordan 9)

SCARTEEN (THE BLACK AND TANS)
Scarteen, Knocklong, Tipperary (Tel: Tipperary 53195)

SHILLELAGH AND DISTRICT
Croneyhorn, Carnew, Co. Wicklow (Tel: Carnew 76)

SOUTH UNION
Coolmore, Carrigaline, Co. Cork (Tel: 882311)

STRABANE AND DONEGAL
The Windmill Farm, Ballindrait, Co. Donegal (Tel: Lifford 83)

TIPPERARY
Tullamaine, Fethard, Co. Tipperary (Tel: 052 31368)

TIPPERARY, NORTH
Kilteelagh, Dromineer, Nenagh, Co. Tipperary (Tel: Puckane 45)

UNITED HUNT CLUB
Knockgriffin, Midleton, Co. Cork
(Tel: Midleton 63171)

WATERFORD
Woodhouse, Stradbally, Co. Waterford (Tel: 051 93110)

WATERFORD, WEST
Bishopstown, Lismore (Tel: Lismore 058 54323)

WESTMEATH
Knockdrin, Mullinger (Tel: Mullinger 8252)

WEXFORD
Moorfields, Ballinaboola, Co. Wexford (Tel: 051 24352)

WICKLOW
Raheenagurran West, Gorey, Co. Wexford (Tel: 055 21128)

UNITED STATES OF AMERICA

AMWELL VALLEY
Clover Hill, New Jersey

ANTIETAM HUNT
Burkittsville, Maryland

ARAPAHOE
Littleton, Colorado

AUSTIN HUNT
Austin Plantation, Lake Cormorant, and Sandhill, Rankin County, Mississippi

BATTLE CREEK
Augusta, Michigan

BEAUFORT
Hummelstown, Pennsylvania

BEDFORD COUNTY
Cifax area of Bedford County

BELLE MEADE
Thomson, Georgia

BLUE RIDGE
Millwood, Clarke County, Virginia

BRADBURY
Escoheag, Rhode Island

BRANDYWINE
Northbrook Pennsylvania
BRIDLESPUR
New Melle, Missouri
BULL RUN
Manassas, Virginia
CAMARGO
Moscow, Ohio
CAMDEN
Camden, South Carolina
CASANOVA
Casanova, Virginia
CEDAR KNOB FOXHOUNDS
Taft, Tennessee
CHAGRIN VALLEY
Gates Mills, Ohio
DEEP RUN
Manakin, Virginia
DE LA BROOKE FOXHOUNDS W
Mechanicsville, Maryland
THE EARLY GROVE HUNT
Moscow, Tennessee
ELKRIDGE-HARFORD
Taylor, Maryland
ESSEX
Peapack, New Jersey
FAIRFAX
Ashburn, Virginia
FAIRFIELD COUNTY
Newtown, Connecticut
FARMINGTON
Charlottesville, Virginia
FORT LEAVENWORTH
Fort Leavenworth, Kansas
FOXCATCHER HOUNDS
Fair Hill, Maryland
FOX RIVER VALLEY
Barrington, Illinois
GENESEE VALLEY
Geneseo, New York
GLENMORE
Staunton, Augusta County, Virginia
GOLDEN'S BRIDGE
North Salem, New York
GOSHEN
Derwood, Maryland
GREEN SPRING VALLEY
Glyndon, Maryland
GREENVILLE COUNTY
Gowensville, South Carolina
MR. HAIGHT, JR'S LITCHFIELD COUNTY
Litchfield, Connecticut
HICKORY CREEK HUNT
Dallas, Texas
HILLSBORO
Inglehame Farm, Tennessee
HOPPER HILLS (1974)
Victor, New York
HOUND AND HORN
Cedar Lake, Indiana
HOWARD COUNTY
Glenelg, Howard County, Maryland
MR. HUBBARD'S KENT COUNTY
Chestertown, Maryland
HUNTINGDON VALLEY HUNT
Furlong, Bucks County, Pennsylvania
IRON BRIDGE
Laurel, Maryland
IROQUOIS
Lexington, Kentucky
MR. JEFFORDS' ANDREWS BRIDGE
Christiana, Pennsylvania
KESWICK
Gordonsville, Virginia

LAURAY
Bath, Ohio
LICKING RIVER HOUNDS
Carlisle, Kentucky
LIMEKILN
Reading, Pennsylvania
LIMESTONE CREEK (1974)
Manlius, New York
LIVE OAK HOUNDS
Thomasville, Georgia
LONG LAKE
Hamel, Minnesota
LONGREEN
Rossville, Tennessee
LONG RUN
Prospect, Kentucky
LOS ALTOS
Paicines, California
LOST HOUND
Edmond, Oklahoma
LOUDOUN
Leesburg and Hamilton, Virginia
MARLBOROUGH
Upper Marlboro, Maryland
MECKLENBURG
Matthews, North Carolina
MELLS
Waco, Tennessee
METAMORA
Metamora, Michigan
MIAMI VALLEY
Spring Valley, Ohio
MIDDLEBURG
Middleburg, Virginia
MIDDLEBURY
Middlebury, Connecticut
MIDDLETON PLACE HOUNDS
Charleston, South Carolina
MIDDLETOWN VALLEY HUNT
Middletown, Maryland
MIDLAND
Midland, Georgia and Fitzpatrick, Alabama
MILLBROOK
Millbrook, New York
MILL CREEK
Wadsworth, Illinois
MISSION VALLEY
Stilwell, Kansas
MONMOUTH COUNTY
Allentown, New Jersey
MONTPELIER
Montpelier Station, Virginia
MOORE COUNTY
Southern Pines, North Carolina
MOORELAND
Madison, Alabama
NASHOBA VALLEY
Pepperell, Massachusetts
NEW BRITTON
Spencer, Indiana
NEW MARKET HOUNDS
New Market, Maryland
NORFOLK
Dover, Massachusetts
NORTH HILLS
Omaha, Nebraska
OAK BROOK
Bryon, Illinois
OAK GROVE (1975)
Germantown, Tennessee
OLD CHATHAM
Old Chatham, New York
OLD DOMINION
Orlean, Virginia
OLD NORTH BRIDGE HOUNDS
Concord, Massachusetts
OLD STONINGTON HOUNDS
Taylorville, Illinois

ORANGE COUNTY
The Plains, Fauquier County, Virginia
PICKERING
Chester Springs, Pennsylvania
PIEDMONT
Upperville, Fauquier County, Virginia
PINE VALLEY HOUNDS
Pine Valley, California
POTOMAC
Potomac, Maryland
PRINCESS ANNE
Virginia Beach, Virginia
RADNOR
White Horse, Chester County, Pennsylvania
RAPPAHANNOCK
Sperryville, Virginia
ROARING FORK
Carbondale, Colorado
ROCKBRIDGE
Glasgow, Virginia
ROCKY FORK HEADLEY
Gahanna, Ohio
ROLLING ROCK – WESTMORELAND
Ligonier, Pennsylvania
ROMBOUT
Staatsburg, New York
ROMWELL FOX HOUNDS
Romney, Indiana
ROSE TREE
Brogue, York County, Pennsylvania
SANTA FE
El Cajon, California
SANTA YNEZ VALLEY HUNT
Los Olivos, California
SEDGEFIELD
Brown Summit, N. Carolina
SHAKERAG
North Fulton County, Georgia
SMITHTOWN
Stony Brook, New York
SOUTHERN ILLINOIS OPEN
Carbondale, Illinois
MR. STEWART'S CHESHIRE
Unionville, Chester County, Pennsylvania
TRADERS POINT
Royalton, Indiana
TRIANGLE
Bahama, North Carolina
TRI-COUNTY
Milner, Georgia
TRYON (1975)
Tryon, North Carolina
TWO RIVERS
Zephyrhills, Florida
VICMEAD
Middletown, Delaware
WARRENTON
Ridglea, Warrenton, Virginia
WATERLOO
Grass Lake, Michigan
WAYNE-DUPAGE
Wayne, DuPage County, Illinois
WEST HILLS
Chatsworth, California
WICOMICO HUNT
Salisbury, Maryland
WINDY HOLLOW
Florida, New York
WOLF CREEK HOUNDS
Goreville, Illinois
WYE RIVER HOUNDS
Easton, Maryland